FAITHFUL
CHANGE

◆

FAITHFUL CHANGE

◆

The Personal and Public Challenges of Postmodern Life

◆

JAMES W. FOWLER

ABINGDON PRESS
NASHVILLE

FAITHFUL CHANGE
THE PERSONAL AND PUBLIC CHALLENGES OF POSTMODERN LIFE

Library of Congress Cataloging-in-Publication Data

Fowler, James W., 1940–
    Faithful change : the personal and public challenges of postmodern
life / James W. Fowler.
        p. cm.
    Includes bibliographical references.
    ISBN 0-687-01730-0 (alk. paper)
    1. Faith development.   2. Life change events—Religious aspects—
Christianity.   3. Postmodernism—Religious aspects—Christianity.
    I. Title.
BV4637.F658   1996
248—dc20   96-5991
                                                                                    CIP

Scripture quotations noted NASB are from the New American Standard Bible, © The
Lockman Foundation 1960, 1962, 1968, 1971, 1972, 1973, 1975, 1977. Used by permission.

Scripture quotations noted NRSV are from the New Revised Standard Version Bible,
copyright © 1989, by the Division of Christian Education of the National Council of the
Churches of Christ in America.

This book is printed on acid-free recycled paper.

96 97 98 99 00 01 02 03 04 05 — 10 9 8 7 6 5 4 3 2 1

Manufactured in the United States of America

*This book is for our daughters
and the men they married*

Joan and Larry   Margaret and Jeff

CONTENTS

INTRODUCTION

Human beings in every generation must have felt in some ways that they lived in unprecedented times. This seems so despite the fact that the doctrine of progress—the idea that history moves forward with the potential for continued expansion and improvement—only emerged in the seventeenth century. Each new generation experiences the full range of challenges of human living for the first time. We may rely upon education, our observations, and the experience of others as it is transmitted in stories. But change is continual, and many of the choices we must make have to address new beachheads of challenge.

The need for change in our lives comes from at least three sources. First, we experience the imperative of developmental changes. We are *bodies*. Our bodies take form in embryo according to the ground plan of a genetic code. When the fetus emerges into extrauterine life, the child begins a journey of physical, emotional, cognitive, and spiritual growth and change. Our bodies include the neurophysiological potential for the realization of the full range of human capacities. Our bodies gradually mature, take their adult forms, and then eventually begin an inevitable process of gradual decline toward death. The processes, the changes, this waxing and waning of our lives as bodies, is integral to our spiritual lives. Courage and faith are required for this journey of growth and change, of struggle and development. We can call this first source and type of change—universal among humans—*developmental change.*

9

Second, as a species we are fragile during the challenging early phases of our growth. Where our brother and sister animals in other species are equipped with instincts and guidance systems evolved over millions of years, we construct more individually distinct patterns of emotion and mind. We are shaped by the characters and the patterns of interaction already in process on the stages where our life dramas begin. The constructions we make of our experiences of the world bear the particular marks of our native languages. Stories, symbols, and rituals in our cultures and religious traditions shape our emotions and our convictional moorings.

But there is more: The social process of shaping our life orientations inevitably results in our growing into adulthood with emotions that are wounded or distorted in some degree. Involuntarily we learn to hide these wounds from ourselves with what the psychoanalytic tradition has taught us to call defenses. Our defenses enable us to mask our wounds from ourselves, and to some degree, from others. As our lives unfold there come critical times of transition or loss, perplexity or success, that upset the fragile balance of mind and spirit we have maintained. We lose a job or are required to move. A child dies or a marriage breaks up. Or we succeed remarkably at some venture and must come to terms with the impact of our success on others who are close to us or are our competitors. Or we find at age thirty, forty, or fifty that we have somehow pursued a path, with whatever success or satisfaction, that we did not choose for ourselves. We may enter a "neutral zone" time in our lives and begin to try to find our own deeper hearts' yearnings—to find and follow our *bliss*. We may think of such times as these as times of "breakdown" or "breakthrough," when we must heal or rework some of the underlying patterns of our emotional or relational lives. This second source and type of change we can call *healing* or *reconstructive change*.

Third, we experience changes that result from our participation in the broader range of social, economic, and political processes of our societies. From the terrible dislocations and losses that come with wars and times of economic depression, to the changes required to accommodate new technological capacities in the workplace or society, we and those around us must periodically relinquish old patterns and horizons of expectations and develop

10

new ones. Old habits and assumptions, serviceable and well-practiced, have to give way. New skills, perceptions, and attitudes may need to be nurtured. Even our convictions and the deepest elements of our systems of beliefs and values may require reexamination and reworking. To be faithful in times of change we must find grounds for hope and trust as we embrace the need to rework our ways of holding and living our convictions. "New occasions teach new duties," as the modern hymn says. And we are called to learn new skills and to form new frames of consciousness and perception. This third source of change in our lives we may call *change due to disruptions and modifications of the systems that shape our lives.*

Faithful Change addresses these three areas and types of change we experience. Part I of the book explores the dynamics of faith and change using the framework of faith development research and theory. From earliest childhood through old age, from the faith of the infant through the faith of world-transforming mystics and militants, the three chapters of part I look at the stages and transitions of ongoing development and change in faith. Chapter 1 opens up the intriguing mysteries of the role of childhood experiences and development in shaping our adult stances of faith. The revisionist work of Daniel Stern on infant development provides a suggestive perspective from which to look at the building block experiences of faith and spirit. Chapter 2 focuses on the emotional dynamics of development in faith. It brings research on faith development into lively interplay with perspectives on human development derived from ego and self-psychology. It concludes with vignettes from research that carry us into some times and textures of transition in persons' lives. Chapter 3 looks at the relationships between the more or less predictable experiences of transitional growth in faith, and the more dramatic transformations many experience in conversions or in mystical ecstasy. Here we bring faith development research into dialogue with the classic psychology of religion of William James. Giving fresh attention to our emotional lives in relation to faith, the whole of part I points to the underlying role faith plays in helping us embrace the challenges of change, while making clear how the patterns and contents of our faith, themselves, must also inevitably evolve and change.

Part II invites an exploration and understanding of one of the most neglected of the human emotions in twentieth-century Western societies—the emotion of shame. In this period, on the threshold of a new millennium, shame has reemerged as an emotion we must learn to recognize and address. The anthropologist Ruth Benedict, in her classic study *The Chrysanthemum and the Sword,* formulated a thesis that ruled as a largely unquestioned cliché for more than thirty years. Eastern societies, she said (meaning Japan, China, and Korea), are *shame*-oriented cultures; while Western societies (meaning Europe and North America) are *guilt*-oriented societies. It is true that Eastern societies, much more than Western societies, have highly elaborated descriptions of shame, of the conditions where one should feel it, and prescriptions for how shame must be faced or remedied—up to and including ritual suicide. In shame-oriented societies one experiences the pain of acting wrongly or irresponsibly as a loss of respect due to the bad reflection one brings upon one's family or people. Shame involves a painful sense of exposure through which the whole collectivity of which one is a part suffers embarrassment. In guilt-oriented societies the pain of acting wrongly comes from the recognition that one has acted against a principle or a law that one acknowledges as normative. Guilt is felt as a negative judgment on the self as an individual actor rather than on one's family or tribe as a whole. While guilt is about something one *does,* shame is about something one *is.* While guilt brings the judgment of an inner voice for something one has done, shame involves the sense of being seen and exposed as defective or flawed. My contention in part II of this book will be that though shame has been more invisible in Western societies in this century, especially in the United States, it pervades our personal and collective lives in ways that underlie a great deal of the self-destructive and violent patterns of our society. Moreover, shame plays a central role in the high rates of depression and of substance use and abuse among us.

The five chapters that make up part II will bring a bodily and neurophysiological perspective to the understanding of shame. We will start with shame as a genetically inherited affect or emotion system, which has evolved in humans to help us maintain the relations that are most important to us. Shame plays an indispensable role in the formation of *conscience,* and therefore in ethical sensibility and judgment. But the same neurophysiological affect systems that make us sensitive to the threat of ostracism or loss of relations can also make us over-conforming. In the deep unconscious need to live up to the "programs of worth" in our families or communities of origin, we can lose access to the truth of our own hearts and desires, our own experiences and callings. We can give our energies over to the creation and maintenance of "false selves."

These chapters aim to make shame visible in this society and in our lives. We will see that there is a spectrum of shame experiences, differing in intensity, depth, and distorting power. We will look at "healthy shame," which is the custodian of our most significant relations, and the basis of conscience. We will look at "perfectionist shame," the distortion of shame a child suffers when self-worth depends too much on meeting conditions imposed by those socializing the child. "Shame due to enforced minority status" can cut across each of the other types of shame, making one feel disvalued, as a member of a group subjected to prejudice and subordination. Finally "toxic shame" and the condition of "shamelessness" will be examined. Each of these five types of shame will be illustrated with the stories of people who have been enmeshed in them.

Part II ends with a revisiting of the creation and fall story in the third chapter of Genesis. The interpretation it offers invites us to see the consequence of our foremother and forefather's sin more in terms of shame and alienation than in terms of guilt. It focuses on the essential role of grace in enabling us to embrace the challenges of growth in relation to both personal and social shame.

Part III of *Faithful Change* explicitly addresses the themes suggested by the subtitle of the book: *The Personal and Public Challenges of Postmodern Life.* The term *postmodern* rings of controversy. It has entered academic and, more recently, popular discussions as what the Germans call a *Streitbegriff,* an idea or concept to fight over. In the last two decades the term has taken on three broad meanings: (1) It is used as a term—somewhat apocalyptic in tone—to designate the transitional time in history and culture in which we presently live. (2) It is used as an aesthetic descriptor, suggesting a type of contemporary art and representation that is permeated with material interest, commercial distortion, and self-conscious intent to reshape perceptions. (3) The term refers to a broad development in contemporary thought that engages in deep going criticism of the Enlightenment with its trust in the possibility of a universal reason and its focus on meta-narratives such as belief in human progress and universal groundings for ethical principles or standards.

In these pages, we will deal primarily with the third of these meanings—that is, the sense that the leading assumptions and ideas of the eighteenth-century Enlightenment have lost their power to provide the intellectual grounding for our most basic and foundational ideas about science and human rationality; our ideas about the philosophical foundations of our ethical and legal philosophies; and our assumptions about human nature itself. Postmodernists assert that the concept of a universal reason, thought to be the grounding for the possibility of articulating rationally certain knowledge of the natural world, is the basis for but one *form* or *type* of rationality. Concepts of justice and right derived from the Enlightenment ideal of reason, they suggest, are also partial and particular notions, which have tended to favor the interests of the dominant classes in societies and to serve the needs of early modern nation states. These ideas, postmodernists contend, may no longer be adequate for pluralistic societies or for adjudicating the differences between classes or nations.

The argument also usually has a sociological aspect. It points to the cumulative impacts of the technological developments of the twentieth century: rapid transportation, telecommunications, and computer technologies that make possible the humming webs of dedicated lines that knit persons and groups in instantaneous exchange across oceans and continents or with the building next door. With the affluence produced by the new international industries spawned by these technologies, people are constructing new forms of consciousness, learning to think in new paradigms and frames. We are shaping new forms of knowing and new concepts of "truth."

Curiously, but importantly, while postmodern approaches shift our attention from unifying notions of universal truth, they tend to open the way to reclaim the value of more particular and local traditions and ways of knowing. While Enlightenment philosophies tended to try to justify morality and religion by appeals to universal reason, postmodern perspectives allow for fresh recognition of the value of concrete religious traditions, traditions of folk wisdom, and of commonsense approaches to ethics. Postmodern thinking, when it allows itself to be practical, reclaims the local, the commonsense, and the wise, as they are grounded in symbol, myth, and metaphor.

Part III builds on the thesis that whether the average person in today's societies has a *theory* of postmodern experience or not, we are—*willy nilly*—finding ourselves living in and developing forms of *practical postmodern consciousness*. Chapter 9 focuses on the Enlightenment and the liberating impacts it made in the early period that we call *modernity*. Using the faith development theory we explored in part I, it sees the Enlightenment as a movement in history in which humankind, in a collective evolution of consciousness, began a serious shift in forms of knowing and ways of holding faith. The concluding sections of that chapter present the thesis that we are, at the end of the twentieth century, engaged in another evolutionary shifting of the forms of consciousness and faith, every bit as far-reaching as that of the eighteenth-century Enlightenment. But now it is happening far more rapidly, and on a global basis.

Times of transition in cultural consciousness are characterized by ferment and conflict. Chapter 10 employs faith development theory to clarify the political and social conflicts some interpreters have called "culture wars." This chapter offers models of premodern, modern, and postmodern consciousness. Based on these models, I seek to illumine the social, political, and religious tensions that have emerged in this time of paradigm shift. Conflicts become sharp as we experience the ways in which both premodern and modern patterns of consciousness seem to fail to enable us to grasp and work responsibly with the challenges of the twenty-first century.

Chapters 11 and 12 explore how Christian theology can offer fresh resources for shaping and guiding our efforts to embrace the challenges of postmodern experience. These chapters pay special attention to how we may understand God's presence and influence—God's *providence*—in the changed thought frames of postmodern experience. Chapter 11 examines four theological approaches that address the emerging experiences of postmodernity. Chapter 12 asks, "Who is the god who is dying in the emergent postmodern consciousness?" It then offers a constructive approach to imaging the providence of God in dialogue with practical postmodern experience. Calling God's providence the *praxis of God,* we ask, How can humans, drawing from biblical faith, discern God's patterns and influence in this systemic world, and how can we try to shape our personal and corporate lives and vocations so as to be part of God's work in this new era?

The final two chapters of part III become truly local and practical. They look at the challenges we face in moral education and religious formation in our pluralistic, increasingly violent and morally corrosive society. Chapter 13 focuses on the challenges of keeping faith with *all* our children, preparing them for life in postmodern terms. It pays special attention to the challenges of education in our troubled inner cities. Chapter 14 looks more broadly at the challenges of Christian education for faithfulness in the contexts of our postmodern, secularizing, yet religiously intense time in history.

What a time to be alive! Controversy flares as we try to address the challenges of reform of our health-care delivery systems, our ways of maintaining temporary social and economic safety nets for all citizens, and as we wrestle with how to reshape our approaches to education. Complexity calls for our best efforts to frame adequate methods of management and ethical responsiveness in the midst of global systems of communications, economic exchange, and environmental threat. Religious communities and communities of moral concern cannot afford to offer simple nostrums and deceptive slogans as solutions to the complexities we face. We must embrace the challenges of systems thinking and of developing the new and responsive forms of organization required to address and manage increasingly rapid and pervasive processes of change. The faith to change is indispensable for us in this transitional time. In faithful change we make ourselves available for callings that aim to embrace vital relationship to the movements and power of the one whose providence creates, sustains, judges, and pours out love to redeem and fulfill creation. As those who are formed in the divine image, may we be enabled to become, in new ways, partners with God in caring for the dynamic—and dangerous—becoming of the earth.

PART I

CHANGE AND THE DYNAMICS OF FAITH

Faith development research has studied how people form their deepest and most personal sense of relatedness to God and the meanings that are foundational for their ways of living. In the first of the three chapters of Faithful Change, we explore the awakening of images and emotions of faith in earliest childhood. We ponder the ways that babies, before they use verbal language, form mutualities of shared meanings with those closest to them. We attend to how they form their earliest ways of imaging God, and the original spirituality they shape in encounter with the stories they hear, the rituals they participate in, and the active processes of making meaning in which they engage.

Building beyond childhood, we look at the forming and changing of stages of faith across the life cycle. This journey, while personal, is not solitary. To understand faith development we must keep in view the relationships, the roles, the social and cultural "materials at hand" that stimulate and sustain the forming of our central meanings. We must claim and interpret the processes and significance of change in the journey of faith. Developmental change shapes the focus of chapter 2. Transformational and conversional change comes to the fore in chapter 3.

Throughout the chapters of part I our goal is to feel the texture of the dynamics of faith, to clarify its patterns and processes, and to invite the reader to reflect on and re-member her or his own journey in faith in new ways.

CHAPTER ONE

BEGINNINGS

PRELUDE

THE BEGINNING OF A JOURNEY

In the quietness
In the quietness
In the dark warm-watery comfort
Sensing—ka-flum, ka-flum, ka-flum—
    the heart's nearby steady beating
And the whisper of her breathing
A basic rocking rhythm.
Arpeggios of changing moods and motions
Play refrains somatic and biochemical
In harmony with vibrations
From the patterned timbre of her voice.

A seed growing silently.
In the spacious limbic pool
Embryonic acrobatics turn to
Kicking, probing restlessness
As term-time comes.

Restlessness, stilled by constriction,
Ooops into pushing sliding advance
Opening the narrow tunnel of passage.
Did ever love squeeze so hard?
Or life demand such bruising?

Head squeezed to cone-shape,
Tiny nose pressed flat,
Closed eyes squinting in the unaccustomed light
The gasping cry sputters with fluid
And the first lung-filling drags
Of on-earth-air.

> Touch and handling
> Towels and tenderness
> Then stretched out gently
> On mother's tum.
> Soon, nipple with breast or bottle
> And welcoming, ecstatic smiles
> Celebrate
>
> The Beginning of a Journey.

N o other period of our life compares with the first two years in terms of the rapidity and explosiveness of developmental change. During the first nine months we are far more dependent upon the care of parents or their surrogates than most other species. At the same time, we may well double or triple in body size and weight in the first year. If Daniel Stern is right (Stern is one of the principal students of early childhood we will draw upon in this chapter), we will have already entered three different dimensions of the experience of being a self before we reach the twelve-month mark, and we will be on the verge of another—the verbal self. Both for faith and for our readiness to embrace and deal with change, the experiences and relations of the first five years of our rapid growth and formation of selfhood have special importance. This opening chapter invites you to retrace that early journey, seeing its paths and turns, and perhaps *re-membering* some of its quality.

FAITH AND SELFHOOD

Let us begin by defining our key terms: By *selfhood* I mean the evolving subjective experience of becoming and being a person in relation. By *evolving* I mean unfolding, changing, undergoing continuing growth and development. I use the term *subjective* to describe the experience of the subject, the one who experiences each stage as he or she goes through this process of evolving, of being and becoming a person in relation. We are indelibly social selves. Only through that deep social experience of being within the womb and then emerging to a new quality of relatedness can we begin the journey of becoming selves. Eventually through maturation and continuing interaction with others, we attain *selfhood:* we become *reflective selves*—persons in relation.

And then there is *faith*—another mystery. Like selfhood, faith involves the formation of an evolving sense of relatedness to other persons. But it also involves our composing an evolving sense of what we may term *spirit*. Spirit gives meaning and coherence to our lives. Through spirit we participate in an *ultimate environment*. In many cultures, people find symbolic representation of this sense of an ultimate environment by seeing their lives as grounded in or related to God. The term "God" brings with it a set of symbols that evoke an image of ultimate being and of our relation to ultimate reality. In the love, the awesomeness, and the moral valuing involved in our sense of relatedness to the power and spirit of an ultimate environment, our ways of relating to the world, to our neighbors, and to ourselves are deeply shaped. This pattern of our relatedness to self, others, and our world in light of our relatedness to ultimacy we call faith. Faith, then, is a dynamic, evolving pattern of the ways our souls find and make meanings for our lives. (See Fowler 1995, 1-36.)

The faith relations by which we live take on a triadic pattern, a covenantal pattern. By "triadic" I mean that faith involves a relationship in which we as selves are related to others in mutual ties of trust and loyalty, of reliance and care; but that dyad is grounded in our common relatedness to a third member, a center of value and power that bears the weight of ultimacy for us. Our relatedness to a spiritually engaging center affects all the other relations of our lives. Our ways of symbolizing the center or centers of transcending worth and power in our lives most often involve symbols, stories, rituals, and beliefs that we share with others and that make us members of communities of faith.

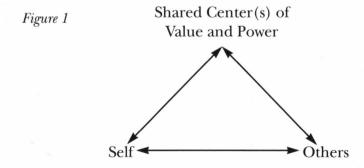

Figure 1

Shared Center(s) of
Value and Power

Self ⟷ Others

There is a triadic structure or pattern to our selfhood and a triadic pattern to our being in faith. Self and others, related in mutual trust in and loyalty to shared centers of meaning, value, and power—these are the spiritual dynamics of faith. In this chapter and those that follow we will explore the origins and development of selfhood and faith in our lives and the lives of others. To prepare for this work we need to sketch the foundational research of others who have studied and written on early childhood, tracing its dynamics in such ways as to open windows toward our relation to spirit. In so doing, they have contributed to our understanding of the dynamics of faith.

EARLY CHILDHOOD: THREE ORIENTING PERSPECTIVES

The seminal work of Erik H. Erikson on psychosocial development has helped us look at the formation of basic trust in the first year or year-and-a-half of life as it struggles against a sense of anxiety and basic mistrust (Erikson 1963, 1982, 1987). If we emerge from that first year or so of life with a balance, on the whole, of trust over mistrust, then a basic *virtue* emerges—a basic strength of selfhood and faith, which Erikson calls the strength of *hope*. The philosopher Santayana refers to what Erikson speaks of as hope as "animal faith"—a kind of ground trust that one can be at home in the world, and that there is a future for this being we are, that we have some title to a life. We begin with a ground sense of hope.

Between eighteen and thirty-six months Erikson sees the emergence of another pivotal crisis in our lives. Now able to stand on our own two feet—however wobbly—we struggle with a new sense of *autonomy*, of being a separate self, while maintaining enough connectedness to avoid feeling overly powerless or dominated. With sufficient autonomy we do not give in to what Erikson calls "shame and doubt" in the self. Where shame and doubt are excessive they can constitute a pervasive sense of unworth, of incapacity, or of inadequacy. How vulnerable the child is to an environment that, by its evaluations or demands, leads him or her to form a sense of being organismically, fundamentally lacking. Where autonomy wins a victory over shame and doubt (though it never totally banishes it, and shouldn't), there emerges the virtue or the strength of personhood and faith that Erikson calls *will*—the ability to assert oneself, to claim the space one needs in order to *be*, and to claim for the self the respect it is due. With autonomy the child learns to say "I" with conviction, and to lay claims with the terms "my" and "mine."

Erikson points to an age, roughly three to five years, as a period for the centrality of a crisis that he names *initiative versus guilt*. This is the capacity of the young child, now able to move and control its limbs and to have purposes and ideas. He or she now competes with others, conspires with and against siblings, and enters the dramas of a play world, the world of imagination and anticipation of future roles. At the same time the child must come to a firm resolution or recognition that he or she is not the permanent and exclusive partner of the parent of the opposite sex. This means dealing with the guilt that one feels about those contemplated desires. It means, on the whole, the child's shaping sense of freedom and initiative that gives rise to the virtue of *purpose*. In this stage we see the emergence of that aspect of *conscience* that involves the internalization of the norms and the values that are important for the communities of which one is a part.

Jean Piaget has been very helpful to us in understanding the early awakening of the child's mind and reasoning—the cognitive development of the child (Piaget 1962, 1967, 1970, 1976; Piaget and Inhelder 1969). A child in the first year and a half of life orders his or her experience of the world largely through bodily experience of that world, in a stage or a phase Piaget calls *sensory-motor knowing*. Knowing in this early stage arises in the child's physical interactions with objects and persons. It activates his or her capacities for constructing the permanence of the object world. This way of ordering the world of objects and of persons occurs prior to language.

By about eighteen months there begins to occur that revolution in which language becomes important in the shaping and communicating of our experience of the world. Here we begin to use symbols to represent objects and persons, feelings and states. We enter into a stage or a phase that Piaget characterizes as "*pre-operational knowing and thinking.*" The child's imagination runs free and ranges over his or her total experience. In this stage we encounter novelties each day and hold together, in episodic constructions, our efforts to grasp the meaning world. Here feeling and perception dominate the child's ways of knowing and believing. Fantasy and make-believe are as real to children as what they encounter in everyday life. Piaget's account of the drama of cognitive development in early childhood contributes to the background of interest in spiritual development, our development in selfhood and faith.

As a final orientation to our focus I need to report on the research I and my associates have pursued in what has come to be known as faith development theory (Fowler and Keen 1980; Fowler 1987, 1991, 1995). In ways that are resonant with Erikson and Piaget, we have identified two early childhood stages in the development of selfhood and faith. The first of these, the stage of *Primal Faith,* marks the period in which the infant enters into bonding with caretakers, usually working out a mutuality in which the child forms a sense of trust and learns a rudimentary kind of relatedness in love to those who are close. In ways that are somatic (bodily) and interactive (shared rituals, both formal and informal) children begin to participate in and share the meanings and values of those who welcome and socialize them to the world.

There follows a stage that begins at about the eighteenth month with the transition to language acquisition and use. We call this the *Intuitive-Projective* stage of faith. In this period, the three- to five-year-old can form deep going and long-lasting images of spirit and of the powers that shape and surround his or her experience world. The child encounters death and awakens to the penumbra of mystery that surrounds and often penetrates life. Identifications with the qualities and values of trusted adults or older children can make significant contributions to the shaping of a self. Stories, told or enacted in play or ritual, provide horizons of meaning in this pregnant time of the child's first constructions of the world, its spiritual mysteries and meanings.

Now that we have sketched the background of these three psychological perspectives on childhood and its forming of self-hood and faith, we are ready to embrace the deeper challenges this chapter needs to engage. We will go behind these familiar perspectives on early childhood, with their various holistic de-scriptions of this period, and try to find more precise and de-tailed accounts, particularly of early infancy. In that effort, let us turn to the work of a theorist of early childhood development, Daniel N. Stern. The source I want to work with now is Stern's *The Interpersonal World of the Infant.* Let me give some orientation to what makes Stern's work very special in my view. There are three features.

First of all, Stern is trained as a psychoanalyst, a psychiatrist. He has a medical background, and he stands in that tradition of psychoanalytic thinkers who try to reconstruct infant experience from the standpoint of their work with adult patients. This psycho-analytic approach tries to reconstruct babies' experiences on the basis of work with adult patients and their retrospective memories. In writing his book on Luther as a young man, Erik Erikson said, "At times, we will have to try to describe what will prove to have had to have been the case about a child's early experiences on the basis of clinical insight" (Erikson 1963, 50). In a sense, psychoanalytic theories have reconstructed infancy on the basis of what presum-ably must have happened in order for the patterns of adult person-ality they work with to exist.

Second, Stern has paid careful attention and contributed to the developmental psychological study of actual infants in the process of their interaction with others and their environments. He works with laboratory research and observational studies with young children, catching them in the act of becoming persons and mak-ing meaning. Daniel Stern's work pulls together these two perspec-tives on infancy and keeps them in a kind of mutually correcting and enriching tension. With Stern, we get a three-dimensional view of infancy that is very rich and suggestive.

In the third place, Stern's work is helpful for us in our interest in selfhood and faith because he provides strong evidence of what I call *innate pre-potentiation* for selfhood and relation, on the one hand, and for faith and spirit on the other. Innate pre-potentiation is an important concept, though a little difficult to communicate easily: "Innate" means coming with the infant, genetically given, a part of the evolutionary equipment of the neonate. "Pre-potentiation" means "pre-ready" for relatedness, "pre-ready" to meet an environment in the process of constructing shared meanings. It does not mean that this development is automatic, or that it is all genetically determined. Rather, it means that there is a readiness that depends upon the environment's ways of activating it—of meeting it in a mutuality of stimulation and active responsiveness. One might say that the seeds or the patterns for the operations of knowing and imagining others, self, and world are "standard equipment" for human babies.

We are born with capacities ready to be activated for linking our emotions with spirit. Where that mutuality of relation is present and consistent, the infant shows a strong predisposition to form bonds, to recruit the love and care of adults, to grow toward healthy relationships. Children come with the potentials to grow in the construction of a coherent and life-sustaining sense of faith and meaning.

EMERGENT SELFHOOD AND THE GENESIS OF FAITH

What does Stern offer us? He gives us a picture of four emergent senses of the self that constitute the infant's first experiences of becoming a self. Now let me say a word about "senses" of the self: Earlier I characterized selfhood as the "subjective experience of becoming a person in relation." Stern has tried to help us enter the baby's experience of the earliest months of life, and to give us access to it as the infant experiences it. We find it too easy to project back onto the child feelings and meanings based on our adult experience. We often look at infant experience with adult eyes and through the lenses of adult experience. Stern has tried as much as possible to get behind our memory screens and projections and to help us enter the world of the child. As we examine what he and his sources can teach us about the infant's experience of growth in selfhood and faith, I will ask you to refer regularly to figure 2.

Figure 2

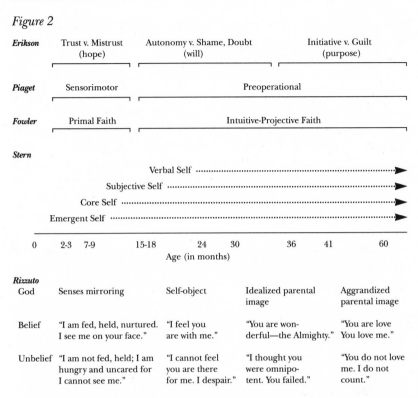

Erikson	Trust v. Mistrust (hope)	Autonomy v. Shame, Doubt (will)		Initiative v. Guilt (purpose)
Piaget	Sensorimotor	Preoperational		
Fowler	Primal Faith	Intuitive-Projective Faith		

Stern

Verbal Self ....➤
Subjective Self ....➤
Core Self ....➤
Emergent Self ....➤

0	2-3	7-9	15-18	24	30	36	41	60

Age (in months)

Rizzuto

God	Senses mirroring	Self-object	Idealized parental image	Aggrandized parental image
Belief	"I am fed, held, nurtured. I see me on your face."	"I feel you are with me."	"You are wonderful—the Almighty."	"You are love You love me."
Unbelief	"I am not fed, held; I am hungry and uncared for I cannot see me."	"I cannot feel you are there for me. I despair."	"I thought you were omnipotent. You failed."	"You do not love me. I do not count."

Let us look briefly at an overview of the four early senses of self in infancy you will find named in the middle section of figure 2. Momentarily I will return to them so that we can go into them in more detail. Please understand that Stern believes that these earliest senses of self have separable or distinct futures. That is to say, these different senses of self do not become homogenized or blended into one. Rather, each of these senses of self has its own future strand of integrity that will interrelate with the others. Let's look at these senses of self.

First, there's the sense of the *emergent self,* beginning from birth to about two months (Stern 1985, chap. 1). I think of this as the slender trunk of a tree that will continue to grow. Here the child starts to construct, from the beginning, a world that is different from the self. She experiences other persons as different from herself and responds to them in ways that indicate that she is already exercising capacities to create a permanent and stable "otherness." This is apparent whether it relates to the otherness of persons or the otherness of objects. In a moment we will see that babies show particular interest in the otherness of *persons,* even in the first two months.

Next, Stern points to a sense of a *core self.* One way to understand this, I think, is to see it as a *body self,* the infant's experience of being a body that is integral and coherent. This experience comes in the period of roughly two to six months.

Then there is a third sense of self that he calls the *subjective self,* or at times the *inter-subjective self.* This sense of self arises in the period of roughly seven to fifteen months. Here we have the emergence of an awareness of emotion, an awareness of feeling, in the self and others, and the beginning of the infant's concern to *attune* her feelings with those of others. This points to a first step in the child's ability to initiate and participate in experiences of emotional intimacy.

And finally there is the sense of the *verbal self:* Here Stern, as Erikson and Piaget did before him, attends to the revolution that occurs in the child's relations to others, self, and world that comes with language. Language acquisition brings a readiness for the communication and memory of experiences and meanings.

Each of these four senses of self has its own future. When he works with adult patients in psychiatry, Stern listens very carefully not just to the expressions of the verbal self, but also for the silences and for the themes that would indicate where repair is needed at the level of the *body self,* even for the adult. It may be that repair is needed for the *inter-subjective* or *core self,* neither of which is initially available to the verbal self. So each of these emergent selves has its own future, and each continues to be an important part of the knowing, the selfhood, the relating, and the faith of adult persons.

EMERGENT SELF AND THE BIRTH OF IMAGINATION

For our understanding of the child's growth in spiritual responsiveness and faith, I invite you to look with me more carefully at each these senses of self: Let us look first at the *emergent self* (Stern 1985, chap. 3). Perhaps you've begun to discern that the picture that Stern gives us of infancy differs in some important ways from the picture that Piaget and Erikson give us of the infant as a kind of undifferentiated entity in its environment. Piaget and Erikson write as though the infant is embedded in the relationship with Mother, Father, caretakers, and the objects of the world and does not attend to them as separate from the self. This is Piaget's *à dualistic* self-other relation. In contrast to what we have thought for a long time, Stern tells us that initially this is not so. From the beginning, Stern contends, the baby has a primal sense of separateness and otherness from those persons or objects that are not the self. What evidence do we have for this? Infants recognize, Stern finds, certain invariant properties of those persons who care for them. For example, newborns can distinguish smiling faces from surprised faces. In research, the infant will habituate to the smiling face and then will be intrigued, amused, or disturbed by the contrast provided by the surprised face. This provides evidence that babies conserve in memory the features that constitute those expressions on faces. Infants recognize certain properties of the smile, but they appear to have an innate preference for whole facial configurations. The young baby, prior to two months, evaluates the social world in terms of its conformity to or its discrepancy from previous patterns of experience. So from the beginning, it seems, we are constructing some sense of what is regular and what is to be depended on in the environment, and we note that which surprises us or deviates from our expectations.

Furthermore, there is good evidence that for babies the human form is more than a perceptual array in a kind of neutral sense. It is very early preferred by the child over nonhuman forms. By one month, infants prefer live faces to geometric ones. They seem to respond globally to animation, to complexity, and to the configurations of faces rather than to specific facial features. A smile alone, drawn on a geometric or flat surface, won't evoke very much response from the child. There seems to be an innate preference for the shape of faces. Further, infants under two months discriminate by smell their mothers' milk from the milk of other mothers. They discriminate their own mothers' voices from others, and they seem innately predisposed to select their mothers from all others.

Recently a person who works with very young infants told me about an extremely premature baby that had to be supported for a long period by an incubator. This meant long separations from the mother. But it happened that one of the physicians in the neonatal intensive care unit, a woman who worked with this child, had a voice whose timbre and quality were very similar to the infant's mother's. The medical staff noticed that when this particular physician was on shift, the baby's need for oxygen and other life support diminished markedly. The baby pinkened just at the sound of this particular doctor's voice. Then when this doctor left the shift, the baby sank down again and had to be supported by the machinery. In this very first period of our lives we are forming rudimentary patterns of attachment, and we seem to exert innate preferences for the human face and for *particular* human others.

Stern tells us that study of infant behavior provides further evidence for this construction of a coherent otherness. Infant experience involves *cross-modal* knowing. What do we mean by "cross-modal" knowing? This term refers to a kind of perceptual unity in which we integrate data from different senses, but seem automatically to translate the perceptions gained through one sense into correlation with the perceptions gained through another sense. How do we learn to do this complex activity? This capacity seems to be innately given, an extraordinary gift. As we look into this remarkable ability I suspect that we come close to the genesis of imagination—the creative linking of disparate elements of sensory experience into one. If faith involves the composing of a coherent and meaningful world and a sense of relatedness to a transcendent other, then imagination is an important, even foundational part of faith and spiritual relatedness. In this earliest period of infancy, we see the rudimentary manifestations of imagination—the capacity to link sensory input from one modality with that from another, so as to form an understanding that is not given in perception.

How do we know that children do this cross-modal knowing? Stern draws on experiments, brilliant in their simplicity, to illustrate this point. In one experiment, blindfolded infants are given one or another of two nipples—either a smooth nipple or a knurled nipple. They suck the particular nipple provided them, without having seen it. When the nipples are displayed before them, each infant will visually prefer the particular nipple that he or she was sucking. How does a baby know this? It involves the cross-modal transposition of the *felt* sense of the nipple, formed through tactile knowing with lips and tongue, to the *visual* sense of the nipple as seen.

In a second experiment we learn that at six weeks babies notice discrepancies between speech and lip movements. We've all seen films projected in such a way that the voice is just a little behind the movement of the mouth on the screen. Infants as early as six weeks of age note that lack of synchronization and find the impression it makes very disturbing. They already expect correlation between sound and the sight of lip movement.

THE CORE (BODY) SELF AND THE BIRTH OF RITUALIZATION

Now we turn to a second level of selfhood that awakens in infancy, the emergence of the *core self* (Stern 1985, chap. 4). This is the genesis of the body self. In terms of its contribution to faith and spirituality, I link this to the birth of ritualization. It constitutes the birth of the body's participation in the social construction of meanings. Somewhere between the second month and the eighth month, the infant first experiences abilities to move and control its body. In doing so, he acquires a sense of self as distinct from others. At this period he does not have the self as an object of reflection. This is not a reflective awareness of self. Rather, it is an experience of separateness from the other, and of the "otherness" of the other. Babies begin to experience being an integrated body, able to control their own actions, owning their feelings, and sensing the continuity of their self in relation to others.

Stern points to four basic aspects of this bodily sense of self: (a) There is the experience of *self-agency:* The baby can regularly reach for and bang a rattle and can meaningfully repeat that activity. He has a sense of the control of the body in being able to do that. This provides for (b) the experience of *self-coherence,* that one is a unified body with a kind of integrity. Whether mobile or still, the baby has a sense of being a non-fragmented, physical whole and seems to have a sense of boundaries and to experience a continuous location

31

of action associated with the self. (c) The baby soon begins to focus and be aware of *self-affectivity, self-feeling.* He begins to recognize patterns of feeling and emotion that are tied to the experience of self. Then (d) in a very rudimentary but important way, the baby begins to have a sense of *temporal continuity*—the expectation that things will repeat, that there is an order to things, and that there is a future to come.

All of these are indications of the formation of self as distinct from, or in differentiation from, others. This constitutes the first phase in the emergence of the core self. It comes at age six or seven months.

This second level of selfhood—the core self—involves the first experience of the self in its relationship with others (Stern 1985, chap. 5). Stern reminds us of the fact that from two to six months the experience of the baby—apart from when it is sleeping—is almost exclusively *social.* Perhaps the absence of mobility, the inability to move about on one's own, lends special significance to the social presence of others as being of primary importance to the baby at this age. In its orientation to sociality, the baby seems also to prefer higher-pitched voices and a close proximity of communication. These preferences help the child to succeed in recruiting the parents to participate in baby talk and face making, along with physical cuddling and loving.

This level of core self relatedness gives rise to two very interesting kinds of developments that Stern discerns in the infant's experience. First we learn of the phenomenon Stern calls *Representations of Interactions that have been Generalized* (RIGs). Earlier I likened the core self's emergence to the beginnings of ritualization. Here we see the infant convert regular social interactions into generalized patterns of familiarity and expectation. The baby comes to expect that these activities will be repeated and learns how to participate in them. We are seeing the beginnings of ritualization.

The essential structure of the game "peekaboo" is one of the RIGs that we form early in infancy. The great excitement about peekaboo becomes how to expand that "game" in innovative extensions of its basic pattern. There are many different ways that this kind of ritual interaction can be modified. But further, there is evidence that the infant is constructing RIGs that capture repeated patterns of action experienced with the parents and others with whom she regularly interacts. We can call these constructions *working models* of the parental figures, or significant others. These working models are dynamic. They continue to evolve and change as the infant has new experiences, and as she offers new initiatives in relation to the parents.

The construction of working models of others results in the forming of what Stern calls "evoked companions." The "evoked companion" refers to the child's sense of the self with others, even when the others are absent. The child feels the reassuring sense of the presence of the other, the reassuring other with the self, even when she is alone. The "evoked companion" brings a sense of the invisible presence of a self-other that can make her feel comfortably affirmed in her total self. Such relationships are embedded in specific episodes or interactional rituals that become generalized. Even before the seven- or eight-month time when Piaget tells us object permanence is fully acquired, there is the possibility, it seems, of constructing this evoked companion. This self-other model is not yet a true *transitional object*. To be that it would require more conscious symbolic activity than is possible here. But it is the construction of a reassuring presence. It makes possible a spiritual bond.

Ken Brockenbrough, a child psychologist, has suggested that that which we call the *numinous,* the sense of the presence of a divine, transcendent, and reassuring reality, has its origins in the experience of the "evoked companion." This seems to tie in with Erik Erikson's suggestion that in feeding or in nursing we have prolonged periods in which the infant's face and eyes encounter the mirroring presence of the animated eyes and face of the mother, father, or their substitute. This same presence, with its confirming regard, may be evoked as an antidote to anxiety when the child is alone, or as an exuberant observer when the child is actively engaging its environment.

THE SUBJECTIVE SELF AND THE BIRTH OF THE SOUL

This brings us to a third level of emergent selfhood: the sense of the *subjective self* (Stern 1985, chap. 6). Here we are present at what we may call the "birth of the soul." Until recently the concept of soul had fallen on hard times in the modern period, at least in Protestant Christian culture. We rarely used the term except for those who talked about the "eternal salvation of the soul." As important as that is, it is good that we are reclaiming an older sense of the soul as the seat of emotion, intuition, and receptivity to God, as well as to others, deep within us. Carl Jung and the contemporary Jungians James Hillman and Thomas Moore have contributed powerfully to this recovery. If we take this older understanding of soul seriously, we see that the emergence of the subjective self may properly be called the birth of the soul. Let me remind you that the Greek for "soul" is *"psyche."* So we speak of psychic states, soul states.

What is this subjective self? Here we see the emergence in interpersonal relations of shared frameworks and fantasies. Around seven to nine months, there is the beginning of the first deliberate sharing of psychic space between infants and those who care for them. How do we infer that there is a kind of intersubjectivity taking form here? We recognize mutual constructing and sharing of feelings because we observe infants and mothers demonstrating a shared attention to a third object or a third experience. A mother turns her head to look into another room at something distressing. Immediately the nine-month-old follows her gaze with attentive anxiousness. We also infer this awakening of soul intimacy through the child and mother's use of pre-linguistic expressions of shared intent. Further, we see clear evidences of shared *affect,* communicated both from the child to the parent and from the parent back to the child. And these can be shared in clearly celebrative ways.

Let me try to make these matters clearer. To recognize and share attention, intention, and feelings requires some shared framework of meaning, and some means of communication such as gestures, postures, and facial expressions. Here we are present at the birth of the construction of shared meanings, the juncture in the infant's life where psychic intimacy becomes a real possibility. At the same time, the infant begins to determine the extent of self-disclosure that he seeks. The infant begins to have some control regarding how much of his feelings will be expressed or shared. Again, this is not a conscious reflection and choice. It is more a kind of bodily and psychic response and initiative that the child experiences in an unreflective way.

What evidence supports Stern's emphasis and claims? First of all, we see evidence that infants do enter into experiences of shared *attention* with their caregivers. Murphy and Messer found that nine-month-olds both point and can follow the imaginary line extending from the pointing finger of the mother or others and look in the direction of the point (cited in Stern 1985, 129). Even earlier, infants are found to follow their mother's line of vision when she turns her head. More important, nine-month-olds will look back to the mother to confirm the accuracy of their own gaze. There is, then, a triangulation between two people and an object of their mutual interest and reference.

Second, Stern points to shared *intention:* Prior to language, infants will persistently signal, through some familiar posture or gesture, that an intent is meant to be understood by another. The most basic form of this is the child's reaching and pointing toward an object and saying, "Uh! Uh! Uh!" This may be the true beginning of language. But also babies give the signal for the beginning of familiar games, such as horsie or pat-a-cake. One-year-olds have repeatedly been noted to share some event with an older sibling by laughing, for reasons often unavailable to the adult observers of this mirthful scene. There can be a kind of teasing present here that adults often miss, suggesting shared mental and affective states among the siblings.

And then there is the important matter of shared *affect,* shared feelings. When a twelve-month-old faces an uncertain situation, such as a novel toy or a wall socket, or a steep set of descending stairs, she will likely refer to the gaze of her parent or her caretaker in order to determine how to proceed. If the caretaker's face communicates anxious dread or alarm, the baby's will also, and she will turn away from the new situation. This is true in completely novel situations; it seems not merely to be an associational imitation. Studies that Stern reports suggest that by nine months, infants are aware of the congruence or the fit between the facial expression of another and their own affective state. In one experiment, after a troubling separation from their mothers, children preferred to look at a sad face rather than a happy face. This occurs before many infants have seen or become familiar with their own facial expressions in a mirror. Evidence such as this signals a visual matching of mood and feeling, which is part of the cross-modal perspective taking of the infant. Stern tells us that affective exchange is the most powerful and pervasive of the three shared states during this period of the emergence of the intersubjective self.

This brings us to Stern's discussion of the important phenomenon he calls "affect attunement" (Stern 1985, chap. 7). Stern's most important contribution to our study of faith and selfhood may be his description of affect attunement as a recognition and restatement by the parent of the child's affective state. This is a complex operation and requires several important factors. First, there must be an accurate reading of the baby's behavior by the parent or other caretaker. Second, this requires an intimate history with the child's feelings, giving rise to the ability to participate in those feelings. Third, it requires the ability to respond with different, nonimitative, but accurate behaviors that signal to the infant that his or her affective states are understood. This means offering a response in a different mode, that says, "I'm reading you, and I'm responding in rhythm, in pattern, in resonance, in synchronicity with your feelings." And finally, for emotional attunement to occur the infant must be able to read and understand that response.

Attunement of this sort falls short of true empathy. It is not consciously mediated by cognitive processes that mentally separate the emotional state from the person. However, think how important, in a continuing way in our lives, this kind of affect attunement is, even between persons who are capable of verbal communication. And consider how sometimes our affect attunement gives us insights that our verbal communications obscure or distort. I find it fascinating to look at some of the instances that Stern and others have studied, in order to understand the ways infants interact with their primary caretakers in this business of emotional attunement. Let me give you a few examples: One of the prime ways that we indicate to children that we are resonating with them, or feeling with them, is through matching the intensity of our responses to the intensity of their actions. An example would be when the loudness of a mother's vocal response matches the force of an abrupt arm movement that an infant makes. Let me quote Stern's account here:

> A ten-month-old girl finally gets a piece in a jig saw puzzle. She looks toward her mother, throws her head up in the air, and with a forceful arm flap raises herself partly off the ground in a flurry of exuberance. The mother says, "YES, thatta girl." The "YES" is intoned with much stress. It has an explosive rise that echoes the girl's fling of gesture and posture. (Stern 1985, 141)

The mother's response says, "I see you! I rejoice with you! I share that exuberance!" Following the contour of the response, we see that the changes in intensity exhibited by the infant over time are matched by the changes in intensity of the other who responds. Another instance:

> A ten-month-old girl accomplishes an amusing routine with mother and then looks at her. The girl opens up her face (her mouth opens, her eyes widen, her eyebrows rise) and then closes it back, in a series of changes whose contour can be represented by a smooth arch. Mother responds by intoning, "Yeah," with a pitch line that rises and falls as the volume crescendos and decrescendos. (Stern 1985, 140)

Or take the case of "temporal beat," in which a regular pulsation in time is matched by the response of the parent:

> A nine-month-old boy bangs his hand on a soft toy, at first in some anger but gradually with pleasure, exuberance, and humor. He sets up a steady rhythm. Mother falls into his rhythm and says, "kaaaaa-*bam*, Kaaaaa-*bam*," the "*bam*" falling on the stroke and the "kaaaaa" riding with the preparatory upswing and the suspenseful holding of the arm aloft before it falls. (Stern 1985, 140)

These samples indicate the kind of cross-modal responses that signal attunement and build a mutuality of affect between caring ones and the infants. Attunement is a dynamic, ongoing process, rather than a discrete set of episodes or a categorical affect. In these ritualizations of behavior, we are seeing the emergence of pre-verbal, pre-symbolic, and yet protosymbolic activity. We are seeing communication at work here, through the use of analog and through the use of symbolic motions and movements. We are seeing the ritualization of a more conscious and collaborative sort between caretaker and infant.

The following paragraph from Stern suggests one of the most intriguing possibilities opened by his discussion of affect attunement. Referring to the innovative work of many French and Swiss thinkers regarding affect attunement, he talks about a dimension of this phenomenon that seems to me to have particular reference for faith and the spirit:

> They assert that mother's "meanings" reflect not only what she observes but also her fantasies about who the infant is and is to become. Intersubjectivity, for them, ultimately involves interfantasy. They have asked how the fantasies of the parent come to influence the infant's behavior and ultimately to shape the infant's own fantasies. This reciprocal fantasy interaction is a form of created interpersonal meaning at the covert level. The creation of such meanings has been called "interactions fantasmatique." (Stern 1985, 134)

This business of the mother's fantasies being available for the infant's attunement to them gives special significance to the eighteenth and nineteenth verses of the second chapter of Luke's Gospel. There it says, after the visit of the shepherds to the newborn and the mother, "And all who heard it wondered at the things which were told them by the shepherds. But Mary treasured up all these things, pondering them in her heart" (NASB).

The triadic structure of faith emerges with this intersubjective phase of selfhood. There is an attending to third realities between the parent and child, including shared fantasies as a third reality between them. And there is the sharing of meanings prior to language that relate to those "thirds." It is interesting to speculate on the contribution of the "evoked companion" we mentioned earlier—the reassuring sense of presence emergent at the core self level—to this more complex business of affect attunement and symbolization.

THE VERBAL SELF AND THE BIRTH OF SYMBOLIZATION

We come now to the fourth level of selfhood, the *verbal self* (Stern 1985, chap. 8). With the arrival of experience of the verbal self we can speak about the contribution to faith of the birth of *symbolization*. At age fifteen months, our oldest daughter, Joan—despite Freudian warnings against it—still lived in the bedroom of her mother and father, in a graduate student apartment where there was not another bedroom. She would wake up in the morning at about six o'clock—an annoying time for people who had studied late in the night—and awaken the world. Then she would proceed to reconstitute the world by naming it. She would stand in her crib and point at the light, and say "Yite!" and insist that there be a response from the sleepy Greek chorus in the bed—"Yes, that's a light. . . . " She would name the fifteen or eighteen objects in that room that she knew the names of. With this ritual exuberantly completed, her day could begin. The world had been reconstituted; it had been named; everything was in its place. We had shared this ritual of confirmation, and now we could get on with the day. We see the child making the ecstatic discovery that things *do* have names and that we can refer to them in ways other than pointing or grasping. Persons have names, and we can talk about things that aren't present to us, even about feelings and thoughts. What an exhilarating new step in life the emergence of language and conscious use of symbolization brings!

Note in figure 2 (page 26) that, for all of the theorists we are considering here, the point of the emergence of the verbal self corresponds with a watershed time. Erikson sees it as decisive in the transition from basic trust versus mistrust to autonomy versus shame and doubt. Piaget sees it as the hallmark of the transition from sensorimotor knowing to preoperational knowing. In faith development theory we see it as the threshold of transition from Primal to Intuitive-Projective faith. What is so significant about these beginnings of language, symbol, image, and representation?

The rise and use of verbal symbols is exhilarating and liberating, and yet it is full of potential for alienation, as well as for communication. Consider the power of language. We are no longer limited to pointing, gesturing, or making faces. It is no longer necessary to limit communication to objects that are present and concrete. We may refer to objects or persons who are away from us. We may begin to refer to feelings and to more intangible dimensions of our experience. We may begin to name and represent qualities of persons and relations. Of course all this begins in a rudimentary way; it begins quite concretely. But the capacities we have seen emerging with each of the levels of selfhood have underscored the importance of feelings in communication. They have also pointed to the natural precursors of symbolic communication and representation. We saw anticipations of this in the cross-modal capacities of the pre-linguistic child's shaping of experience. We saw it in the capacity to construct and be comforted by evoked companions. We saw it in the abilities to generalize from events and to shape working models of persons and rituals. And we saw it in the capacities for affect attunement. All of these qualities bespeak the forming of abilities to employ sign and symbol, metaphor and analog, narrative and meter.

Language and symbolization create wonderful new possibilities. They bring the ability to communicate about objects, persons, feelings, and shared understandings. They make possible the shared examination of aspects of our experienced world. They give us the capacity to stop our world and to interrogate it as an object of our experience. We gradually become able to hold dimensions of our experience up for our examination or for joint consideration with others. But our naming and symbolizations of experiences are never fully adequate or fully complete. Always, in our efforts at communicating our experiences, our knowledge, or our feelings, we must deal with a broad gap between what we see and feel, on the one hand, and what we can say, on the other.

Michael Polanyi, in his book *The Tacit Dimension*, states this succinctly: "We *know* more than we can *tell*" (Polanyi 1967, 4). He reminds us that much of our knowing and doing remain inaccessible both to our consciousness and to our ability to communicate. He calls these crucial aspects of our knowing the "tacit dimension." Our sense of self has deep and continuing parts that are preverbal at the levels of the core self and the subjective self. There are aspects of our selves and our meanings that are capable of verbal expression only at the cost of significant distortion and reduction. From eighteen months through early childhood we make remarkable progress at utilizing language and symbols to communicate with others. Nonetheless, in this early period, it remains a beginning process. We work a lifetime to bring our most significant knowing and experiencing to expression. Words and symbols are increasingly helpful to us, but there is always the danger—even the inevitability—that our verbal and symbolic expressions of self and our meanings are too limited to bring to word all of the richness and fullness of what we experience.

LANGUAGE AND SELFHOOD: THE DANGER OF THE FALSE SELF

The subjective self, which Stern has described prior to the advent of language, is experienced by the infant as separate from others. That sense of selfhood, however, is not yet an object for self-recognition. With the advent of symbol and language, the infant has at his or her disposal the tools to objectify, to distort, and to transcend experiences of the self and the world at large. What is this pre-linguistic child's experience of alienation or distortion, in the first year and a half? Stern makes vague references to "narcissistic injuries" experienced within the primary relationships, and he calls these "primitive agonies." These are unnamed agonies we undergo before we have the language to give voice to them, or the capacity to reflect and say, "I'm hurting." We have primitive agonies that we suffer without words, without ways of reflectively communicating about them. In some sense we simply *are* our agonies at this stage. Stern seems to suggest, however, that neurotic experiences of anxiety and the forming of distorting defense mechanisms come only after the experience of the self as object through the use of language. Stern recognizes that a child may experience disruption in core and intersubjective relatedness, but he insists that anxiety as "the fear of ceasing to be" or of ceasing to be loved entails positioning oneself, via representation and objectification, as an object in the immediate future. Therefore, he suggests, true anxiety experiences are a postlinguistic matter. Real anxiety comes after we have acquired a sense of the verbal self. Insofar as I understand Stern's position here, I think I differ with him. It seems to me that each level of emergent selfhood represents a place at which mutuality, worth, shared meanings, and organismic well-being are at stake and at risk for the young child. We are vulnerable at each of these levels. While the child's self-aware grasp of these experiences will not take form until after the advent of language, abuse or serious neglect experienced at any of these levels can have deep and lasting effects on the forming self.

In any case, with the advent of language new potentials for alienation and for the experiences of shame and doubt emerge. At eighteen months a child who has surreptitiously had a red spot of rouge placed on his or her nose will, upon seeing himself reflected in a mirror, point to the rouged spot on his own face. The child shortly afterward will use "I," "me," and "mine" in appropriate ways. Children at this age also will begin to manipulate replicas of family members—sets of dolls, which they will match with family members—and take an interest in family pictures. The child begins to recognize the self as a body self and to hold in memory representations of self and significant others (Stern 1985, 165-67). For the first time in his young life, the child is in a position to negotiate with the parent to determine how psychically transparent or isolated he will become in the quest for mutuality. A child now has the beginnings of reflective choice about what he will and will not disclose—what is safe to disclose and what is not safe to disclose.

The maintenance of one's integrity in the face of inner and outer experiences of threat can be attempted through potentially distorting defense mechanisms such as repression, disavowal, and denial. In each case where these distorting defense mechanisms emerge, a path between experience and feeling, between feeling and language, and between language and experience is broken or blocked. Defenses break the linkages between experience and feeling and language. And we can begin, consciously or unconsciously, in small or large ways, to deceive others and to deceive ourselves. This gives rise to the construction of what some have called a "false self" (D. W. Winnicott and Alice Miller, for instance). By this we mean a representation of self to self and others that makes existence possible and bearable in the midst of mildly or severely depriving, distorting, or abusive relational circumstances. The "false self" can be constituted in a necessary overidentification with the ideal images of self valued by those on whom the child is dependent for love and protection. It can, more seriously, result from the self's conforming to exceedingly harsh prohibitions or taboos on the expression of one's own needs or desires. The false self can adopt the twisted posture required in a family situation that places mutually contradictory demands upon the child—the classic "doublebind" situation.

The "false self" is a strategy for survival in a deeply threatened relational matrix. It severs the child's relation to and reliance upon his or her own preverbal experiences. Its defense strategies require the child's collusion—against a potentially truer self—with the structure of denials and lies of the crippled family's ways of relating. It gives rise to unreality and severe discontinuity between the past experiences of the subjective self and the present experiences of the objective self. If these patterns of defense persist, there is the likelihood that the false self will become ascendant. This may protect the woundedness or lack of the truer, preverbal self, but to some degree the child will be sundered, cut off from below, from those primal experiences of the earlier levels of selfhood that could fund and support further growth. Furthermore, the child will be cut off from above, from the consolidation toward a mutual future—from the formation and internalization of a firm sense of the truer self and the reliable presence of others within the self (see Stern 1985, 209-10, 227-28).

LANGUAGE, RITUALIZATION, AND MEANING

With the emergence of the verbal self, meaning is communicated by language and symbol. Meaning is created *between* others and the child in new levels of mutuality. This is Martin Buber's notion of the spiritual connection that arises and mediates between us in our relationships. This I-Thou quality of relatedness is the essence of symbolic and verbal mutuality. Just as language is a tool for distancing and separation, so also it is a tool for communion. Words represent the medium through which different minds and experience-worlds can be united in episodes of spiritual union and shared meaning. Katherine Nelson, Jerome Brunner, and their colleagues describe an episode where, upon the birth of a younger brother, the two-year-old sister devises all sorts of ways to keep the father present with her at bedtime. At his eventual departure, she adopts his tone and mannerisms in an ongoing monologue. Besides practicing his language patterns, she is demonstrating her internalization of her father's total presence. If successful, the child gains agency—she keeps Dad present. She gains autonomy, being able to relinquish his physical presence. She gains communion, because she now participates in his symbol system and mannerisms, all by way of this simple bedtime ritual (cited in Stern 1985, 172-74). This, then, is the opposite of alienation; it keeps her from having to construct a false self. The emanating power of becoming, coming up from below, meets with the transcendent or the numinous power of the future in language and ritual, and a relatively true self is consolidated in an early interpersonal relationship.

More than any other social scientist, Erikson has suggestively indicated the contribution that each developmental life stage makes to our total capacity as adults to be ritualizers and celebrators of shared meanings (Erikson 1977). In earliest infancy we come to our first awareness in the presence and under the care of powerful ones upon whom we are dependent. We come to awareness in the midst of everyday rituals—of feeding, tending and cleansing, of putting to bed and getting up—through which we are provided with care. But in these everyday rituals we also take the identity that is provided by the names we are given. In the mutuality of *re-cognition,* in which we are called by name and given a name to call our caregivers, we have the primordial experience of what Erikson calls the *numinous:* the mysterious, the transcendent. The experience of the numinous recalls our discussion of the sense of an evoked companion that is transcendent. Religious traditions and the institutions of religions have evolved in societies in order to take principal care of the rituals that relate us to the numinous. About the reenactment and ritual of our earliest experiences of knowing the Other, Erikson writes:

> [T]he believer, by appropriate gestures, confesses his dependence and his childlike faith and seeks, by appropriate offerings, to secure the privilege of being lifted up to the very bosom of the divine which,

indeed, may be seen to graciously respond with the faint smile of an inclined face. (Erikson 1977, 89-90)

For Erikson, one of the most primordial and recurring deep religious nostalgias of the human being is the longing for the face that blesses and the eyes that recognize. When we participate in such rituals as the Christian Eucharist, part of what we hunger for is that sense of recognition by the transcendent and for the blessing that comes through it. Identifying a fundamental and continuing element in all identity and ritualization, Erikson says, "The numinous assures us of a *separateness transcended* and yet also a *distinctiveness confirmed*" (Erikson 1977, 90). A separateness transcended—we really do belong to and participate in something cosmic and ultimate. And a distinctiveness confirmed—we really are separate creatures recognized and blessed as having their own dignity and worth. And both of those are held together. This, suggests Erikson, constitutes the basis of a spiritual sense of an "I" that is renewed by the mutual recognition of all that "Is" and joined in a shared faith in one all-embracing "I am."

If infancy offers our first experiences of the mutuality of ritualization and of the numinous, the next stage of toddlerhood and autonomy sees the emergence of a sense of law and lawfulness, which Erikson associates with the *judicious.* Recently I had occasion to give testimony in a federal courtroom and was struck again by the dignity, the majesty, and the "set-apartness" of the judicious. The judge sat behind a high bar, robed and distant in a kind of remote inaccessibility. We witnesses were kept outside the courtroom until our time to give testimony came. At the appropriate time we were ushered in by an officious bailiff. We solemnly swore to give true testimony; then we were seated in a high place before everyone's view.

This judicious dimension becomes an element in all ritualization; for, as Erikson points out, there is no ritual—up to the last judgment itself—that does not imply a severe discrimination between the sanctioned, the permitted, and the out-of-bounds. In this stage (toddlerhood), the child begins to form the awareness of taboo, the forbidden, the prohibited. The child learns to feel with the forbidden the inner sense of danger that one might become

45

the very kind of person against whom all prohibitions, taboos, and boundaries are established. In relation to these standards the child experiences the potential for falling into a negative identity. Theologically, we are in touch here with the emerging sense of *sins* in the plural, the danger of committing acts that are forbidden. We are also in touch with sinfulness, a pervasive sense of deficiency or defectiveness that threatens to lead us into the walled-off and the prohibited. Central in the ritualizations of this stage are experiences of a judicious authority who sets limits and judges in accordance with them, but who does so on the basis of love and protection, and out of the desire for righteousness—for right relationships.

Now consider the contributions to ritualization of the play age, Erikson's third stage of early childhood. Here fantasy and the children's capacities to pretend enable them to rehearse dramas of heroic and significant possible futures. Says Erikson, "Childhood play, in experimenting with self-images and images of otherness, is most representative of what psychoanalysis calls the *ego ideal.*" What is the ego ideal? Erikson calls it

> that part of ourselves which we can look up to, at least insofar as we can imagine ourselves as ideal actors in an ideal plot, with the appropriate punishment and exclusion of those who do not make the grade. Thus we experiment with and, in a visionary sense, get ready for a *hierarchy of ideal and evil roles* which, of course, go beyond that which daily life could permit us to engage in. (Erikson 1977, 101)

The dramatic and the playful capacities of this stage make us, potentially at least, creative and ready participants at any age in the dramas of sacrament and liturgy. Coupled with the high dignity of the judicious and the transcendent reality of the numinous, the dramatic enables us to join with others in corporate enactments and celebrations of the actuality, the presence, and the power of the holy.

EARLY CHILDHOOD AND THE "BIRTH OF GOD"

No account of the development of faith in childhood would be comprehensive enough if it neglected the formation of our representations of God. Ludwig Feuerbach, Friedrich Nietzsche, and Sigmund Freud offered powerful reductionistic accounts of "God's birth" as accounted for by our tendencies to project our human strength or our dependent needs onto the screen of the universe. For a rich account of our childhood constructions of images of God, I suggest we turn to the work of Ana-Maria Rizzuto and her book *The Birth of the Living God.* Dr. Rizzuto is both a devout Roman Catholic and a devout, but revisionist, Freudian psychoanalyst. For purposes of following this discussion, you may want to return to figure 2 (page 27), the bottom lines of which depict the flow of Rizzuto's thinking. For a moment, however, let me orient you to the principal thrusts of her book *The Birth of the Living God.*

Rizzuto claims that virtually all children, by the age of about six, construct an image or representation of God. Please understand that it is possible for us to have a representation of God in which we do not believe, or which we do not find sustaining. We are not saying that a child necessarily has a positive and a believable image of God—in the sense of having his or her heart attached to that representation. But almost every child, says Rizzuto, constructs such a representation. In our own research we have found this to be true.

One of the most interesting cases from my own research came when we interviewed the six-year-old daughter of a man and a woman who both happened to be the children of clergy. So negative had been this couple's early experiences of faith and church that they resolved that they would try to "protect" their own child from any exposure to religious language. They were going to try to raise a "healthy" child. When we interviewed their daughter, we found that their efforts to eliminate God from their child's environments had not succeeded. She had constructed a very interesting, if somewhat primitive, representation of God. While her spiritual hunger may have been innate, we found that there were two primary sources to stimulate her imagining of God. One was the television show *Bonanza,* then being shown regularly. If you remember that Western, with its story of life on the ranch with Little Joe, Hoss, and Pa Cartwright, occasionally weddings or funerals were depicted there. These apparently made strong impressions on this religion-deprived child. She was intrigued with the question to whom the prayers were offered, and what the hymns were about. Far more satisfying and informative to her was the Lutheran Church in America's *Davy and Goliath*, an animated television series in which a little boy named Davy and his dog Goliath had adventures from week to week. There she saw stories that portrayed the love and care Davy gave to friends and strangers, and she located the source of that care in God. Through listening to the prayers Davy and his parents offered, she formed a firm sense of being a friend of God. In pursuing her forbidden fascination, this little girl illustrated Rizzuto's claim that in our society virtually every child creates some kind of representation of God from a variety of sources.

Second, Rizzuto refutes and rejects Sigmund Freud's claim that the God representation comes from the boy's resolution of the Oedipal struggle and castration anxiety through the projection of a benign but stern father image onto the universe. She agrees that the projection dynamic is an important one to examine, but she rejects Freud's version of it for three reasons. First, it is incomplete in that it gives no account of how and why girls should construct God representations. Second, and equally serious, she claims that the God representation begins to take form before the Oedipal period, and has its origins earlier in the infant's life. Third, and most important, she suggests that God representations, based on her research, partake of both the parental imagoes, both the mother and the father, and perhaps other significant adults who are present in the life of the child as well.

Rizzuto offers a third thesis: The representation of God, she says, takes form in the space between parents and the child. This is the same space in which D. W. Winnicott says we construct "transitional objects." What are transitional objects? This British object-relations terminology provides a very mechanistic language for talking about our relations to the human beings who are most significant to us. When we speak about transitional objects, we are talking about symbolic representations of our relatedness to important other persons. The Linus blanket that the toddler drags around is a transitional object, symbolizing the security, the care, and the assurance of return of his or her parents. The teddy bear can be a transitional object that symbolizes the qualities of steadfastness, innocence, and love the child counts on from parents or extended family. God takes form in that same transitional space, says Rizzuto, and becomes a transcending representative of a dependable presence and confirming "constancy."

What kind of transitional object is God? Rizzuto in her fourth thesis asserts that God is a very particular and unique kind of transitional object. Children construct many others—images of monsters, representations of the devil, depictions of superheroes— all of which are transitional objects that capture their imagination at certain periods in their childhood. But God is different from all of these. This is because with God there is no physically present "other" on which the symbolization can be projected. Of course for Christians there are pictures of Jesus. When we interviewed four-, five-, and six-year-olds from Catholic Christian families and asked them about God, occasionally one would go and get a picture of Jesus and bring it back to show us. The transitional object does have a face for that child. But for many others God does not have a face, as was the case with the four-year-old who, when we asked her about God, said that "God is everywhere; God is like the air." She had no physical representation for God.

There is no tangible model on which God can be based. Another significant difference between God and the other transitional objects we mentioned—the devil, monsters, superheroes, witches, and so forth—is that there is an adult world that takes God very seriously. There are cathedrals, art and architecture, solemn ceremonies, and impressive people standing in resplendent pulpits, wearing elaborate garments, and using their most adult voices, addressing this Other. There are powerful "actualizations" of the reality of God inviting children to construct their mental and emotional representations of God.

At about two and a half, says Rizzuto, at about the time language begins to flourish as a medium for examining the environment, children make the discovery that human beings create and cause things to be. Here begins that line of questions that we are all familiar with. What is this? Who made it? Why? Where did it come from? What's it for? That unending series of questions that children can generate about the origins and reasons for things often leads back to the point where the parent either loses patience or cannot say where this came from, and so we say, "God made it; God is the creator." And the child begins to learn that no one created God. Like Aristotle, the child constructs his or her own notion of the Unmoved Mover, *the primum mobile.*

How does the child construct this transitional object we call God? Rizzuto suggests that when the child looks for analogs of an almighty, mysterious, transcendent, caring, or dangerous Other, the child draws on those experiences he or she has had of those qualities, especially with his or her parents. The composing of the child's representation of God employs the child's experiences with the parents or their surrogates. The child constructs a representation of God that has some of the characteristics of the parental figure or figures.

The God representations children form based on their parental models have not only some of the strengths and virtues but also some of the flaws and blind spots of the parental imagoes. Rizzuto suggests that children do idealize their representations of God so as to correct and compensate for some of the deficiencies of the actual parents. In fact, God representations can do a great deal to replace, restore, and heal the wounds from absent or badly distorting parents. In an early round of interviews about ten years ago, repeatedly we found a certain group of persons who had lost one parent or the other before the age of five. We found that often these persons had constructed a representation of God to which they had attached immense power. So deep going and primal was their attachment to God that we called them "totalizers," persons whose relationship to God was so integral to their selfhood that they could more easily imagine the loss of the self than they could imagine loss of God. The conception of a faith that contained doubt had very little meaning for these persons. This may have occurred because their God-representation had played such a significant part in their finding and maintaining a sense of security after the death of a parent.

Examine now the lower part of figure 2 for a brief look at Rizzuto's account of the relationship between the construction of a God-representation and the possibilities of belief and unbelief from her psychoanalytic standpoint. You see that in the very first stages of infancy, corresponding with the emergent and core self, the experiences on which the child would draw to construct a God-representation involve sensory experience and the mirroring eyes and responses of those who provide primary care. For those who find a God-representation in which they can rest their hearts, in which they can believe, experiences connected with being fed, held, nurtured, and being reflected and mirrored seem to be very important. And the opposite of that seemed to be a factor in those who have a God-representation that is not nurturing and not believable.

At the period of constancy or consolidation of the self, around twenty-four to thirty months, we see a God-representation that in some ways replicates and re-enforces the relationship between the self and the dependable objects, the dependable other persons, in one's life. The constancy that one has experienced or that one longs for with significant caretakers in one's life is projected onto a God-representation, if there has been enough of that constancy to allow that association to occur. And then we begin to have a true "transitional object" relation to God: "I feel you are with me, even when others I rely upon are not." The obverse of that, where that kind of constancy has not been available to the child, brings consistent feelings that "I cannot feel you; I cannot feel that you are there for me; I despair."

Around age four, Rizzuto theorizes, the child finds a kind of objectification of God in symbolic representations that can be *idealized* so as to compensate for parental deficiencies. This makes for a more secure world in the midst of the insecurity of discovering death. We have here God constructed in terms of idealized parental images. "You are wonderful. You are the almighty," or the opposite of that.

And then around age five, a kind of realism about both the parents and the self emerges and God becomes less idealized. God becomes identified, in Rizzuto's view, with the experience of love and being loved or its opposite. There is much more to be said about Rizzuto's account. It offers us a very rich and provocative extension of our look at faith and selfhood in earliest childhood.

51

CONCLUSION

It is our great privilege, as parents, teachers and friends of young children, to be allies of the potential for wholeness with which children are created. I draw, from this extensive examination of various perspectives on early childhood development in selfhood and faith, the following observations:

1. Children are inherently social from conception, and they are evolved and gifted by our Creator—normally—with capacities for recruiting and responding to adults and siblings in relations of true mutuality. Patterns of distortion and dis-ease are deviations from, not manifestations of, children's potentials.

2. Parents and other significant adults are far more important in the earliest months and years of children's lives than many of us have been taught. It is not that we adults "imprint" or mold the child, as some behaviorist psychologies would suggest. All the students of child development we have drawn upon recognize that child development is a profoundly *interactive* matter, the children taking a great deal of constructive initiative in our relations with them. But our initiatives and responses—and our provision of "holding environments" enriched with language, stories, and love—are of immeasurable importance in the development of selfhood and faith.

3. Attention to the preverbal emergence of the different "senses of self" that Stern has identified may provide us with access to the genesis of some of the central dynamics of faith and religious participation. The cross-modal knowing of the infant under two months of age gives us clues to the beginnings of imagination. The generalization of interactions and construction of the "evoked companion" during the emergence of the "core self" suggest the origins of ritual and the sense of the "numinous." Affect attunement in the first and second years of life suggests the genesis of shared meanings and the birth of the soul. The beginning use of language and symbols in the emergence of the verbal self points the origins of symbolization in faith and religious participation.

4. The account of children's composing of the image of God, drawn principally from Rizzuto, helps us to see—without reductionism—how we form the central religious symbol of our culture

and of our lives. Her findings about the ways children's God-representations incorporate aspects of their parents' ways of being underlines the role of adults as means of grace and revelation for children. It also makes us more deeply mindful of how, in our weaknesses, neglect or abuse, we can deeply impair our children's emerging faith and cripple their spirits.

CHAPTER TWO

STAGES OF FAITH AND EMOTIONS

W e have looked at the forming of faith and selfhood in the earliest months and years of childhood. At each of the phases of development we examined, we could see and sense the interplay of emotions and feelings with thought and knowing. We also attended to the vital importance of the child's interactions with others—especially those providing the primal relations of caring for and confirming the child in her or his growth and construction of ways of experiencing and becoming an actor on the stages of their shared life.

I intentionally use the term "stages" in a double sense. First, I use it to refer to the phases or recognizably different levels of activity and understanding the child experiences in psychosocial growth. But second, "stages" also refers to the theaters of interplay and interaction the growing child shares with the significant people in her or his young life.

As one's life continues to unfold, new stages, in both these senses, come into view. The genetic ground plan that equips the maturing person with new capacities, new degrees of readiness, brings the new stages we call toddlerhood, early childhood, the school years, and adolescence, and then on into the stages of adulthood. These developmental stages find their actualization on widening stages of social and institutional interaction. The world widens and becomes more complex as we traverse these stages. We become more self-reflective and aware of ourselves as relating to others; we take on many roles and responsibilities. The dramas on these widened stages give our lives their joys and sorrows, their triumphs and defeats. To participate in these dramas of our lives we both find and help to create the stories we are living. None of us is the sole author of the stories that compose our life. We interlive with others; we find roles in institutions and communities; we emerge onto the stages of our lives entering into dramas that are already underway. We must find our roles and find ways to help shape or reshape the larger stories that embrace us.

Now we turn to a perspective that gives us language and a framework for naming and modeling the changes that faith and selfhood, formed in early childhood, continue to embrace as we progress in age and as we move onto the succession of stages (in both senses) of our lives. In this telling of the story of the stages of our life, the theories of Erikson and Piaget, whom we met in the previous chapter, will continue to help guide us. Other students of human development will be introduced as we proceed. The bulk of the research on which this chapter is based I have carried out, along with many research associates and graduate students, across more than two decades. In this fresh telling of the story of our development in faith, you will find a new explicitness about the emotions and feelings that accompany our shaping and reshaping of the patterns of faith and selfhood that we bring to our lives' stages.

FAITH, SELFHOOD, AND THE MAKING OF MEANING

Faith development theory and research have focused on a multi-dimensional construct for faith that sees it as foundational to social relations, to personal identity, and to the making of personal and cultural meanings (Fowler 1980, 1986a, 1986b, 1987, 1989, 1991, 1995). Faith, we claim, is a generic feature of human beings. In order to make this claim credible, we must take some care to distinguish faith from two related patterns of human action that are often treated as synonymous with faith: *belief* and *religion. Belief,* in the modern period, has come increasingly to mean the giving of intellectual assent to propositional statements that codify the doctrines or ideological claims of a particular tradition or group. While belief may be an aspect of a person's or group's faith, it is only a part. Faith includes unconscious dynamics as well as conscious awareness. It includes deep going emotional dimensions as well as cognitive operations and content. Faith is both more personal and more existentially defining than belief, understood in this modern sense.

Religion, as distinguished from faith, may be thought of as a cumulative tradition composed from the myriad beliefs and practices that have expressed and formed the faith of persons in the past and present. The components of a cumulative tradition can include art and architecture; symbols, rituals, narrative, and myth; scriptures, doctrines, ethical teachings, and music; practices of justice and mercy; and much more. Elements from a cumulative tradition can be the source of awakening and forming for the faith consciousness of persons in the present. A current generation's drawing upon and being formed by elements from a cumulative tradition make for a reciprocity of mutual vitalization and commitment. In the long evolution of humankind the tie between faith and religion has generally been inextricable. It is only in the modern period, in which many persons have separated themselves from religious communities and religious faith, that we need to distinguish between religious faith and faith in a more generic and universal sense.

Faith, understood in this more inclusive sense, may be characterized as an integral, centering process, underlying the formation of beliefs, values, and meanings, that (1) gives coherence and direction to persons' lives, (2) links them in shared trusts and loyalties with others, (3) grounds their personal stances and communal loyalties in a sense of relatedness to a larger frame of reference, and (4) enables them to face and deal with the limit conditions of human life, relying upon that which has the quality of ultimacy in their lives.

The foregoing way of thinking about faith is meant to be as formal and inclusive as possible. It aims to include descriptions of religious faith as well as the less explicit faith orientations of persons and groups who can be described as secular or eclectic in their belief and values orientations. This non-content-specific characterization of faith correlates with the formal intent of the descriptions of the stages of faith we will be looking at in a moment. *The stages aim to describe patterned operations of knowing and valuing that underlie our consciousness.* The varying stages of faith can be differentiated in relation to the degrees of complexity, of comprehensiveness, of internal differentiation, and of flexibility that their operations of knowing and valuing manifest. In continuity with the constructive developmental tradition, faith stages are held to be *invariant, sequential,* and *hierarchical.* I do not claim for these stages *universality.*

STAGES OF FAITH: AN OVERVIEW

In the following descriptions of the faith stages and the changes they bring, I want to acknowledge the complex interplay of factors that must be taken into account if we are to begin to understand faith development. These include biological maturation, emotional and cognitive development, psychosocial experience, and religio-cultural influences. New knowledge of brain functioning in cognitive and emotional behavior is beginning to open a rich field for inquiry regarding neurophysiological dynamics underlying faith. Because development in faith involves aspects of all these sectors of human growth and change, movement from one stage to another is not automatic or assured. Persons may reach chronological and biological adulthood while remaining best defined by structural stages of faith that would most commonly be associated with early or middle childhood or adolescence. Now to descriptions of the faith stages.

Primal Faith (Infancy)

As we look at this brief description of the earliest stage of faith, I hope you will keep in mind the much richer explorations of this stage, and the next, we pursued in the previous chapter. Here we must describe the development of faith and selfhood during the first months of life more telegraphically: In this first stage a pre-linguistic disposition of trust forms in the mutuality of one's relationships with parents and other caregivers to offset the inevitable anxiety and mistrust that result from the succession of cognitive and emotional experiences of separation and self-differentiation that occur during infant development. Experiences combining to form this trusting disposition include body contact and care; vocal and visual interplay; ritualized interactions associated with early play, feeding and tending; and the development of interpersonal affect attunement in the infant's relations with caregivers. Factors such as these activate pre-potentiated capacities for finding coherence and reliability in self and primal others, for forming bonds of attachment with them, and for shaping a predisposition to trust the larger value and meaning commitments conveyed in parental care. Anxiety and mistrust have their own developmental pattern of emergence, which caregivers' consistency and dependability help to offset (Erikson 1963; Stern 1985; Fowler 1989).

Infants only gradually achieve self/object differentiation in the era of Primal faith. Their experiences of mutuality, of consistent and undistorted mirroring, and of the informal rituals that convey meaning and dependability do much to confirm children's sense of being "at home" in their life spaces. Significant deficits and distortions in the relational environments of infants can, of course, undermine or put at risk bodily and emotional well-being and give rise to a foundational mistrust of self, others, and the larger environment.

Intuitive-Projective Faith (Early Childhood)

From the time children begin to use language to communicate about self and objects in the world, we see the emergence of a style of meaning making based upon an emotional and perceptual ordering of experience. Imagination, not yet disciplined by consistent logical operations, responds to story, symbol, dream, and experience. It attempts to form images that can hold and order the mixture of feelings and impressions evoked by the child's encounters with the newness of both everyday reality and the penumbra of mystery that surrounds and pervades it. Death becomes a conscious focus as a source of danger and mystery. Experiences of power and powerlessness orient children to a frequently deep existential concern about questions of security, safety, and the power of those upon whom they rely for protection. Due to naive cognitive egocentrism, children do not consistently differentiate their perspectives from those of others. Lacking simple perspective-taking skills and the ability to reverse operations, children do not understand cause-and-effect relations well. They construct and reconstruct events in episodic fashion. Fantasy and make-believe are not distinguished from factuality. Constructions of faith are drawn to symbols and images of visible power and size. Stories that represent the powers of good and evil in unambiguous fashion are prized; they make it possible for children to symbolize and acknowledge the threatening urges and impulses that both fascinate and terrify them, while providing an identification with the vicarious triumphs of good over evil that such stories as fairy tales can provide (Bettelheim 1977). There is in this stage the possibility of aligning powerful religious symbols and images with deep feelings of terror and guilt, as well as of love and companionship. Such possibilities give this stage the potential for forming deep going and long lasting emotional and imaginal orientations—both for good and for ill.

From psychodynamic perspectives this stage begins with the time of first self-consciousness. Standing on one's own two feet, being aware of being seen and evaluated by others, and being attentive to standards for how things are supposed to be makes the child especially sensitive to the twin polarities of pride and shame. At about this time, children undertake the construction of their first representations of God. As we saw earlier, Ana-Maria Rizzuto's research suggests that these earliest God representations are populated with the dominant emotional characteristics children have experienced in their relations with those all-powerful ones upon whom they feel absolutely dependent—namely, the imagoes of their parents. Where defenses like splitting and dissociation have been necessitated by parental or other abuse or neglect, either God is likely to undergo splitting as well or the child constructs images of the "bad" self as being the deserving recipient of the inevitable—and deserved—punishment of a demanding but justifiably angry God. Where inadequate mirroring in the previous stage has resulted in an empty or incoherent sense of self, or where conditions of worth and esteem are such that the child must suppress his or her own processing of truth and experience, we often see the forming of a "false self" (Kohut 1977; Miller 1981; Winnicott 1971). In faith terms this can correlate with constructions of God along the lines of a taskmaster deity who requires performance and perfection, or shame and guilt about failures, for one to qualify for grace and approval.

Mythic-Literal Faith (Middle Childhood and Beyond)

Though the emotive and imaginal funding of the previous stage is still operative in this newly emerging stage, concrete operational thinking (Piaget) makes possible more stable forms of conscious interpretation and shaping of experience and meanings. Operations of thought can now be reversed, which means that cause-and-effect relations are now more clearly understood. Simple perspective taking emerges, which ensures that the differentiation of one's own experiences and perspectives from those of others becomes a dependable acquisition. The young person constructs the world in terms of a new "linearity" and predictability. Though still a potent source of feelings, the previous stage's store of images gets "sealed over," and its episodic, intuitive forms of knowing are subordinated to more logical and prosaic modes.

In this Mythic-Literal stage the child, adolescent, or adult does not yet construct the interiority—the feelings, attitudes, and internal guiding processes—of the self or others. Similarly, one does not construct God in particularly personal terms, or attribute to God highly differentiated internal emotions and interpersonal sensitivities. In making sense of the larger order of things, therefore, this stage typically structures the ultimate environment—the cosmic pattern of God's rule or control of the universe—along the lines of simple fairness and moral reciprocity. God is constructed on the model of a consistent, caring, but just ruler or parent. Goodness is rewarded; badness is punished.

In gathering its meanings, this stage employs narrative. Story (and stories) is as close as the Mythic-Literal stage comes to reflective synthesis. Persons at this stage, whether children, adolescents, or adults, do not carry out extensive synthetic reflection upon their stories. They offer narratives from the middle of the flowing streams of their lives. They do not step out upon the banks to reflect upon where the streams have come from, where they are going, or what larger meanings might give connection and integrated intelligibility to their collection of experiences and stories. In this stage, the use of symbols and concepts remains largely concrete and literal. The Mythic-Literal stage begins to wane with the discovery that ours is not a "quick payoff" universe—in other words, evil or bad persons do not necessarily suffer for their transgressions, and often "bad things happen to good people." We have coined the term "eleven-year-old atheists" for children who, in having this latter experience, temporarily or permanently give up belief in a God built along the lines of simple cosmic moral retribution.

Synthetic-Conventional Faith (Adolescence and Beyond)

Accompanying the exploding physical, glandular, and sexual changes brought on by adolescence, there can also be revolutions in cognitive functioning and in interpersonal perspective taking. With the emergence of early formal operational thinking (Piaget and Inhelder 1969) a young person's thought and reasoning take wings. Capable of using and appreciating abstract concepts, young persons begin to think about their thinking, to reflect upon their stories, and to name and synthesize their meanings.

In this period we see the emergence of mutual interpersonal perspective taking (Selman 1974, 1976). "I see you seeing me; I see the me I think you see." And the obverse can also be appreciated: "You see you according to me; you see the you you think I see." This capacity can make youths acutely sensitive to the meanings they seem to have to others and to the evaluations those meanings imply. Identity and personal interiority—one's own and others'—become absorbing concerns. *Personality,* both as style and as substance, becomes a conscious issue. From within this stage youth construct the ultimate environment in terms of the personal. God-representations can be populated with personal qualities of accepting love, understanding, loyalty, and support during times of crisis. During this stage youths develop attachments to beliefs, values, and elements of personal style that link them in conforming relations with the most significant others among their peers, family, and other adults. Identity, beliefs, and values are strongly felt, even when they contain contradictory elements. However, they tend to be espoused in tacit rather than explicit formulations. At this stage, one's ideology or worldview is lived and asserted; it is not yet a matter of critical and reflective articulation.

Where earlier deficits in the self, its emotional life, and its patterns of object relations have not been worked through and healed, they become factors that can inhibit the use of cognitive abilities in the tasks of identity and ideology construction in adolescence. Between the emotional and cognitive functioning of adolescents or adults, we frequently see splits that are directly attributable to such unresolved issues and relations from early childhood. Sometimes the potential of God as a constructive self-object must be jettisoned because God can only be emotionally populated with the shaming or narcissistic qualities of our earliest and most salient object relations.

One decisive limit of the Synthetic-Conventional stage is its lack of *third-person perspective taking.* This means that in its dependence upon significant others for confirmation and clarity about its identity and meaning to them, the self does not yet have a transcendental perspective from which it can see and evaluate self-other *relations.* In the Synthetic-Conventional stage the young person or adult can remain trapped in the "Tyranny of the They." We will deal with this issue and its implications for therapeutic work in the next section.

Individuative-Reflective Faith (Young Adulthood and Beyond)

For this stage to emerge, two important movements must occur, together or in sequence: First, the previous stage's tacit system of beliefs, values, and commitments must be critically examined. The configuration of meanings assembled to support one's selfhood in its roles and relations must now be allowed to become problematic. Evocative symbols and stories by which lives have been oriented will now be critically weighed and interpreted. Second, the self, previously constituted and sustained by its roles and relationships, must struggle with the question of identity and worth apart from its previously defining connections. This means that persons must take into themselves much of the authority they previously invested in others for determining and sanctioning their goals and values. It means that definitions of the self that are dependent upon roles and relationships with others and with groups must now be regrounded in terms of a new quality of responsibility that the self takes for defining itself and orchestrating its roles and relations.

At the heart of this double movement in the transition to the Individuative-Reflective stage is the emergence of *third-person perspective taking*. This capacity generally emerges out of the conflict of voices of external or internalized authorities. With its transcendental view of one's self-other relations, the third-person perspective allows one a standpoint from which conflicting expectations can be adjudicated and one's own inner authorization can be strengthened.

To sustain their reflective identities, persons in this stage compose (or ratify) meaning frames that are conscious of their own boundaries and inner connections and aware of themselves as worldviews. Utilizing their capacities of procedural knowing and critical reflection, persons of the Individuative-Reflective stage "demythologize" symbols, rituals, and myths, typically translating their meanings into conceptual formulations. Frequently overconfident in their conscious awareness, persons of this stage attend minimally to unconscious factors that influence their judgments and behavior. This excessive confidence in the conscious mind and in critical thought can lead to a kind of "cognitive narcissism" in which the now clearly bounded, reflective self over-assimilates "reality" and the perspectives of others into its worldview.

We see a fair number of persons—most frequently though not exclusively men—whose emotional development exhibits arrest at a stage at least as limited as the operations of the Mythic-Literal stage. At the same time, their cognitive functioning exhibits the selective use of operations that correlate with the Individuative-Reflective stage. Confident and authoritative in their professional and occupational domains, these persons are often unaware of the sharp limits of their empathy and their abilities to construct and identify with the interior feelings and processes of others. Religiously, these persons are often drawn to the rigidities and seemingly unambiguous teachings of Fundamentalism and of authoritarian leaders. (We should remind ourselves that there are liberals and radicals as well as conservatives with Fundamentalist spirits.) As spouses, parents, and bosses, such persons are at best insensitive and at worst rigid, authoritarian, and emotionally abusive.

Lack of attention and access to their own unconscious processes often brings persons best described by the Individuative-Reflective stage to a place of emotional burnout due to the burdens of the continual conscious process of maintaining the self and its boundaries. This especially characterizes those who in early childhood constructed a successful "false self" that has served as a life script for their journey well into adulthood. The wear and tear of maintaining personal boundaries, without access to the "heart" they suppressed in adopting the parental or cultural program, becomes a serious drain. Only through therapeutic and spiritual interventions that invite the naming of, the grieving over, and the expression of anger at the terrible price they have paid for approval can the energy tied up in defenses and the maintenance of the false self be released. These are prerequisite steps to restoring access to the recovered heart and spirit, and to beginning to claim the reconstituted will and energy required for the healthy narcissism of midlife (Kohut 1977, 1984).

Conjunctive Faith (Early Midlife and Beyond)

The name of this stage implies a rejoining or a union of that which previously has been separated. The name comes from Nicolas of Cusa (1401–64), who wrote about what he called the *coincidentia oppositorum,* the "coincidence of opposites" in our apprehensions of truth. The confident clarity about the boundaries of self and faith that the Individuative-Reflective stage worked so hard to achieve must be relinquished in the move to the Conjunctive stage. The executive ego, which claims authority for its own decisions and selectively affirms values and beliefs that it finds acceptable, must come to terms with the fact that its confidence is based at least in part upon illusion or upon seriously incomplete self-knowledge. We are many selves: We *have* a conscious mind, but we also *are* a great deal of patterned action and reaction that is largely unconscious. These powerful and important unconscious aspects of selfhood are personal, social, cultural, and perhaps archetypal in origin. We are driven and pushed, as well as funded, from underneath by motives, desires, hungers, and lures of the spirit, which we have difficulty recognizing and integrating.

In the transition to the Conjunctive stage one begins to make peace with the tension arising from the realization that truth must be approached from a number of different directions and angles of vision. Faith must learn to maintain the tensions between these multiple perspectives, refusing to collapse them in one direction or another. In this sense, faith must begin to come to terms with indissoluble paradoxes: the strength found in apparent weakness; the leadership that is possible from the margins of societies and groups but not from the center; the immanence *and* the transcendence of God.

Conjunctive faith exhibits a kind of epistemological humility. The realities that religious rituals, symbols, and metaphors seek to bring into our reach spill over in excess and recede behind them in simultaneous disclosure and concealment. This stage marks a movement beyond the demythologizing strategy of the Individuative-Reflective stage. Acknowledging the multidimensionality and density of symbols and myth, persons in the Conjunctive stage learn to enter into symbolic realities, allowing them to exert their illuminating and mediating power. Instead of "reading" and "analyzing" the symbols, metaphors, and narratives, they learn to submit to the "reading" and illumination of their situations that these and other elements of tradition can offer. In what Paul Ricoeur has called a "second" or a "willed" naiveté, persons of the Conjunctive stage manifest a readiness to enter into the rich dwellings of meaning that true symbols, ritual, and myth offer. As a correlate of these qualities, this stage exhibits a principled openness to the truths of other religious and faith traditions.

Until recently, only the Jungian traditions, among analytic perspectives, provided much help in the transition to the Conjunctive stage. Overimpressed with autonomous individualism and with the rejection of the neuroses associated with conventional religion, humanistic psychologies tended to run out at this point of transition. Freud illumined many of the paradoxes that arise from trying to strengthen the slender abilities of rationality to mediate between the imperious demands of the id and the harsh constraints of the superego. But his vision of maturity scarcely got beyond the maintenance of a kind of armed truce.

While Jung may have underestimated the wily resistance and cunning conservatism of the personal unconscious and its defenses, his teachings about the midlife process of individuation have much to commend them. His notions and teachings about how to work at integrating such archetypal complexes as the shadow, the contrasexual element, the wise elder, and the archetype of the Self itself are important. Transition to the Conjunctive stage involves the embrace of what Carlyle Marney once called a necessary "ego leak." It requires nurturing methods of meditation and therapy that nurture a safe permeability of the defensive membrane that separates conscious from the nonconscious. There must be a context of love and grace that makes it safe to bring the deepest insults of body and soul from previous experience into the sunlight of a presence that can dissolve the strain of bypassed shame, even as it is being named, raged over, and grieved. Such psychotherapy cannot do its work, I believe, without acknowledging the spiritual nature of its task, and without reliance upon a spirit of love and acceptance, of healing and forgiveness, beyond the powers of humans alone.

Universalizing Faith (Midlife and Beyond)

This stage involves persons moving beyond the paradoxical awareness and embrace of polar opposites that are hallmarks of the Conjunctive stage. The structuring of this stage derives from the radical completion of a process of de-centration from self that proceeds throughout the sequence of stages. From the non-differentiation of self and objects in the earliest phases of infancy to the naive egocentrism of the Intuitive-Projective stage, each successsive stage marks a steady widening in social perspective taking. Gradually the circle of "those who count" in faith, meaning making, and justice has expanded until, at the Conjunctive stage, it extends well beyond the bounds of social class, nation, race, gender, ideological affinity, and religious tradition. In Universalizing faith this process comes to a kind of completion. In the previous stage persons continue to live in the tension between their rootedness in and loyalties to their segment of the existing order, on the one hand, and the inclusiveness and transformation of their visions toward a new ultimate order, on the other. The Conjunctive self is a tensional self.

Persons found in the Universalizing stage are relatively rare. What I am going to say about the qualities they exhibit may remind some of you of William James's discussion of "Saintliness" in lectures 11-15 in *The Varieties of Religious Experience*. Psychodynamically, the self in this Universalizing stage moves beyond usual forms of defensiveness and exhibits an openness based on groundedness in the being, love, and regard of God. I need to say that such persons continue to be finite creatures. They have blind spots, inconsistencies, and they still exhibit some distorted capacities for relations with others. Nonetheless, if they have done the work of healing and reintegration that the previous stages require, they cannot be confused with those dangerously charismatic figures who exhibit the kind of manipulative dissociations and psychotic pseudo-authority we have seen in the Jonestown and Waco tragedies. A good test for distinguishing the authentic faithful leader from the dangerously charismatic copy is whether the leader requires regressive dependence and relinquishing of personal responsibility from his or her followers. Similarly, the authentic spirituality of the Universalizing stage avoids polarizing the world between the "saved" and the "damned." Persons of this stage are as concerned with the transformation of those they oppose as with the bringing about of justice and reform.

SHIFTING STAGES: THE CHALLENGES OF TRANSITION AND CHANGE

In the preceding section, I have described the stages of faith almost as though they were snapshots in a photo album, rather than connected scenes in an unfolding drama, depicting our movement from one stage to another, involving struggle and "dark nights of the soul." Yet I have claimed that faith is a dynamic process, close to the center of the self, that continually works to enable us to deal with the challenges and changes life presents us. It is now time to speak of these *dynamics* of faith—the transitions and the transformations of faith.

To be "in" a given stage of faith means to have a characteristic way of finding and giving meaning to everyday life. One has a "worldview" with a particular "take" on things. One has a set of values—both conscious and unconscious—that find expression in what one gives priority to in decision making and life planning. But a person also has a *locus of authority*—a reference point or points, either resting on an external source or sources, or residing in one's own soul's judgment. Moreover, a person's heart is attached to certain stories, symbols, and myths that mediate the person's sense of what is good, true, and beautiful, as well as what is despicable and unworthy. And as we saw earlier, to be in a faith stage is to be a member of a community or class of persons who tacitly or explicitly share many elements of the substance and style of one's faith. With such communities there may be shared rituals and patterns of interaction through which faith is shared and periodically renewed.

A transition from one faith stage to another does not necessarily mean a change in the *content* or the *direction* of one's faith. It does mean, however, changes in the ways one holds, understands, and takes responsibility for living one's faith. Let's consider some examples.

When a child enters the period from about five to seven years of age, he or she likely begins a two-year or longer process of transition from the Intuitive-Projective stage of faith to the Mythic-Literal stage. We already know that this means relinquishing the *preoperational* thought world, dominated by feeling, perception, and imagination, and beginning to enter the more linear and predictable experience of everyday life constructed by *concrete operational* patterns of thought and logic. What we have not attended to so far is the experience and the feeling of such a transitional time and the emotional dislocations and relocations it requires.

Consider the following illustration: A five-year-old boy, big for his age but naive in other ways, sat with three seven-year-old boys. The seven-year-olds had been teaching the younger boy to "cuss" (to use mild profanity and "dirty" terms). Glad at feeling included and "big" with his newfound vocabulary, the younger boy made a crucial mistake. He asked the older boys what Santa Claus was going to bring them for Christmas. Scoffing, the seven-year-olds said, "You don't believe in Santa Claus do you Tommy?" "Naw," answered Tommy, absorbing crushing news. While Tommy struggled internally to accommodate a newly flattened and secularized world, Billy, on whose front steps they were sitting, went into his house and returned with a small green parakeet his aunt had given him. The parakeet was sick. As Billy held it in his fat, freckled hand, its head kept falling to one side. After the boys contemplated the sad looking bird for a few moments, Dickie, the slyest and most hard-hearted of the older boys, said, "Let's kill it. It's going to die anyway. We might as well put it out of its misery." Buddy, a handsome, soft-eyed lad, looked at the bird and then at its owner. He asked, "Do you want to kill it?" After a pause, Billy, who only recently had become the bird's owner, said, "Yeah! Let's kill it." Tommy wasn't consulted about the matter, and after his earlier experience of embarrassment was not about to speak. He watched as Billy tightened his grip on the frail body of the bird and then forcefully slapped its listing head against the cement step. "Thwack . . . Thwack . . . Thwack, Thwack, Thwack, Thwack, Thwack." And there was death, broken-necked, pop-eyed, and limp.

In young Tommy's life and faith, this sequence of events, occurring with older boys he admired, initiated a period of transition out of the Intuitive-Projective stage and into the construction of a Mythic-Literal stage. It also marked the beginning of his move from a life stage defined by the fairly controlled drama of family and preschool into the more diverse, rough-and-tumble stage of public school. Tommy's dramatic experiences and learnings on that December afternoon began a process, deeply fraught with emotion, of looking in new ways at many things his family and church had taught him. He began to think in new ways about God, death, and the evil good people can do. If Santa Claus was not real, then what else had he been taught and imagined that might now also need to be recognized as naive or wrong? Which world was truer or more valuable: the world of peer solidarity, incorporating the dirty talk and violence he had begun to experience with his older peers, or the world of his family and teachers, at home, at school, and at church? How could he move back and forth between these worlds? Which of the other stories people told him could be depended upon? Did God make the world in seven days? Was there a devil? What sense was he to make of the terrible nightmare about a big, dark, red, male figure, with dangerous strength and glowing eyes, who beckoned to him menacingly across a black boiling river of flowing, smoking tar? A boy's experience of the onset of transition.

Or take someone at the other end of the life cycle: A sixty-seven-year-old woman had recently retired from a long and successful career as an officer high in the leadership ranks of an international-aid organization. Her demanding work and fast-rising career, and the international travel and residence periods they required, had led her to pass up the several opportunities to marry that had come to her earlier in life. Satisfied with her career, she settled into retirement in the city where she had grown up more than five decades ago. She affiliated with a church and some other community organizations because she had few friends and no family left in the city after her many years of international travels and living abroad. Through her church she was contacted by a German student in his early twenties studying theology in a local seminary on an exchange year. He had an assignment to do an in-depth interview with an adult regarding the formation and changes in his or her worldview and faith. He had met her at the church they both attended, and was attracted to her international experience. Would she be willing to spend time with him for the interview? Ms. M. agreed to the interview and on a Sunday afternoon he called at her condominium. The interview, which was to be tape-recorded for later analysis, was scheduled to take about an hour and a half. At the end of two hours, it became clear that there was much more that they needed to talk about. The visiting student approached his professor on Monday and explained that Ms. M. seemed to need to talk more about the matters discussed in the interview. Some of these matters, he sensed, would involve dealing with pain, grief, and the struggle of making meaning. He already had more than enough interview content to fulfill the assignment, but he felt a sense of responsibility not to end the conversations until both Ms. M. and he felt they had finished their work. The professor encouraged him to go back on a weekly basis for a time to continue the talks, and promised to support him in processing and working with the issues their conversations surfaced.

Their conversations lasted about six Sundays. Ms. M., it turned out, had felt an immediate closeness to the student because he reminded her of her nephew, a man whose education she had encouraged and supported. And because of her time in Europe, she felt very comfortable speaking with a German—and a Lutheran—about matters that were close to her heart. As the student and professor met each week to process the interview experience it became very clear that this young man had entered Ms. M.'s life precisely at a time when she seemed to need to work through a long-postponed stage transition in her selfhood and faith. As they talked, she dismantled the strong conventional faith she had formed as an adolescent and young adult in her Lutheran church many years ago. In the light of her long years of service in other societies and countries, her encounters with other religious traditions, her confrontation of evil and tragedy in human affairs, and her long, career-absorbed avoidance of facing her own deep loneliness, she needed to revisit and fundamentally rework her faith. In the six weeks of conversation between them, and the days in between their visits, she effectively worked out a new intellectual and emotional stance of faith and selfhood. The structured intimacy of their relationship and the framework of the interview facilitated a long overdue transition from a mature Synthetic-Conventional stage of faith to the more reflective and critical structuring of an emerging Individuative-Reflective stage. In her professional life she had already developed many of the patterns of intellect and emotion required for the Individuative-Reflective stage. But there had been no safe space, no "holding environment" prior to this, where she could take her deepest beliefs and convictional grounding and bring them into critical interchange with the rich range of her life experiences and some deep sources of pain and grief they held.

THE TEXTURE OF TRANSITIONS

In any significant time of transition in our sense of selfhood and faith we engage in a protracted time of dis-ease and disequilibration. Such periods are precipitated either by interruptive events and experiences, or by the realization that many of the ways one has been living and making meaning no longer "make sense." The maintenance of selfhood and faith in meaning and plausibility is profoundly relational. The pressures for change come both from within and from without—from internal processes of trying to "keep our balance," and from external influences that impact and threaten the balance we try to maintain. Piaget, using a biological analogy, saw an equilibrated or balanced time *in* a stage as one in which we can more or less *assimilate* the events and challenges of our relationships and environments to our existing patterns and operations of knowing and valuing—the existing patterns of our faith. Times of transition, on the other hand, are initiated by the awareness that our existing structures are no longer sufficient for dealing with the shape and content coming to us from our experience-world. At such times, Piaget would say, we find we must *accommodate* the new challenges by constructing new patterns of knowing and valuing in order to deal with them. Transitional times in life and faith are times of constructing new patterns of knowing and valuing, giving us new capacities for dealing with the life issues we face. This is what Piaget means by *accommodation*.

Times of major, reconstructive transition in our lives are marked by three phases. There is the phase that inaugurates the change, a phase that is marked by *endings*. In Tommy's life the period of transition we looked at began with the ending of an era of naiveté in his relation to older boys he admired and was learning to know. For Ms. M. transition began with retirement and the endings associated with career, administrative responsibility, and the heavy week in, week out pattern of continuous activity. For each of these persons, in different ways, *endings* involved four interrelated aspects: (1) disengagement, (2) disidentfication, (3) disenchantment, and (4) disorientation.[1]

Disengagement begins whenever we give up a significant connection to some context of relationship and shared meanings that has helped to constitute our sense of self. Extreme experiences of disengagement include deaths, divorces, and the catastrophic destruction of a home and its belongings. Lesser forms come with job changes, moves, illness, the end of a school year, and the like. For

---

1. The terms introduced here, as well as the three phases of change to be discussed below, are adapted from William Bridges, *Transitions: Making Sense of Life's Changes* (Reading, Mass.: Addison-Wesley, 1980). For my own treatment of these ideas see Fowler, *Faith Development and Pastoral Care* (Minneapolis: Fortress Press, 1987), chap. 6.

Tommy, disengagement began with his giving up the naive assumption that his older friends shared the same values and honored the same standards as he had been taught in his family and at preschool. To join them, he had to qualify his previous relations. For Ms. M., retirement had represented a major disengagement, initiating an inevitable process of change.

Disidentification results from breaking or losing old connections with the world, which means the loss of important ways of self-definition. Some part of our identity must be given up or changed. Disidentification is the internal side of the disengagement process. For Tommy, it was impossible to turn back to his previous sense of himself. He had acquired dangerous knowledge and experience; he could no longer experience himself as one who does not know these things. Ms. M. may have felt a significant sense of loss of identity as she relinquished the long-term leadership position she had occupied. Part of her transition to a new stage involved the effort to find a grounding for her sense of self and identity that no longer depended upon her institutional and social role.

Disenchantment means giving up or enduring the loss of some part of our previous constructions of reality. For Tommy, Santa Claus was revealed as fiction. This led to the destabilization of other elements of his assumptive and belief-full world. For Ms. M., the perspectives on God, the Scriptures, and the meanings of sin and forgiveness she had maintained from her adolescent religious experiences and training had to be acknowledged as inadequate for her critical and reflective reviewing of her activist life. In order to change and reconstruct her faith, she had to recognize that some significant part of her old faith reality was in her head but didn't coincide with the realities she had experienced. Disenchantment can bring feelings of grief, loss, guilt, shame, lostness, and confusion. It can also bring a sense of liberation and empowerment.

Disorientation, in a sense, is the cumulative impact of the three other aspects of our experience of endings. For a time, we feel that we have lost our mental and emotional maps, charts, plans, and sense of direction. A great deal of emotional energy is diffusely expended in trying to grasp what has happened to us. In the cumulative impact of our experiences of endings we find ourselves in what William Bridges calls the *neutral zone*.

This second phase of any major time of transition, the *neutral zone,* we experience as a time out of ordinary time. The anthropologist Victor Turner refers to such times as experiences of the *antistructure.* Robert Kegan, a distinguished psychologist and author and a colleague of mine, used to say to persons in transition, "No, you are not going crazy, but you may be out of your mind" (see Kegan 1982, 1994). To be in the neutral zone is to be out of one's mind. It means experiencing the dismantling or disintegration of a way of seeing and being in the world, and living through the ragged period of struggling to compose a new and more adequate meaning. Saint John of the Cross's great image of the "dark night of the soul" captures the emotional sense of dislocation, and sometimes desolation, such deep going times of transition can bring.

Times in these neutral zones often mark the transition to a new stage. There are aspects of knowing and wisdom that can come only from our embracing these "times out of time" in our lives. We see the structures of everyday life in quite different terms from the vantage point of the antistructure. When we return we bring some of that wisdom and the new patterns of understanding and processing of reality we have won or been given by the neutral zone time.

When our time in the neutral zone has done its work, we begin to find the clues or the signposts that point toward the shaping of *new beginnings.* In this phase of new beginnings it is important not to rush. A comprehensive, gradual reintegration of life in light of the newness that has come from the neutral zone must take place. We need "holding environments" in therapy, spiritual direction, or membership in communities of faith that can help us pace our reentry and reintegration in a new stage or place, protecting the fragile new beginnings against the power of old patterns or the premature forging of new ones.

CHAPTER THREE

ONCE-BORN/TWICE-BORN: FAITH AND TRANSFORMATION

Our focus on "faithful change" has led us through chapters on the early formation of faith in childhood and an overview of the stages of faith from the earliest to the latest. In chapter 2, we explored the changes faith undergoes in times of developmental transition and, implicitly at least, the faith that sustains us through the neutral zone times of our engaging in developmental change. In the introduction of this book, we made a distinction between *developmental change* and a second type that I called *healing or reconstructive change*. This second type of change will engage us in the present chapter.

William James undoubtedly ranks as the best-known psychologist of religion of the twentieth century. This status rests most centrally on his classic work *The Varieties of Religious Experience*. The purpose of this chapter is to bring the faith development perspective, with its research and theory on the predictable stages and transitions of faith, into comparative dialogue with James's great book. James made a distinction between the "once-born" and the "twice-born" patterns of change brought about by religious experience. Our stress in the previous chapter was on the sequence of transitions envisioned by faith development theory. Placing that perspective in dialogue with James's work will help us to see what it means to embrace the challenges of transforming or "twice-born" religious experiences. What follows will presume a reading of chapter 2. I will attempt to give the reader who is unfamiliar with James's work a reliable sense of the power and drama with which he writes about religious experience and transformation.

JAMES AND *THE VARIETIES OF RELIGIOUS EXPERIENCE*

In writing *The Varieties of Religious Experience,* William James combined remarkable capacities for finding descriptive accounts of various aspects of religious experience with an ongoing process of assessment based upon his primary philosophical methods and commitments. His commitment to the sense of a "pluralistic universe" allowed him to honor difference, variety, and multiplicity regarding types and excellences of religious experience. His commitment to pragmatism allowed him to reshape the question of the "truth" of religious experiences, practices and beliefs. Instead of addressing questions of truth epistemologically, metaphysically, or theologically, his analysis consistently sought to appraise the veridical character of religious experience by assessing its impact on the intensity of human action and on the shaping of human welfare. James clearly valued religion and religious experience for the zest, the drive, the inspiration it provided for the heroic and strenuous life. Inclined to melancholy and vocational indecision in his early life, he valued the ebullient energy and higher sense of purpose religion provided for many. While admiring the equanimity and poise of the "once-born" type of person and the optimistic rationality of the "healthy-minded," James was well aware of their blindness to the presence of real and deep going evil in nature and the human community. Over their shallow optimism and bland idealism he favored the subconscious ferment and emotional upheaval of the "twice-born" type.

Like the nineteenth-century German theologian Friedrich Schleiermacher, James saw the essence of religion in *feeling*—the feeling of solemnity, the feeling of seriousness, the feeling of relatedness to transcendence or what he called the *more.* James's own existential search gives compelling power to his wrestle with the pragmatic questions of religion's truth and usefulness, as well as its plurality of manifestations. His personal questions fuel his investigations of conversion, saintliness, and mysticism. His courageous commitment to a non-reductionistic examination of the topics of a psychology of religion appropriately leads, in the end, to his bringing his readers face to face with the mystery that lies on the "farther side" of religious experiences and their practical consequences. James does, indeed, anticipate Freud with his suggestion that

> the "more" with which in religious experience we feel ourselves connected is on its *hither* side the subconscious continuation of our conscious life. . . . At the same time the theologian's contention that the religious man is moved by an external power is vindicated, for it is one of the peculiarities of invasions from the subconscious region to take on objective appearances, and to suggest to the Subject an external control. In the religious life the control is felt as "higher"; but since . . . it is primarily the higher faculties of our own hidden mind which are controlling, the sense of union with the power beyond us is a sense of something, not merely apparently, but literally true. (James 1961, 396-97)

James leaves us with a sketch of his own "overbeliefs," as he calls them, which express the conviction that "confining ourselves to what is common and generic, we have in *the fact that the conscious person is continuous with a wider self through which saving experiences come,* a positive content of religious experience which, it seems to me, *is literally and objectively true as far as it goes.*" When we commune with the wider self—which for James plunges us "into an altogether other dimension of existence from the sensible and merely 'understandable' world"—we are affected and changed. When we commune with this "other dimension," he says, "work is actually done upon our finite personality, for we are turned into new men, and consequences in the way of conduct follow in the natural world upon our regenerative change. . . . [T]hat which produces effects within another reality must be termed a reality itself, so I feel as if we had no philosophic excuse for calling the unseen or mystical world unreal." Having thus removed the excuse for dismissing the reality of an unseen dimension, James proceeds to utilize the name "God" for it. "We and God have business with each other; and in opening ourselves to his influence our deepest destiny is fulfilled. The universe, at those parts of it which our personal being constitutes, takes a turn genuinely for the worse or for the better in proportion as each one of us fulfills or evades God's demands. . . . God is real since he produces real effects" (James 1961, 398-400).

This brief characterization of James's classic merely intends to remind you of some of his characteristic concerns, his passion, and a flavor of his conclusions. It is bracing to reenter his thought world and its social-historic location. His phenomenological accounts of conversion experiences, of the aspects of saintly existence, and of mystical rapture are rich beyond comparison with most of what you will find in the faith development literature. Although the foci and questions fueling James's work have significant differences with those of faith development theory, there are significant similarities as well. To follow these comparisons, the reader may need to refer to the preceding chapter for its underlying distinctions of faith, belief, and religion, and for its account of the stages of faith.

SOME SIMILARITIES BETWEEN JAMES AND FAITH DEVELOPMENT THEORY

1. *Both Mean to Be Non-Reductionistic and Are Indirectly Apologetic.* Earlier James was likened to Schleiermacher in relation to his focus on feeling and emotion. James's psychology of religion also shows a relatedness to Schleiermacher in its forceful address to "the cultured among the despisers" of religion. Of course, James is writing in such a way that his text, appearing just after the cresting of the revivalist period in late nineteenth-century America, would have broad popular appeal. But the text was written for a university audience, and in psychology it aimed to counter the emerging positivist passion for making psychology an exclusively laboratory science. At the time of this writing, James was increasingly defining himself as a philosopher. As such, he makes a strong case for honoring the sui generis character of religious experience. While it anticipates Freud's account of religion based upon the projection of unconscious needs, James's account affirms the indispensability of this activating role of the "subconscious," as he calls it. He pointedly insists on leaving open the question of how the subconscious dynamics of our experiences of the Holy connect us with a genuine transcendence.

Faith development theory is grounded in a conviction that humans have evolved into an ontological vocation for responsiveness to God. This approach claims that the orientation to centers of value, the construing of meaning as the context for relationships and our life projects, is generic to human beings. Like the works on faith of Paul Tillich and H. Richard Niebuhr, which so influenced its underlying theological approach, faith development theory may be said to have an apologetic aim of demonstrating that this central act of meaning making, of shared commitment to centering values, and joint living by core stories, is indispensable and integral to human survival and flourishing. Like James, I have sought to make this case in ways that commend the research and theory to university audiences. Also like James, I have written to and addressed a wider audience from this perspective. *Both perspectives aim to be non-reductionistic; both are indirectly apologetic.*

2. Each Approach Is Empirical, Though in Different Senses of the Term. A central characteristic of pragmatist philosophy is that it puts conceptual categories at risk in relation to the dynamic contours of experience. This is the sense, I believe, in which James's *Varieties* may be said to be both pragmatist and empirical. Through the use of case accounts and texts of autobiography and biography, he builds up shared experience of dimensions of religious life. Then he retrieves categories from religious and psychological traditions and both fills them and reworks them to convey and order his rich, reflective sense of their role in religion and in the lives of those who experience them. Unlike Max Weber, who claimed that he was not "religiously musical," James has an acute ear and feel for the nuances and emotions of religious experience. His own vicarious participation in the experiences he recounts from others—despite his disclaimers of any significantly original personal experiences of his own—makes his empirical method one full of the risk and passion of his own involvement. The reader participates, through James, in the "strenuous mode" of reconstructing and evaluating experience.

Faith development theory and research can also rightfully claim to be empirical, in some ways that overlap with James. But in other respects, it is empirical in more typical social scientific senses of the term. The stage theory had its origins in my joint leadership of intensive group experiences where participants were invited to share their life and faith pilgrimages with each other in an unusual context of intense leisure. The hermeneutical framework of Erikson's psychosocial developmental theory initially helped me order what I was hearing. Later, teaching a course at Harvard Divinity School called "Theology as the Symbolization of Experience," I broadened the interpretative framework to include the works of Freud, Jung, Durkheim, Bellah, and eventually Piaget and Kohlberg. With grant money, I was able, during the 1970s, to work with students and a research team that helped me carry out three major waves of empirical work. We used semi-structured interviews, on which we based the analyses that led to successive stages of reconstruction and elaboration of the stages of faith. While increasingly detailed and clarified descriptions of stages and transitions emerged from this empirical and constructive process, the theory was also being presented to university audiences and gatherings of professionals in religious education, ministry, and pastoral care. The empirical evidences of resonance and dissonance with the reflective experience of these professionals has been a significant factor for me as the primary author of this work. And, like James, the personal quest for orientation and truth about these matters has been a continuing source of motivation and energy in this project. *Each of these approaches is empirical, though in different senses of the term.*

3. *Both Point to a Generic Unity Underlying the Many Manifestations of Religion and Faith.* James's contention for a pluralistic universe is well known, and the very title *The Varieties of Religious Experience* advertises his commitment to the honoring of difference. Later I will say more about James and pluralism. Here, however, as we enumerate similarities between James and faith development theory, I want to emphasize an underlying unity each of these approaches finds behind the diversity. "The pivot round which the religious life, as we have traced it, revolves," says James in his "Conclusions," "is the interest of the individual in his private personal destiny" (James 1961, 381). Destiny here, I take it, refers not only to our ultimate destiny—what becomes of us after death—but also to the question of the unfolding of our lives and the meaning and purpose of our striving. James poses to himself the question, "Is there, under all the discrepancies of the creeds, a

common nucleus to which they bear their testimony unanimously?"
He gives an affirmative answer:

> The warring gods and formulas of the religions do indeed cancel
> each other, but there is a certain uniform deliverance in which
> religions all appear to meet. It consists of two parts—
> 1. An uneasiness; and
> 2. Its solution.
> 1. The uneasiness, reduced to its simplest terms, is a sense that
> there is *something wrong about us* as we naturally stand.
> 2. The solution is a sense that *we are saved from the wrongness* by
> making proper connection with the higher powers. (James 1961,
> 303)

This statement manifests James's commitment to the twice-born
paradigm as fundamental and generic for human beings. In this
he confirms the puritan and evangelical heritage mediated
through his father and renders the Emersonian and Unitarian
influences of the Transcendentalist movement secondary. Religion, in all its guises and manifestations, is fundamentally about
concern for one's personal destiny and finding an adequate solu-
tion for the fundamental dis-ease of human existence found in its
natural forms.

For the faith development perspective, the generic unity underlying the many manifestations of religion and faith has to do with
the universal need for meaning and orientation in life, in the face
of its ultimate limits and conditions; and, secondarily, the sense of
meaning and significance for the expenditures of one's life energies and capacities for commitment. Fundamental, then, are the
making or finding of life meaning and sustaining networks of
valuing and commitment. *Both perspectives point to a generic unity
underlying the great variety of religious and faith orientations.*

4. *Each Combines a Pragmatist and Functional Approach with Normative Evaluative Criteria.* In keeping with his pragmatist orientation,
James consistently focuses his eye on the differences in life and
living that religious experiences and convictions tend to make.
With his passion for the strenuous life, for the zest and energy that
make for an audacious engagement with the challenges of life, he
often seems temporarily to subordinate questions of the moral

worth of religious experience to questions of its vividness, vitality, and impact. On the whole, however, *truth,* in relation to religious experience, consists in the combination of its vividness and power to transform a life and in the linking of its subject more clearly in his or her unique relation to the "higher powers." In a fine unpublished dissertation, Brian James Mahan has identified three criteria he finds in James for the functional truth of religious experiences and their impacts: (1) response to immediate luminousness; (2) philosophical reasonableness; and (3) moral helpfulness. For James, no substantive content of religious experience or belief can qualify as truth unless all three of these criteria are met in the assessment of its functional shaping of the lives of persons (Mahan 1989, 136-41).

Faith development theory also takes a functionalist approach, which it combines with normative criteria. Its primary attention rests upon the patterning of knowing and valuing by which persons compose and commit to meanings, and to the ways their faith perspectives shape their patterns of relating and interpreting experience. The functionalism of faith development theory is much more related to persons' ways of construing and interpreting experience than it is to the energy and motivation for action they engender. However, it does argue, on the bases of aesthetic, rational, and ethical criteria, that the constructive patterns of the later stages of faith are more adequate, more "true," than those employed in earlier stages. *Each combines a pragmatist and functional approach with normative evaluative criteria* in its approach to religion and faith.

SOME DIFFERENCES BETWEEN JAMES AND FAITH DEVELOPMENT THEORY

1. *Two Different Responses to Pluralism in Faith and Religious Experience.* James asks in his "Conclusions": "Ought it to be assumed that in all men the mixture of religion with other elements should be identical? Ought it, indeed, to be assumed that the lives of all men should show identical religious elements?" In answer to his own question he writes:

The divine can mean no single quality, it must mean a group of qualities, by being champions of which in alternation, different men may all find worthy missions. Each attitude being a syllable in human nature's total message, it takes the whole of us to spell the meaning out completely. So a "god of battles" must be allowed to be the god for one kind of person, a god of peace and heaven and home, the god for another. We must frankly recognize the fact that we live in partial systems, and that parts are not interchangeable in the spiritual life. If we are peevish and jealous, destruction of the self must be an element of our religion; why need it be one if we are good and sympathetic from the outset? If we are sick souls, we require a religion of deliverance; but why think so much of deliverance, if we are healthy-minded? (James 1961, 378-79)

The varieties of faith and religious experience, for James, seem to be equivalent to the variety of personality types and patterns of need. This likely means that from James's point of view, the stage theory of faith development might present a far too confining frame, a Procrustean bed, into which to force the rich welter of various types of religious folk. His accounts of the differing expressions of sainthood and its distortions, alone, suggest the range and variations of religious personality that attracted his interest. Yet he does give some hint of interest in evolutionary or developmental perspectives, or at least characterizations of higher degrees of religious experience. He writes: "Unquestionably, some men have the completer experience and the higher vocation, here just as in the social world." But then he adds, "But for each man to stay in his own experience, whate'er it be, and for others to tolerate him there, is surely best" (James 1961, 379).

Faith development theory deals with what I have sometimes called "vertical pluralism." The same person, across a life cycle, may well construct his or her faith perspective in a predictable range of three to seven different stages. In any average group of adults one may find persons in any of the stages from the Mythic Literal to the Conjunctive or the Universalizing stage. In this sense, faith development theory is a "reception theory." It shows the range and variations of ways in which persons appropriate religious traditions or correlate meanings with eclectic or secular ideological perspectives.

In a therapeutic context, James's work may help one identify a once-born or twice-born person; it may invite attention to similarities and differences of conversion experiences or particular forms of melancholy or levels of energy. Faith development theory serves diagnostic aims by providing a frame to characterize qualitatively different ways of construing self, others, and self-other relations, including one's relation with God. It offers some precision to knowledgeable therapists in identifying the stage or transition that best characterizes a given help-seeker's way of making meaning. Faith development theory offers an implicit model of evolving selfhood, constituted by its characteristic patterns of construing self, and self-other, self-world, and self-ultimate relations.

2. *The Feeling Self and the Construing Self.* Given James's account of the self in his book *Psychology,* we should not expect that he would give an essentialist or substantivist account of the self. Nor does he, like his student George Herbert Mead, provide a social and relational account of the self. For James, we might rephrase Descartes' famous statement: "I feel, therefore I am." Or more adequately, "I am moved by the flow of my affections toward centers of value that capture my will and focus my passions." With Jonathan Edwards, James might say, "The will is as its strongest motive is." James uses the term *feeling* in a sense broad enough to include both the perceptive and the cognitive processes that it orients and presses into its service. But clearly it is feeling that is fundamental for motivation and orientation. Cognitive processes follow feeling and attempt to bring to consciousness, thought, and word what one has experienced so powerfully.

Faith development theory stands in a tradition in which cognition and affection or emotion tend to be distinguished and theoretically separated. Piaget acknowledged that one always observes the presence and influence of affections in thought and action. But his theory clearly privileges cognition and the modes of discursive rationality that can balance and guide the emotions. In contrast to Piaget and Kohlberg, in my work I have tried from the beginning to include the role of emotion and valuing in the construing activity by which a person finds or makes meaning and grounds the self in its relatedness to others, to self, and to an ultimate environment. This has meant arguing for a "logic of conviction"—a kind of reasoning *in faith*—as more primal than Piaget's "logic of rational certainty." We may say that James privileges the self as constituted by its life-shaping feelings and affections, with cognitive processes giving account and elaborating their meanings in derivative ways. The faith development approach, by contrast, privileges the self as constituted by patterns of construing, but tries to incorporate the affections and valuing into these patterns of construing, which we call stages.

3. *Development and Conversion: Contrast in the "Once-Born/Twice-Born" Distinction.* From a superficial standpoint, it would seem obvious that James's psychology of religious transformation centers in conversion and the "twice-born" orientation, while faith development theory centers in the progressive movement of one stage to another in an expansive working out of the "once-born" orientation. But the situation is more complex than that. In *Stages of Faith,* I characterize conversion as "a significant recentering of one's previous conscious or unconscious images of value and power, and the conscious adoption of a new set of master stories in the commitment to reshape one's life in a new community of interpretation and action" (Fowler 1995, 281-82). In that definition, and in the account I give of conversion experience in the book, one can detect the lines of transformation that James, with his imagery of the rupture of the "hard rind" of the subconscious, and "the expulsive power of a new affection," paints more vividly. The major difference lies in situating the conversion phenomena in a sequence of developmental stages having to do with the structuring of faith. James, on the one hand, is more interested in the *quantitative* impact of conversion—the power of a new direction, the energy of a new centering loyalty and affection. In writing *Stages of Faith,* on the other hand, I was clearly more interested in the impact of a new set of affections and their object on the overall process of making and sustaining life-orienting meanings. My interest is more *qualitative* than quantitative, in the sense that I understand conversion as occurring at different stages for the same or different people, and as being interpreted and integrated in quite different ways depending upon a person's present stage or transition.

4. *Grounding Convictions and Overbeliefs.* As we have seen, *The Varieties of Religious Experience* and *Stages of Faith* have both some

striking similarities and some vivid differences. Both books, despite the undergirdings they share in scholarly research, are very personal books. The authorial voice in each book is a personal voice. *Varieties* was prepared as a set of lectures. One can almost hear the sibilant intake of breath and the rise and fall of a voice close at hand as one reads it. I lectured many parts of *Stages* before giving it integrated form in a final written version. In writing *Stages*, I frequently experienced the presence of remembered audiences, recognizing the need for a narrative or an explanation from the remembrance of frowning brows or glazed eyes at particular junctures.

By virtue of personal voice and a certain existential passion, both books convey, I think, the conviction that their subject matter is important, for them and for their readers. Each, in its own way, weaves a holding environment where transactions between the soul of persons and a reality or realities on the further side of human experience can be explored and honored as intrinsically valuable and indispensable in human experience. Separated by nearly eighty years, both books address the readers with rich maps of essential areas of human experience, and with a certain pressure to locate themselves in recognition and decision. Both books, in complex ways, combine empirical descriptiveness with an undeniable normativity.

Both James and I rely on the convictions James called "overbeliefs" to resolve deep going tensions between science and faith. James finds the linkage with God in the self's relation to its own "transmarginal" or "subconscious" depths. Straightforwardly, he affirms that the sense of an objective and truly "other" entity encountered in religious experience can be identified with aspects of our subconscious self. With some intellectual sleight of hand, James—in the spirit of his essay "The Will to Believe"—leaves standing the conviction that through this encounter with aspects of our subconscious mind, we are (or may well be) experiencing relatedness to the *more*—the Higher Powers on the further side of religious experience. This conviction, left standing because nothing else accounts for the data of experience, gives James's pluralistic universe its complex but final integrity. This is not a static integrity, but rather an integrity in the midst of process—the process of the self, the process of myriad human beings and other organisms embracing and experiencing relatedness in a great variety of ways.

In *Stages of Faith,* a more straightforwardly expressed conviction affirms a oneness that encompasses and preserves the expanding, manifold processes of nature and history. A theologian at base, I affirm the priority in being, valuing, and power of God. My anthropology affirms that humans have evolved with pre-potentiated capacities that underlie the structuring activities of faith and equip us for our ontological callings to relatedness to and partnership with God. Also emphasizing process, but less radically than James, I see the self as being constituted in fundamental ways by this ontological vocation—which, of course, humans may embrace, neglect, or struggle against.

The structure and temper of our overbeliefs help explain why James struggles between the once-born and the twice-born pattern of experience as normative, and I dominantly attend to a kind of once-born series of transforming reconfigurations of the continuously dynamic relationships of faith. I am glad that we do not have to negate one of these options in the study of religious experience and faith in order to embrace and affirm the other, for both perspectives make indispensable contributions to our understanding of the ways faith changes and the qualities that constitute the faith to change.

PART II

FAITH AND THE FAULT LINES
OF SHAME

P art I has led us on a journey from birth and earliest childhood through a succession of stages of faith that mark aspects of our potential for growth in relatedness to God and neighbor. In our mapping of that journey we have sought to honor the role of emotions, imagination, and the gradual emergence of "knowing" in the development of faith. With William James, we examined the dynamics of conversion and transformation in faith and religious experience. James's contrast of the "once-born" and the "twice-born" paths in faith leads well into part II of our study of faith and change.

To be faithful, whether in human relations or in our relations to the Holy, means to maintain a certain sensitivity, a responsiveness, a suppleness of spirit in relation to the self and others. Faithfulness involves attending to the Other or to others, while also attending to ourselves. This "attending" in faith is about right relatedness. It is about living in relation to self and others with regard and reverence for their (and our) value and worth. It is about trust and trustworthiness; it is about loyalty and "keeping faith."

In our study of earliest childhood in the company of Daniel Stern, Erik Erikson, Ana-Maria Rizzuto, and others, we saw the importance, for faith, of the early developmental crises of trust versus mistrust and of autonomy versus shame and doubt. In part II, I want to lead you into a deeper exploration of these vitally important "places of the heart," especially as they affect our ways of being faithful in the midst of change.

Much has been written and spoken about shame in recent years. There have been few efforts, however, to link our recovered and new awareness of the importance of this emotion to the life and dynamics of faith. This is the task we undertake in these pages. To read and find ourselves in these pages may bring pain. To embrace our pain and woundedness is prereq-

uisite to genuine acceptance of grace and the transformation of healing. Grace—the grace of God and the grace mediated through the love and acceptance of humans—is the antidote to and the healing power for shame. From Adam and Eve to Nietzsche, from developmental psychology to the parables and parabolic actions of Jesus, this part of our book is about the dynamics of shame and grace.

CHAPTER FOUR

SHAME AND THE BROKEN HEART:
FAULT LINES AND CULTURE

Now that I have eyes for it, I see it everywhere: It hangs like a limp banner over the debutante ball where young women, with half a lung and half a heart, ambivalently try to project enjoyment and comfort in roles chosen for them by parents trying to confirm or establish their social standing. It curls like a wounded snake in the homeless shelter where a skilled thirty-seven-year-old graphic artist comes to terms with being replaced by a new wave of computer-based drafting technology that renders his job, and those of thousands like him, obsolete. His story—of unemployment insurance dribbling out, family deterioration and marital breakup, loss of contact with his children, and now life on the streets—radiates it. In universities it intrudes through the abrupt halt in the flow of the abstracted prose of a gifted graduate student in a seminar as she experiences the emergence of images and words that disclose some personal feeling from the heart. The face reddens, the shoulders slump, the articulate flow ceases, the mind temporarily shuts down like a computer in a power outage. I hear it in the talk of folk who, in fidelity to religious traditions that require close monitoring of attitudes and behavior as conditions of worth and worthiness, pepper their self-descriptions with frequent terms of self-debilitation. Curiously, I have seen it among corporate leaders or political incumbents, usually men, whose studied toughness masks questions about their own inner fiber and firmness: "Am I capable of doing what has to be done?" "Can I order the permanent layoff of three thousand workers without flinching or losing sleep at night?" Shame. Each of these windows gives us a glimpse of this painful yet centrally human experience.

Shame is an emotion of self-assessment. Alongside shame, guilt takes its place as an emotion of negative self-assessment. On the positive side, pride and self-esteem reflect favorable assessments of the self. Of the two emotions of negative assessment, shame is the harder to acknowledge and claim. Frequently we use less painful terms to describe the moments when shame blips on the radar screens of our hearts: "uncomfortable," "awkward," "embarrassed," or "stupid." These softening descriptions of such moments give us important clues to the nature of shame. Shame is the awareness of the self as disclosed to others, or to the self, as being defective, lacking, or inadequate. Shame involves a painful self-consciousness in which we feel exposed to others and to ourselves as deficient, weak, or helpless—and, at worst, contemptible.

Guilt has less global impact on our feelings about ourselves than shame. Generally speaking, guilt can be described as a feeling of regret or remorse at something I have done that violates a principle or rule that I acknowledge to be right or appropriate. In guilt, pain flows from some action that violates a norm of behavior to which I assent. In guilt, my action can be separated from my character or my worth as a self: I can do wrong things and still think of myself as a good or worthy person. With shame, however, the negative self-evaluation is more holistic: It is the self *I am* that I now must perceive as flawed or unworthy.

Spiritually, shame is related to the deepest places of truth in our souls. Shame cuts to the heart. In its healthy forms, it helps to form and inform the heart. Shame provides a primary foundation for conscience and for the instinctive sense of what is worthy or unworthy, right or wrong. Shame, as an emotion, relates to the sensitive feelings touched in love and deep communion with others. Shame protects the intimacy of our closest relations with friends, lovers, spouses, or children. It surrounds our relation with the Holy or the domain of what is sacred to us. Shame, in its positive influence, is the caretaker of our worthy selves and identities. When we listen attentively to the voice of our healthy shame, we speak and act from our "center." We respond and act with authenticity, with integrity, with identity. Shame has a special role to play in matters of attending to the spirit and in the care and nurture of the soul.

In its distorted forms, however, shame can misshape or "break" the heart. It can cut off sensitive access to the place of truth and transcendence in our own hearts. It can lead us to create "false selves" in order to meet the conditions of worth in our families of origin, or in our workplaces, social roles, or even in our churches or synagogues. Shame distorts our relations whenever power discrepancies based upon class, gender, race, sexual orientation, or religious commitments become established and taken for granted. In its most distorted forms, excessive shame can lead to the "shameless" orientations of sociopaths or to the super-narcissism we see embodied in some political dictators, money magnates, and celebrities in our world.

There is no path toward spiritual aliveness and integrity in today's society that does not embrace the challenge of working with this most elusive and painful emotion. Serious embrace of the challenges of dealing with shame leads in the direction of vitality, intimacy, responsiveness, and attentiveness to what is truly important to us. It leads to a passion for respecting self as well as others, and for living toward recognition of equal worth with others that reflects our common origin as creatures of God. To deal with our distorted shame leads to empowerment and courage to face the social and economic injustices of our common lives. This comes from recovery of a deep trust in our own "good-enoughness"—a sufficiency based on our true worth—and in our effective power to make this a better world.

Shame starts with experiences of the body and expressions of the face. Shame is one of a limited number of neurophysiological affects with which we are born. We need to recognize these earliest bodily and emotional foundations of shame and see how they become linked with personal, familial, and cultural meanings in the period of early childhood. This is where we will begin. In this first set of reflections on shame, we will explore its important role in the formation of conscience, see how it is present in our earliest experiences of self-consciousness, and see how the fragile calibration of worth and self-worth can be thrown awry.

Shame, as it were, "goes to school." Almost from birth, we begin to populate our experiences of emotions with meanings that are shaped by culture—by language, stories, symbols, and ideas that are offered in the social environments where we grow. In this section of the book we will inquire into aspects of our culture and this society that seem particularly potent in shaping and transmitting experiences of shame. All societies have patterns that guide the social construction of what it means to be a successful man or woman. We have powerful and pervasive—though often unrecognized—norms for the shaping of gender and gender relations. Race, class, and socioeconomic status are formed and reinforced by codes we internalize along with our mothers' milk and our families' compositions and lifestyles. Authority relations make subtle but effective use of shame and shaming as sanctions for ensuring employee or subordinate compliance. Religion, when it functions as one of the means of social control, can be a potent employer and sanctioner of shaming. Nietzsche characterized Christianity as a "slave religion." He saw it as calling the followers of Christ to accept lowly lives of solidarity with the poor and the oppressed. He was outraged at its separating of spirit and flesh, and its objection to the passions of heroism and willful domination. As central shapers of Western culture, Christianity and the churches deserve our attention as we look at the transmission of shame in culture and society.

When we take shame seriously we begin to see its pervasive and powerful influences in personal and collective life. It may be instructive to see how present tensions in this society over religious authority, sexual orientation, gender construction, and attitudes toward public policy regarding support and empowerment of the poor are related to the dynamics of shame. Such an inquiry has implications for how politics need to change if we begin to act on what we are learning about shame. The upsurge of violence and interethnic conflict in this nation and the world can be illumined more broadly by attention to shame in interpersonal and intergroup relations.

In the nineteenth century and before, shame played a prominent role in the philosophical and anthropological understandings of key novelists, essayists, and students of human evolution. Charles Darwin devoted the climactic chapter of his *The Expression of the Emotions in Man and Animals* to "Self-Attention, Shame, Shyness, Modesty: Blushing." Friedrich Nietzsche's flurried writings were permeated with a deep understanding of shame, both in its sense of preserving the honor and dignity of the person of noble being (the *Übermensch*) and in its distorted, false form in the cringing adherents of "slave religion." Nietzsche understood brilliantly the need for shame to protect the private, intimate aspects of life, the vulnerable emergent creations of the artist, and the sacred. Havelock Ellis's pioneering work on the psychology of sex contained an essay on "The Evolution of Modesty," and philosopher Max Scheler wrote a penetrating study of shame in his essay "Über Scham und Shamgefühl."[1]

In the first half of the twentieth century, philosophical and psychological attention to shame went into eclipse. Freud and his movement made the fateful choice to focus on the instincts or drives as the basic source of motives for human action. As a result, emotions came to be seen primarily in terms of their interfering with the slender capacities of reason in its effort to umpire the conflict between the imperious demands of the drives of the id and the harsh constraints of civilization as encoded in the superego. Freud focused on guilt, not on shame. Moreover, working with hysterics in a sexually repressive age, he paid particular attention to *neurotic* guilt, coming to see a primary role for analysis in ferreting out symptoms of bondage to guilt in this false sense. Behaviorism in psychology, with its studied ignoring of internal processes of mind and emotion, certainly did little to acknowledge or illumine the role of shame or any other emotions in human motivation and action. Humanistic psychology, reacting to the Freudian overattention to unconscious defenses and the deeply conflicted psyche, failed to penetrate deeply into either the defenses or the complexities of the dynamics of shame.

At mid-century, pioneering writers such as Erik Erikson, Gerhart Piers and Milton Singer, Helen Merrell Lynd, and Helen Block Lewis began to redirect attention to shame as a central factor in the formation of identity and in the dynamics of human relations. In the 1980s, a host of psychoanalytic writers, many of whom studied with Helen Block Lewis, began to attend carefully to the phenomenon of shame, in both literature and history, and in the context

---

1. In *Shame, Exposure, and Privacy* (Schneider 1992), Carl Schneider offers a thorough analysis of the concept of shame in the work of these nineteenth-century thinkers.

and conduct of psychoanalytic treatment (see Wurmser, Nathanson, Morrison, Broucek, A. Miller). Coalescing with writings from the "object-relations" school of psychoanalysis (see St. Clair 1986) and especially with the "self-psychology" of Heinz Kohut and his followers, in the late seventies and eighties attention to shame, its relation to narcissism, and its key place among the emotions that shape the deepest and earliest patterns of our personalities began to come to the fore.

The concern with shame has claimed widespread public attention in the United States since 1988 through the media presentations and writings of John Bradshaw, as well as a host of family therapists, addictions counselors, and interpreters of Twelve Step programs. In this popular emergence, and the self-help literature issuing from it, the primary focus has been on understanding and breaking the hold of what is often called "toxic" shame. Other dynamics and functions of shame have been largely neglected.

A number of authors have written insightful books on aspects of shame in the last decade. We will encounter many of them and their ideas in these pages. Few of them, however, have made concern with shame the gateway to a recovery of spirit and spiritedness in our personal and collective lives.[2] The chapters that follow intend to open up some fresh and fruitful perspectives on how this place of response to truth in our lives that we call shame can be the place of engagement with a healing and restoration of soul we desperately need as we look toward a new century and a new millennium.

---

2. Two notable exceptions deserve mention: Rita Nakashima Brock, *Journeys by Heart: A Christology of Erotic Power* (New York: Crossroad, 1988), and Lewis B. Smedes, *Shame and Grace: Healing the Shame We Don't Deserve* (San Francisco: HarperSanFrancisco, 1993).

CHAPTER FIVE

OUR BODIES AND SHAME

A n infant in diapers, just old enough to sit alone, plays with a bright, smooth plastic doll. Alternately looking at it, manipulating it, and tasting it with her tongue and lips, the baby shows the bright eyes and energetic engagement that communicate enjoyment and interest. Without warning, an older brother, maybe three, approaches the baby from the side and slightly behind. Intruding between the doll and the infant's face, he plants a juicy kiss below her right ear. The baby's face drops and turns away. The eyes turn downward. The shoulders and neck begin to slump. The mouth, open and sagging at the sides, shows a slight protrusion of the lower lip. The baby lets the hand holding the doll drop between her outstretched legs. Enjoyment and interest interrupted, the change in this baby's facial expressions and body posture communicates to us watchers—and to the infant herself—the affect shame.

According to the theory of emotions propounded across thirty years by research psychologist Silvan Tomkins, there are a handful of basic affects that are innate and universal features of human beings.[1] Affects, for Tomkins, denote

> sets of muscular, glandular, and skin receptor responses located in the face (and also widely distributed throughout the body) that generate sensory feedback to a system that finds them either inherently "acceptable" or "unacceptable." These organized sets of responses are triggered at subcortical centers where specific "programs" for each distinct affect are stored, programs that are innately endowed and have been genetically inherited. They are

---

1. I want to acknowledge my appreciation to Donald L. Nathanson, MD, whose writings have greatly aided and guided my reading and understanding of the work of Silvan Tomkins. See Nathanson 1987 and 1992.

capable, when activated, of simultaneously capturing such widely distributed structures as the face, the heart, and the endocrine glands and imposing on them a specific pattern of correlated responses. One does not learn to be afraid or to cry or to startle, any more than one learns to feel pain or to gasp for air. (Tomkins 1987, 137)

Tomkins is boldly aware of the significance, both for psychology and for our understanding of human action more generally, of the theory of the affects he is proposing. He writes:

Contrary to Freud, I do not view human beings as the battle-ground for their imperious drives, which urge them on blindly to pleasure and violence, to be contained only by a repressive society and its representations within—the ego and the superego. Rather, I see affect or feeling as *the primary innate biological motivating mechanism*, more urgent than drive deprivation and pleasure, and more urgent even than physical pain. Without its amplification, nothing else matters, and with its amplification anything can matter. It thus combines urgency, abstractness, and generality. It lends its power to memory, to perception, to thought, and to action no less than to the drives. (Tomkins 1987, 137)

From the outset we need to understand that for Tomkins affects consist centrally of "face work." Common sense suggests that we "have" or "feel" an emotion, and then we express it with our facial expressions, body gestures, and overall demeanor. Tomkins's approach contends otherwise. The innate affects—these pre-programmed sets of muscular, glandular, and skin receptor responses—are triggered as analogs to certain kinds of experiences. The face, with its highly articulated musculature, its eyes that can dilate widely, and its capacities to blanch pale or redden hotly, is the prime place of the person's own awareness and experience of the affects. In Tomkins's view, the affects take shape first in the face and the correlated glandular and neurophysiological sequences. Then they "go in" to register psychically.

The face is also the primary place of nonverbal communication of affect to others. Long before bodily needs, relational reactions and feeling states can be articulated with words, the face and the affects play primary roles in communication between children and their caregivers. Universally, the facial and bodily expressions provide a crucial substratum of communication between persons and groups. The system of affects, for Tomkins, is somewhat analogous to Chomsky's theory of the universal presence in human groups of innate structural potentials for language acquisition and use. Tomkins holds that the affects are a universally evolved set of psychobiological programs designed to amplify persons' awareness of factors that threaten or can enhance the well-being of the self. In serving this critical function, they offer vital communication, both to the experiencer and to those with whom he or she interacts.

Tomkins identifies nine basic affect sets. Three of these are positive; four are negative; and two are what he calls "drive auxiliaries." In each of the first seven affects he identifies two levels of intensity—the first mild and the second more intense. Each affect set has its unique patterns of facial and bodily expressions.

Let us examine the positive affect sets. First there is the set identified as *interest* or *excitement.* Here we observe the eyebrows down, the mouth partially open, and the gaze riveted in tracking an object or fixed on it. Second, there is *enjoyment* or *joy,* expressed with a bright and shining face, muscles relaxed, lips open and widened in the smiling response. Third, Tomkins names *surprise* or *startle,* shown on the face with mouth open in astonishment, eyebrows raised, and eyes wide and blinking.

There are four negative affects. First, *distress* or *anguish,* expressed with eyebrows pulled together, the corners of the lips pulled down, and with tears or dilated eyes. Second, *fear* or *terror,* in which the eyes may be frozen open in a fixed stare or moving away from the dreaded object to the side, the skin pale, cold, and sweating, the muscles trembling, the hair on the face and neck standing on end. Third, *shame* or *humiliation,* with eyes averted and downcast, neck and shoulders slumping, and head lowered. Fourth, we note *anger* or *rage,* with a frown, clenched jaw, narrowed eyes, and red face.

The two drive auxiliary affects derive their names from the senses the human body employs to avoid ingesting non-palatable or toxic substances to satisfy the hunger drive—taste and smell. *Disgust* is expressed with the head forward, the mouth shaped as if spitting out distasteful food. Tomkins coined the term *dissmell* for the expression of contempt captured with the raised upper lip, head drawn back, and wrinkles alongside the nose that indicate contact with a foul, repugnant odor. Both these affect sets generalize widely to enable persons to communicate economic but powerful negative evaluations of situations or of other persons and relationships. Both affects suggest expressions or judgments of repugnance, disdain, or contempt. Delivered from a position of actual or claimed superiority, they are capable of separating and distancing persons from each other and of evoking a sense of disvalue in those targeted by them. As we shall see, these affects, when employed in parent-child relations, have particular power to evoke experiences of shame that can toxically tincture the core of the self.

In Tomkins's scheme, *shame-humiliation* is also thought of as an *auxiliary* affect. Rather than being an auxiliary to a drive, however—as *disgust* and *dissmell*—shame as an affect interacts with and is auxiliary to the positive affects of *interest-excitement* and *enjoyment-joy*. As disgust operates only after something has been taken in, shame operates only after interest or enjoyment has been activated. It inhibits one or the other or both. As Tomkins puts it:

> The innate activator of shame is the incomplete reduction of interest or joy. Such a barrier might arise because one is suddenly looked at by another who is strange; or because one wishes to look at, or commune with, another person but suddenly cannot because s/he is strange; or one expected him to be familiar but he suddenly appears unfamiliar; or one started to smile but found one was smiling at a stranger. It might also arise as a consequence of discouragement after having tried and failed, and then lowered one's head in apparent "defeat." . . . Discouragement, shyness, shame, and guilt are identical as affects, though not so experienced because of differential coassembly of perceived causes and consequences. (Tomkins 1987, 143)

The affect set *shame-humiliation* operates to interfere with enjoyment-joy or interest-excitement in circumstances where the self's balance, self-esteem, or standing with others is threatened. The threat can arise from the "strangeness" of another. It can arise from responses of others suggesting the likelihood of their rejection or disvaluing. An illustration will help: In a study employing what has come to be called the "still face" experiment, two-and-a-half- to three-month-old infants and their mothers were filmed in face-to-face interaction under closely replicated circumstances (Tronick et al. 1978). In the first phase of the experiment, the mother is instructed to behave normally while sitting face to face with her infant in pleasant surroundings. Viewed in slow motion, the films show the absorbed interest with which the mother and infant view each other, and the flow of rapidly shifting expressions that occur between them. In the next phase of the experiment, researchers ask the mother to leave the room for a few minutes. They instruct her upon returning to sit down before her infant, just as before, only now she is to make her face as neutral and noncommunicative as possible. Although making eye contact, she is asked to refrain from making any facial expression or gesture. Donald Nathanson, a psychoanalyst and influential interpreter of Tomkins's work on shame, reports a conversation about these films in which child researcher Virginia Demos gave her interpretation of the babies' responses. Nathanson says that for a short time the babies

> will exhibit a number of facial expressions in an apparent attempt to engage the mother in the mode of interaction normal for that dyad. After a while . . . the infant exhibits one of two characteristic behaviors. Some children will cry in distress, but many will slump down in the chair with a sudden loss of body tonus, turning the head downward and to one side, averting their eyes from the mother's face. Viewing such films in slow motion, Demos felt it was difficult to avoid the interpretation that this latter group of children was exhibiting a primitive shame response. Here was a situation that seemed to fit Tomkins's criteria: Shame affect operated to interrupt the affect interest that had been powering the child's attempted interchange with the mother, shame triggered by some signal related to the maternal refusal to participate in the expected interchange. (Nathanson 1987, 21)

The baby involved in this experiment experiences the neurophysiological response that can be triggered by the disruption of the affects of enjoyment-joy and interest-excitement. Notice that this disruption has the peculiar effect of reversing the flow of the baby's attending. From fixation on the mother's face—with its accustomed array of responsive brightness—the infant's pleasurable engagement ceases. Now the baby's attending, suddenly and reflexively, comes to focus on the sensations of his or her own face. This may include the flush of blood to the skin of face and neck, the involuntary dropping of the head and eyes, and the spontaneous aversion of the face. Only after a few seconds will the infant "have" the feelings of confusion, dis-ease, and dislocation that this sudden reversal of attending and abrupt refocusing of it in the self occasions.

This account provides us with an important set of clues about the nature and power—and functions—of the shame-humiliation affect. (1) The shame-humiliation affect occurs in the context of face-to-face relations. (2) It is triggered when something occurring in the relation suggests that the person may experience rejection, disapproval, or exclusion. (3) It registers by means of a set of affective sensations that recall one's attention from the other and redirect it into heightened awareness of self. And (4) it brings a set of disturbing and painful feelings that include confusion, self-doubt, and a sense of unworthiness.

The shame-humiliation affect, I am suggesting, has a unique role among the affects Tomkins identifies in that it is *reflexive* in direction. It gives rise to neurophysiological responses and accompanying feelings that reference and amplify awareness of the *self*. The other eight affects he identifies, in contrast, point to neurophysiological reactions that amplify awareness of states of affairs external to us, registering whether they are threatening, repugnant, interesting, enjoyable, or the like. The shame-humiliation affect, we begin to see, makes foundational contributions to the emergent processes of self-awareness and self-consciousness. It provides powerful motivations for the generation of the cognitive operations involved in constructing the perspectives of others, and especially for constructing their perspectives upon—their construals and evaluations of—the self.

Shame-humiliation does not act alone as an affect amplifying self-awareness and self-evaluation. I believe that there is at least one other central self-reflexive affect of which we need to take account.

Tomkins fails to identify this affect set, though interpreters and extenders of his theory, such as Robert Emde and Donald Nathanson, have done important work with it. I have in mind the affect we can call *confidence-pride*. In confidence-pride, the head is uplifted, the eyes meet and hold the gaze of others, the face reflects ease and gladness. The body feels coherent and supple, and may exhibit the flush of excitement and pleasure. As is shame-humiliation, confidence-pride is probably best thought of as an auxiliary affect. The primary affects interest-excitement and enjoyment-joy seem to be basic to confidence-pride. In this regard, however, they are reflexive affects experienced as being confirmed in one's relations and as amplifying one's sense of well-being and of being valued. Later, as we come to discuss the role of shame-humiliation both in the functioning of conscience and in relation to sin, I will elaborate further on this complementary reflexive affect, confidence-pride, which is in many ways the obverse of shame.

CHAPTER SIX

SHAME, GUILT, AND CONSCIENCE

Shame, we have seen, begins as a non-pathological innate neurobiological affect program in humans. It is one of a number of such affect sets. Gradually in the course of infant and early childhood development the shame-humiliation affect comes to be associated with certain patterns of feeling. With shame, manifested to others and to the self by the lowered head, downcast eyes, averted face, and blush, the accompanying feelings are usually experienced as a sudden jolt, a painful inner jarring, bringing a wince, a smart, or a sting (Lewis 1971, 233-50). Reflexively, the self becomes the object of one's own attention. At the same time, there is some degree of painful awareness that one's self is also the object of others' attention—particularly others' *evaluative* attention.

In a moment, I want to turn to a closer accounting of the development of shame from affect to feelings and from complexes of feelings to full-fledged sets of guiding and evaluative emotions in our lives. As background and context for that task, however, I want to propose that shame has evolved—in our species and potentially, at least, in each of us as persons—into two forms: *discretionary shame* and *disgrace shame.*[1] Each of these forms serves its own distinct function.

Discretionary shame evolves to maintain and strengthen the bonds between persons and the communities of which they are a part. This variant of shame includes tact, sensitivity, respect for others, and respect for the values that the self shares with those to whom he or she prizes connection. This dimension of shame serves as the custodian of a self worthy of respected membership in the group

---

1. The terms "discretionary" and "disgrace" shame are taken from Carl Schneider (1977, 1992). See his important discussion showing that many European languages provide different terms in order to make verbal distinctions between these two types and functions of shame.

or groups that are essential to one's self-esteem and self-worth. Discretionary shame protects those qualities of personhood that are grounds for esteem in the eyes of others and for honest confidence and pride in the self. The jolt, the jarring, the wince or sting of this form of shame can interrupt one's involvement in an activity or relationship that might threaten one's membership in a valued group. In the reflexive turn back into the self occasioned by the dropped head, downcast eyes, slackened neck and shoulders, and flushed face, one experiences emotions connected with the chagrin of imagining one's present pursuit as played out before the eyes of valued others who would disapprove. In the development of shame, from feeling to full-fledged emotion, cognitions and memories enable one to sense in anticipatory ways which potential actions, situations, and relations are likely to bring the pain of shame. These become the source of internal promptings of shame and are constitutive of discretionary shame.

Discretionary shame comes into play in seemingly trivial as well as in very significant decisions and choices in our lives. From deciding what clothes to wear on a particular occasion to purchasing a car, part of our thinking and weighing concerns the statement our choices make about our values, our tastes, our priorities, our character. We recognize that such choices and priorities, cumulatively taken, not only build our "image" in the eyes of others whom we value as associates and friends, but also build and modify our character, the structure of our personhood—both in the eyes of others and in our own inmost eye. Discretionary shame involves both instinctual evaluative responses and the exercise of what we can call moral imagination. This aspect of shame plays a central positive role in the formation and strength of *conscience.*

If discretionary shame is premonitory and anticipatory, *disgrace shame* evolves as the painful set of emotions in which one feels exposed as unworthy, as defective, or as having failed to meet some set of standards necessary for the esteem of important others and of the self. The standards by which one fears or recognizes personal failure may be both moral and nonmoral. These are standards for character, for qualities of personhood, and as such they imply devaluation of the total self. Disgrace shame can involve gaffes, misjudgments in taste, the display of weaknesses, or the demonstration of an ignorance or a naiveté one ought not have. It may also be the pained response one has to the recognition of some overall pattern in one's own behavior that reveals as reprehensible the motives and underlying aspects of one's way of living.

In the category of gaffes and disclosures of painful naiveté, I remember my first dinner date as a sixteen-year-old. Dressed in my best attire, I had asked my current girlfriend to go with me to the Town House, the most expensive and sophisticated restaurant my small mountain town afforded. Among the appetizers listed on the impressive menu was "Soup Tureen." Imagining this to be a delicate French soup, but not knowing its contents, I asked the server to tell us about "Soup Tureen." "Oh," he said, "it just means a large soup bowl from which you serve yourself. It's right over there. The soup tonight is French Onion." I took my red face and embarrassed pride to get a bowl of this mysterious substance.

One gets over disgrace shame in this form of simple embarrassment. But disgrace shame is most devastating when a person experiences public exposure of the fact and consequences of a pattern of action or a way of being that has gone on for a long time. I am speaking here not of a one-time lapse, an inadvertent mistake due to poor judgment—devastatingly embarrassing as these can be—but rather of an ongoing, deliberate action. Take the case of a respected minister, entrusted for twenty-five years with the operations and investment management of a voluntary retirement program for his fellow clergy. Now as his colleagues are reaching the age when they can withdraw their funds, it is discovered that their assets have disappeared. Audits show that the minister has embezzled over a half-million dollars over a period of years. Suddenly one whose character had been thought to be beyond reproach is revealed as being self-deceived and a deceiver and betrayer of others. The disgrace shame pours over him, his wife, their children, his church and colleagues in ministry, his profession.

Disgrace shame is to be differentiated from guilt. Shame brings a global sense of being seen by the self and others as defective or flawed as a person. This is recognized in the form of painful self-consciousness formed through the responses of others and through one's own self-recognition and self-accusation. Guilt, on the other hand, represents self-judgment occasioned by a particular act or a specific response to a situation. In guilt, one can separate the self and questions of its overall worthiness from its actions. The latter can be evaluated as good or bad, right or wrong, without necessarily raising the question of the basic worthiness of the total self. In guilt there is honest self-condemnation of specific acts, based upon the specific violation of a principle or standard to which one is committed. Guilt can be addressed by repentance, apology, restitution (where possible), and forgiveness. In shame, however, it is a question of coming to terms with a lack, deficit, or defect of the self *qua* self. Release from a pervasive sense of disgrace shame requires acknowledgment and exposure of the defect or lack to a trusted other or others and the undertaking of substantial change in one's way of being a self.[2] It is clear that disgrace shame plays a foundational role in what we may call the punitive and self-reformative aspect of conscience.

We have identified two major faces of shame, as it functions to guard a sense of personal worthiness and membership in valued communities. We have suggested the contributions these two faces of shame make to the operations of conscience. What do we know about the movement of shame from affect to feelings, and from feeling to the emotional complexes fundamental to the character or personality structure of the self? How do the patterns and content of shame take form in a person's life?

More than forty years ago, Erik Erikson first offered his revision and expansion of Freud's psychosexual stages of development (Erikson 1963, 63). The first two of his eight psychosocial stages are of enduring importance for understanding the forming role of shame in the development of the self. In the first year of life, Erikson says, the infant's ego deals with the challenge of developing a sense of basic trust. This means a sense of being "at home" in its new environment, a feeling of the trustworthiness of its caretakers, and of being a welcomed and valued newcomer. The quality of mutuality between caregivers and the baby is marked by consistency and ease of feeding, and by the mirroring in which the infant

---

2. Twelve Step programs, especially in the original formulations found in the approach of Alcoholics Anonymous, provide a profoundly wise approach to the process of acknowledging the bases and patterns of disgrace shame in one's life, and for accepting group support for and during the process of fundamental change in one's ways of being a self.

develops a confirmed sense of coherence and worth through the eyes and responsive communication it enjoys with its primal others. Psychoanalytic writers since Erikson, such as Heinz Kohut (1977), Alice Miller (1981), and others, have elaborated the mirroring process further and have clarified our understandings of the dangers of "narcissistic deprivation." This occurs when, either through anxiety or distraction or through the narcissistic deficiencies of the caregivers, the child is seen and mirrored with reference to the needs and anxieties of the caregivers and not in such a way as to experience a confirming acknowledgment of the child's separate and uniquely valuable selfhood. In this latter situation, Erikson says, a ratio of mistrust over trust can emerge, leaving the child vulnerable to self-doubt and to feelings of unworthiness and anxiousness.

Recall that Daniel Stern's work (Stern 1985) combines cognitive and psychosocial theories of development with recent research psychology findings on infants. He offers valuable refinements of the Eriksonian perspective. Through the four sub-phases of infant development we traced in chapter 1, Stern traces the infant's emergent sense of the firmness and initiative of the self through growingly complex patterns of interaction with caregivers. Especially important is his insight that before the emergence of language as a means of expressing feelings and encoding memories, the child has significant experiences of communication with caregivers through body and gesture and through the production, reading, and matching of affects. Prior to language, the infant in optimal development has learned to participate in nonverbal games or rituals (peekaboo, goodnight, and so on) and in what we discussed as "affect attunement." In affect attunement, as we saw, the infant (often playfully) expresses an affect, which the parent "reads" and responds to with an affect pattern that is different from but resonant with that produced by the child. The child, in turn, "reading" the parent's answering message—"I see you. I *feel* with you!"—responds with increased affective exuberance. Plainly, the same skills that make such joyful interchanges possible also make possible the child's reading of painful or contemptuous parental affect such as that expressed by the gestures and facial expressions that signal *disgust* or *dissmell.*

Stern's perspective provides observational bases that account for the dynamics of "mirroring" as discussed by Kohut, Alice Miller, and the self-psychologists. Through his work we have a deepened appreciation of how, prior to language and prior to conscious and retrievable memory, the child forms and stores cognitions and affect messages that coalesce to form the mixed feelings of trust and basic mistrust that fund the child's emergence into the use of language and into Erikson's second stage. Even prior to language acquisition, residues from the affective interchanges between infants and those upon whom they are completely dependent have formed. Erikson's global language of "trust versus mistrust," understood dynamically, points to the infant's location on a continuum between the subjective experience of incoherent/disvalued/non-mirrored selfhood, at one end, and coherent/cherished/accurately mirrored selfhood, on the other. A particular child's location on that continuum would identify the balance already taking unconscious form in the child's sense of self, between the reflexive affects of confidence-pride and shame-humiliation.

Showing an early appreciation of the foundational importance of shame, Erikson identified his second stage as the crisis of *autonomy* versus *shame and doubt.* Occurring between eighteen months and three years, entry into this stage is marked by the child's being able to "stand on her own two feet." It coincides with the maturation of the sphincter muscles and with the cultural expectations that children will learn to control the release of bladder and bowels. At the same time that caregivers are trying to establish limits and curb their children's angry outbursts, children are feeling urges to explore their environments and to claim exclusive ownership of interesting toys anytime they want to enjoy them.

Erikson says that shame is visual and has to do with a sense of being exposed and seen by others before one is ready. Between eighteen and twenty months, most children recognize that the image they see in a mirror is themselves. Some observers claim that frequently children this age, unaware of being observed, will look at themselves in an available mirror and exhibit a momentary shudder, accompanied with the physiological symptoms of shame-humiliation (Nathanson 1992). It is as though the child is experiencing a first explicit sense of self-consciousness—an awareness of being seen or being on display to others. This is coupled, say researchers Jerome Kagan (Kagan 1984) and Judy Dunn (Dunn 1987), with an emergent attentiveness to standards for the way things are supposed to be. Not restricted to rules regarding morality or fairness, this interest in standards can be seen in the child's distress at seeing soiled clothing, a broken toy, or a stuffed animal with a severed head.

Similar distress that shows concern for standards can be evoked when children observe actions that hurt another child or person. Kagan attributes this distress to the child's capacity for empathy and its identification with the discomfort that comes from being hit, spanked, or bruised (Kagan 1984, 126). In a further illustration of the young child's concern with standards, Kagan reports that, in an experiment, two-year-olds become very upset if they are unable to meet a standard for mastery imposed by another person. In the experiment, a woman approaches a child, picks up some toys, and uses them to act out some brief sequences that are difficult to remember or to implement. Then she returns to her chair. In response, Kagan says, children from diverse cultural settings will immediately cry or protest. Kagan explains this response:

> I believe that the child invents an obligation to duplicate the adult's actions and, additionally, knows that she is unable to do so. The combination of awareness of a standard for a performance to be met with an inability to meet that standard is the basis for the crying and protest. However, children who do meet a self-imposed standard will show signs of joy: the two-year-old typically smiles spontaneously after spending several minutes building a six-block tower or finishing a difficult puzzle. . . . [The smile] is a private response reflecting the recognition that she has met the standard she set for herself. (Kagan 1984, 127)

This qualitatively new sense of self-awareness, combined with concern about standards, helps us see that the two-year-old is poised in a place of great vulnerability as regards shame, selfhood, and conscience. It is a time before there is sufficient cognitive ability or experience to fully understand the standards the child recognizes as implicit in parental or adult admonitions to be a "good boy" or a "good girl." Newly aware of self, newly aware that others are observing and evaluating the self one is, the child is vulnerable, to the very core, to the expectations, messages, and affects communicated by those upon whose approval and love the child is still absolutely dependent. Their affective messages of approval and disapproval can register powerfully on the very finely calibrated scale of self-worth taking form in the child's inmost heart. At the same time, parents and their surrogates are setting limits, insisting on new behaviors, and beginning to assign blame or responsibility for acts or impulsive behaviors of the child. Experiences of conflict with socializing adults and with siblings bring the full range of affects into play. With language and memory now in the picture, this full range of affects—both of conflict and of intimacy—are being populated with specific feelings, cognitions, interpretations, and memories. Drawing upon such consistent experiences of the affect confidence and pride as the child may have, and upon her growing understanding of standards and expectations, she is constructing an ideal image of the self—what the psychoanalytic tradition calls an *ego ideal.* She is also constructing—partially at a conscious level—images of a shadow self, the rudiments of a negative identity, composed from the experiences of shame-humiliation affect and the fragments of painful meanings attached to them in the family setting or its surrogate.

In this conscious and unconscious process of constructing images of the ideal and the shadow self, what we call conscience is taking form in the child. The assembly of affects and feelings that constitute shame, in both its discretionary and its disgrace modes, contribute foundational elements in the formation of conscience, as in the forming sense of self.

Throughout this chapter in which we have dealt with shame as the custodian of personal worthiness I have meant to portray the essentially positive role that both discretionary and disgrace shame play in the forming and maintenance of a sense of balance and worthiness in the emerging self. These windows into early childhood development have begun to convey the extraordinary way humans have evolved the affective building blocks for the emotional complexes that ground the felt sense of self, and that help to maintain the sense of worth and competence necessary for feeling oneself to be a valued and integral member of one's primary groups. Any system so sensitively calibrated for registering and monitoring factors that could threaten the self's sense of worth and worthiness for relationship can surely be exploited and distorted. We turn now to a brief examination of several types and degrees of distortion to which shame is susceptible.

CHAPTER SEVEN

CROSSING THE SPECTRUM OF SHAME

In the burst of attention to shame in recent years most concern has focused on "toxic shame." Mediated by the televised lectures of John Bradshaw and by the proliferating influence of Twelve Step programs, the language of "dysfunctional" family life and the dynamics of "codependence" have become part of our daily conversations. Toxic shame refers to the poisonous impact on early childhood experience of families organized to accommodate one or more leaders who are incapacitated by drug or alcohol abuse, or involved in afflicting spouse or children with emotional, physical, or sexual abuse. In this book we will not neglect the attempt to understand the spiritual impact of—and the possibilities of healing—toxic shame.

There are, however, other types and degrees of shame experience. We will be looking in depth at some of these other dynamics of shame in these pages. I find it helpful to organize types of shame experience along a continuum. These types are separated from each other primarily by differences in the intensity and comprehensiveness of shame experience each represents and by the resulting degrees of distortion and use of psychic energy required to compensate for or suppress the crippling impact of shame.

Along the continuum of shame experiences I locate the following five types and degrees of shame, arranged in a sequence that moves from healthy or "normal" shame toward increasingly distorting variations:

1. *Healthy Shame.* The capacity for healthy shame has evolved with human beings and is essential for protecting our relations with people and groups whom we love and upon whom we are dependent. Healthy shame serves as an essential guardian of our desire to be worthy persons. In chapter 6 we identified two crucial functions

of healthy shame. We called them discretionary shame and disgrace shame. Discretionary shame gives us an almost instinctual "early warning system" that something we are feeling or thinking of doing could lead to the diminishment of self-respect, and if known to others, a decrease in their confidence and care in our direction. Disgrace shame, on the other hand, is the pervasive sense of self-disapproval we feel when we have inadvertently or by design done something that reveals us to others—and to ourselves—as unworthy or less than we want to be. Healthy shame in both these modes constitutes an indispensable foundation for conscience.

2. *Perfectionist Shame.* Second on the continuum of shame experiences, this type often fuels those in its grip to high achievement and to the gaining of approval and success. In perfectionist shame, as in all distorting shame experiences, however, there is a significant measure of suppression of access to the place of truth in the heart or soul of the ones who bear it. In order to gain the approval and affirmation of the people the young child most depends upon, he focuses attention upon meeting the program, values, and behaviors they require. This approval, so indispensable to the child's sense of worth, comes at great cost. The child pays the price for this approval and esteem in neglect of his own evaluation of experiences and his developing sense of inner guidance and desire. Following D. W. Winnicott, Alice Miller, and others, I call this set of responses in perfectionist shame the creation of a "false self." It represents a loss of access to one's own "heart." Much so-called burnout in the adult years can be traced to a person's need to free the self from the parental or child-culture script or program he adopted to meet his family's and social group's conditions of worth. Healing comes through his being helped to reclaim access to his own suppressed heart and crippled will.

Perfectionist shame usually has its earliest rootage in the first year of life. To some significant degree the child is likely to have experienced inconsistent or inadequate mirroring in relation to the primary caregiver or caregivers. Depression, distraction, or the emotional or physical absence of a primary caregiver can be factors in this lack of consistent mutuality or mirroring. Narcissistic deprivation in the childhood of a parent or parents can lead to clumsy or inattentive interaction with the child, or to "tone-deaf" participation in situations that could provide occasions for "affect attunement." A primary caregiver could be so insecure in that role, so anxious about making mistakes, that he or she does not see and sense the rhythms and needs of the actual baby. Rather, he or she fixes attention on guidelines and procedures prescribed by some expert or another. Worse, the caregiver, instead of serving as a mirror for the forming sense of self in the infant, can require that the infant serve the function of ratifying and gratifying his or her own deep neediness.

Patterns of interaction of this sort can lead to a subjective sense in the infant of incoherent selfhood, coupled with a feeling of unclear boundaries. The infant has accumulated the residues of interrupted enjoyment-joy affect brought about by experiences of shame-humiliation. He or she lacks a sense of trust and confidence and of self *rely-ability* as regards the self's reactions and initiatives in relations with others.

In a real sense the lack of mirroring just described results in a loss or diminishment of "face." When the child emerges toward the self-awareness in the second year, she will be likely to tilt the construction of the experience of being seen and evaluated by those who matter in anxious or negative directions. Fearing the threat of devaluation and unworthiness, she becomes particularly sensitive to the standards implicit in parental expressions of approval and disapproval. The ego ideal of the parent (or, frequently, the *superego* of the parent) supplants any constructions of the ideal self that the child might make for herself. Instead, the child tries to construct a way of being a self designed to fulfill and exceed the parental ideals of worthiness and competence. Distrusting her own fragmentary evaluations and experiences, the child suppresses her potentials for guidance, along with the pain of feeling unworthy and unacknowledged. Often the false self-identity—the perfectionist self—is reinforced by the parents, with the sanctions of religious and class ideals of moral superiority. Such children, rewarded by the conditional regard of their parents, often succeed well in the other socializing environments through which they move. Often it is not until much later in their lives that they begin to come to terms with the alienation from their own core self—from their own authentic heart—that resulted from their years of living out the perfectionist program they took on to meet the conditions of worth in the first little battalion of the family. The following window into the life of a forty-three-year-old woman provides an informative instance of coming to terms with early perfectionist shame and some elements of a false self.

"Susan," now in her early forties, enjoys respect and success in her profession. She is highly effective as a mother and wife, and she is recognized as a leader in the religious denomination to which she belongs. It was in her role as leader in this latter context that I heard her give an extraordinary public talk. Asked to speak about the "foundations of her faith," Susan fulfilled her assignment with a quality of rare candor and painful insight, born of being deeply in touch with her experiences during a time of profound transition in her inner life.

Susan began her talk by evoking scenes from her childhood. She told of growing up in a small midwestern town where the summers lasted a long time. Her father had built a small structure she called "the hut" where she and friends spent a lot of time. She said, "I would spend hours in the hut, sweeping the dirt floor. It was as hard-polished by my feet as those pioneer homes I learned about in school. My dreaming was in rhythm with the rustling of wind through the tall corn stalks in the garden that was in the front of the hut. . . . Do you remember how corn leaves feel, snagging your fingers when you rub them the wrong way? I could hear it in the wind, and it was woven into my dreams."

One day, Susan remembers, she and a friend—both about seven—went over to play in the yard of a family that had a big double garden. The garden ran alongside an irrigation ditch separating the vegetables from an apple tree and a giant wild rose bush. "While we were trailing our feet in the ditch and examining the tiny green apples," she said, "Mrs. White, who was an old gray-haired woman (and was only that to me—an old gray-haired woman), called to us and told us she had something special to give us. Her present was an old-fashioned baby doll with blue porcelain eyes. We giggled and thanked her. And then we ran back to the ditch, still snickering quietly. Burdened with a gift we didn't want, we dug a hole under the apple tree, and we buried the doll."

Susan told us that her talk would involve, metaphorically at least, a resurrection of that doll buried so long ago and a revisioning of its reception and burial. Retrieving the doll, it became apparent, would serve as a symbol for her effort to reclaim some long-buried part of her own deeper self. We began to grasp this as Susan told us the following:

> I'm not the person who was asked to give [this] talk. I'm actually here under false pretenses. That person had a clear-cut value system, personality, and style of presentation that pleased other people and sometimes herself. But during the last two months, I've discovered that in many ways, that self was a mask I had created over time. She could have told you charmingly about the amusing way she's decorated the foundations of her faith with clever hints acquired at homemaking meetings as well as literature and film conferences. She knew God loved her, found pleasure and congruence with a great deal of her religious community's culture and theology. I'm resisting the great temptation to put on that mask, to become that person, and to let her deliver her version of the foundations of faith.
> . . . Right now I'm caught. Caught in a paradigm shift, flat-footed in a period of self-examination triggered by major surgery followed by four weeks of isolation and introspection with ten hours of sleep a day and no children.

Her surgery involved a hysterectomy. In healing the incision from this surgery, she said, she found that there were other, less visible wounds that had to be healed, or at least recognized in some ways. It was as though the deep structures of her identity and faith had crumbled, leaving the "temple of identity" floating above her, sustained by nothing, yet still operative and functioning. But inside, everything had changed. She remarked: "Every relationship, every attitude, every memory seems different, calling out for examination and re-definition. I'm only interested in feelings—*my* feelings. And ideas and other people only as they relate to those feelings. Sometimes when I meet friends or engage in daily tasks, I feel, "Who is this person anyway?" I feel defined by my past, a prisoner of personality. I want to be loved, I want to be cherished, but I'm very suspicious of past strategies I've used to evoke those feelings from other people, from God, and from myself."

Susan gave insightful articulation of the insights she found emerging from her time of dismantling and beginning the reconstruction of her identity and faith. Especially significant here is the discovery she put this way: "There is an identity beneath all the belief systems that have dissolved. Although this process has been filled with fear and with pain, I haven't dissolved. . . . There is something undeniably 'me' present, constituted by the pain, as well as the denial of that pain. And the revisioning generates assurance of this identity at the very same time it threatens it." Allied with this irreducible sense of an authentic self, Susan seemed to be finding an awareness of unique purpose or dynamic source of direction from within. Referring to a book by Joseph Campbell she had been given, she said, "He speaks of the real power of the left-hand path, of following your bliss, instead of instructions. Our demons, he says, are our own limitations, which shut us off from the realization of the ubiquity of the spirit. . . . With his words I caught a glimmer of what had been happening to me. I had been launched on a vision quest. But mine had led backward, first, revisioning the original visions I had disowned, that I had buried."

Susan closed her statement with a return to the metaphor of retrieving the doll buried thirty-five years ago in her childhood. "The latest image I know I need to revision is that little girl I used to be. The one who buried the baby doll an old woman gave her. I'm sure that doll had something to do with losing my uterus and my ovaries, but I only know that intellectually. Now I'm on a vision quest, to dig up the doll, wipe the dirt from her porcelain blue eyes, look deep into them, and hold her close. After we rock together quietly under the apple tree, smelling the wild roses, I'll inquire of her why I buried her, what she learned while she was underground, and why every day I look more and more like the old woman who gave her to me."

3. *Shame Due to Enforced Minority Status.* Shame arises in a child's first experiences of social self-consciousness. Between eighteen and twenty-four months of age, children recognize themselves in the mirror and are suddenly aware that they are being seen and evaluated. For the first time they become consciously attentive to the evaluations others make of them. With the finely sensitive calibrations of their just-forming sense of self and self-worth, they bring great vulnerability. Parents and caretakers transmit the quality of their own self-esteem as they nurture the children in their

care. Sadly, where social discriminations based on minority status have become part of a child's familial identity, even before venturing forth into the world beyond the family the child will be impacted and will embrace a measure of shame due to enforced minority status. This transmission of parent and familial shame to children is a form of *ascribed* shame. It has little to do with the personal qualities of the family or their children. It has everything to do with the social environment's dis-valuing of some qualities over which they have little or no control. Most potent among the forms of this type of ascribed shame are the distortions due to socioeconomic class, race, ethnic background, sometimes religion, and—most commonly—gender.

The following story graphically discloses shame that combines childhood vulnerability with shame due to enforced minority status in terms of race, gender, and social class. It comes from the opening of the first of Maya Angelou's autobiographical books, *I Know Why the Caged Bird Sings*:

> *"What you looking at me for?*
> *I didn't come to stay . . ."*

I hadn't so much forgot as I couldn't bring myself to remember. Other things were more important.

> *"What you looking at me for?*
> *I didn't come to stay . . ."*

Whether I could remember the rest of the poem or not was immaterial. The truth of the statement was like a wadded-up handkerchief, sopping wet in my fists, and the sooner they accepted it the quicker I could let my hands open and the air would cool my palms.

> *"What you looking at me for . . . ?"*

The children's section of the Colored Methodist Episcopal Church was wiggling and giggling over my well-known forgetfulness.

The dress I wore was lavender taffeta, and each time I breathed it rustled, and now that I was sucking in air to breathe out shame it sounded like crepe paper on the back of hearses.

As I'd watched Momma put ruffles on the hem and cute little

119

tucks around the waist, I knew that once I put it on I'd look like a movie star. (It was silk and that made up for the awful color.) I was going to look like one of the sweet little white girls who were everybody's dream of what was right with the world. Hanging softly over the black Singer sewing machine, it looked like magic, and when people saw me wearing it they were going to run up to me and say, "Marguerite [sometimes it was 'dear Marguerite'], forgive us, please, we didn't know who you were," and I would answer generously, "No, you couldn't have known. Of course I forgive you."

Just thinking about it made me go around with angel's dust sprinkled over my face for days. But Easter's early morning sun had shown the dress to be a plain ugly cut-down from a white woman's once-was-purple throwaway. It was old-lady-long too, but it didn't hide my skinny legs, which had been greased with Blue Seal Vaseline and powdered with the Arkansas red clay. The age-faded color made my skin look dirty like mud, and everyone in the church was looking at my skinny legs.

Wouldn't they be surprised when one day I woke up out of my black ugly dream, and my real hair, which was long and blond, would take the place of the kinky mass that Momma wouldn't let me straighten? My light blue eyes were going to hypnotize them, after all the things they said about "my daddy must of been a Chinaman" (I thought they meant made out of china, like a cup) because my eyes were so small and squinty. Then they would understand why I had never picked up a Southern accent, or spoke the common slang, and why I had to be forced to eat pigs' tails and snouts. Because I was really white and because a cruel fairy stepmother, who was understandably jealous of my beauty, had turned me into a too-big Negro girl, with nappy black hair, broad feet and a space between her teeth that would hold a number-two pencil.

"What you looking . . ." The minister's wife leaned toward me, her long yellow face full of sorry. She whispered, "I just come to tell you, it's Easter Day." I repeated, jamming the words together, "Ijustcometotellyouit'sEasterDay," as low as possible. The giggles hung in the air like melting clouds that were waiting to rain on me. I held up two fingers, close to my chest, which meant that I had to go to the toilet, and tiptoed toward the rear of the church. Dimly, somewhere over my head, I heard ladies saying, "Lord bless the child," and "Praise God." My head was up and my eyes were open, but I didn't see anything. Halfway down the aisle, the church exploded with "Were you there when they crucified my Lord?" and

I tripped over a foot stuck out from the children's pew. I stumbled and started to say something, or maybe to scream, but a green persimmon, or it could have been a lemon, caught me between the legs and squeezed. I tasted the sour on my tongue and felt it in the back of my mouth. Then before I reached the door, the sting was burning down my legs and into my Sunday socks. I tried to hold, to squeeze it back, to keep it from speeding, but when I reached the church porch I knew I'd have to let it go, or it would probably run right back up to my head and my poor head would burst like a dropped watermelon, and all the brains and spit and tongue and eyes would roll all over the place. So I ran down into the yard and let it go. I ran, peeing and crying, not toward the toilet out back but to our house. I'd get a whipping for it, to be sure, and the nasty children would have something new to tease me about. I laughed anyway, partially for the sweet release; still, the greater joy came not only from being liberated from the silly church but from the knowledge that I wouldn't die from a busted head.

If growing up is painful for the Southern Black girl, being aware of her displacement is the rust on the razor that threatens the throat.

It is an unnecessary insult. (Angelou 1970, 3-6)

Shame due to enforced minority status has largely been neglected by the popular discussions of shame. We cannot afford to neglect its potency and destructiveness. When it is compounded with one or more of the other types of shame we are identifying, it gives the persons and groups affected by it terribly crippling disadvantages.[1] To acknowledge shame due to enforced minority status will remind us throughout this book that personal shame cannot be healed just by attention to reworking patterns in one's inner self. This variant of shame cannot be healed without attention to issues of economic and political justice, equality, and the effective affirmation of inclusiveness in societies.

---

1. In this respect, it makes sense to view *shame due to enforced minority status* not so much as a particular form of shame placed on the continuum, as I am discussing it here, but rather as a factor that can be present in accompaniment with any of the types of shame from "healthy" to "perfectionist" to "toxic" shame, and to "shamelessness." As Maya Angelou puts it so graphically, this form of shame, in accompaniment with any of the other forms, "is the rust on the razor that threatens the throat." My former student and now colleague Carol Pitts helped me focus this insight.

4. *Toxic Shame.* All of the forms of distortion that our capacity for healthy shame undergoes are toxic. If this is so, what leads to our giving one of these types separate attention as toxic shame? Remember that we are basing this typology on the degrees and the comprehensiveness of distortion in shame. And we are making distinctions based upon the amount of psychic energy required to suppress the awareness and pain of shaming conditions and memories. Toxic shame arises when children are placed in situations where the conditions of survival depend upon their adhering to unacknowledged "rules" of familial or social life that keep them in "double bind" emotional relationships. For example, the children in a family may get the clear sense that they must ally themselves in support of their mother's continual devaluing and critical belittling of their alcoholic father. At the same time, however, outside the home they are never to speak of his alcoholism and are to respond to any "slighting" remark about him with staunch denial and with a firm defense of his and the family's honor. In these kinds of situations the "false self" is on stage most of the time in a person's life. The core of the self is built around shaping and maintaining a public posture that contradicts in many ways the everyday private realities of the child's life. The public self must be created in significant measure from the observation of others than the child's immediate family. The child's loyalty and love for those nearest and dearest—and for the self—are thereby deeply divided and ambivalent. Considerable psychic energy is required to suppress and defend against the inner pain of this division and ambivalence.

To deepen our understanding of toxic shame, I will build on the metaphor of the "heart" to refer to the core self and to the deepest, felt truth of an authentic self. The degree of shame's distortion we are discussing here may be designated as the "broken heart." The distortions of shame grow in degree of alienation from the core self when the quality of parental care adds significant physical, emotional, and possibly sexual abuse to the lack of adequate mutuality and mirroring in the early years. More pervasively distorting, yet, are contexts where patterns of family life suppress expression of most or all truthful feelings and emotions, in the service of stretching a cover of public acceptability over a pit of damaging and damaged relations. The child coming to a sense of self and of self-value in these more distorting conditions frequently must construct split images of the parents or their surrogates. This splitting, unconsciously carried out, allows the child to preserve the conscious sense of having a loving parent or family. At the same time, however, the child widens a split in the self occasioned by (1) the suppression from consciousness of both the awareness and the memory of his or her suffering and (2) the investment of psychic energy required to maintain the system of defenses. This is "heart-brokenness."

The result of the physical, emotional, and sexual violence children experience in such environments can be properly referred to as "toxic" shame. In such instances it is difficult for a child to develop a sense of clear boundaries for the self. And though the child may develop a brave face to make day-to-day life in public bearable, he or she is likely to feel distant and guarded in any relations requiring or allowing genuine intimacy, maintaining a social cover for a self that feels damaged and of dubious worth.

We are given a courageous and ultimately encouraging window into the sources and the pain of toxic shame through the story shared by a man named Dan. Dan's path to unearthing the suppressed memories he shares began with what he characterized as his extreme reactions to his three-year-old daughter's being molested by a neighborhood boy. By this time a minister and a partner with his father in business, Dan began a journey marked with great pain to unravel a seamless net of lies and deceptions that had protected his "perfect Christian" family of origin. Committed to help others deal with these hidden sources of shame, Dan decided to bring his story into the sunlight of grace and truth.[2]

Seven-year-old Dan was speaking: "God loves you and has a wonderful plan for your life. Let me share what God can do for you. He will give you joy unspeakable, love undeserved, peace in tribulation, and a life filled with happiness." Remembering this as an adult, he says, "For a seven-year-old, my delivery was flawless. Sincerity flowed from my very being. Could this be the day my two

---

2. Dan's story can be found in his essay, "Uncovering the Self: The False Self," which appears in *Escaping the Shadows, Seeking the Light* (Brewer 1991), pp. 23-32. All quotations in this section are from Dan's account.

friends would say yes to Jesus? I was overwhelmed with anticipation." The adult Dan tells us that his boyhood evangelistic efforts were successful. His two friends gave their lives to Jesus. "This event," he says, "would change my life forever. In the years before, I had already learned to view myself as worthless, strange, dirty, and alone. Something was wrong with me. It seemed other kids would play with me only when my mother bribed them with candy, cookies, or doughnuts. As far back as I could remember I had been lonely and confused. I was not really sure why I felt such pain."

Dan told the leader of his outreach group about his success at witnessing. The leader jubilantly told Dan's parents, who were evangelists themselves. Dan received overwhelming affirmation, love, and pride from his parents. But after a week or so, things settled back to normal, and Dan, along with his younger sibling, returned to the lonely life with a nanny provided by the religious organization to which his parents gave their every waking moment.

"As time passed," he says, "I became the best Christian I knew how to be. The only shadow on my faith was the sexual desire I occasionally felt. I remember thinking it must be normal to have pictures of committing sexual acts with my mother swimming in my mind. . . . I knew that as a Christian, I had to learn to control those disturbing desires. I had to put all filthiness out of my mind and never think such thoughts. Nevertheless, the recurring parade of sexual pictures never quit."

Dan tells us that when he was between the ages of eight and sixteen his mother tried to commit suicide seven times. On a number of occasions he wrestled razor blades or drugs away from her, and he remembered accompanying her as she was rushed to the hospital for emergency treatment for slit wrists or a sleeping pill overdose. Once, when she had overdosed and was passing out, his father put the mother, Dan, and his little sister in the car to go to a hospital and instructed Dan to keep slapping his mother to keep her from going under. "We surely did not want anyone in our city to find out, so we drove out of town. As time passed, slapping failed to awaken her, so my father screamed, 'Hit her with your fist, harder! Come on now, harder!' . . . I trembled in panic as I hit my mother and watched the blood trickle down her face."

Finally they reached a hospital two cities away. After several hours alone with his sister in the car, Dan feared that his mother had died. He found a pay phone and tried to call an uncle for help. "Just as I heard ringing on the other end of the line, I felt my body fly across the hallway and then my face slap against the wall. Staggering to my feet, I faced my father. Writhing in anger, he screamed into my face, 'Do you want someone to find out what happened? Don't you realize they will think bad of you? We will *all* look bad. How could you do that to us!'"

In breaking through his suppressed memories, Dan recalled that when he was nine, between episodes of attempted suicide his mother would "blank out" and think that he was her father. "During these times," he says, "she would reenact past experiences using me as a substitute father. When Mom thought I was her father, she would do something to me I couldn't quite remember. But I did know she would beat me afterward." The mother's father had killed himself when she was nineteen. She told Dan that he had sexually molested her. "Years later, when the repressed trauma began surfacing," he said, "I realized that beginning at age three, she would lay me down on the bed and lick my genitals. She would then sob and cry, 'Daddy, Daddy, why did you make me do it?' Then she would beat me."

Though troubled by feelings of deficiency and lack, adults whose childhoods have included relations and experiences like those of Dan can shape and pursue challenging paths of self-improvement and striving for success that promise compensatory vindication for the self. They have to deal with legacies from their childhoods that function as undertows to their aspirations. The denied, unconscious sense of violation and worthlessness they carry from the past may work like an inner saboteur, undermining their confidence and performance at crucial times. Worse, as parents themselves they may recycle the violence and abuse of their own childhoods due to unconscious identification with the parental aggressors of their own experience and the unrecognized and unaddressed pool of anger carried deep in the memory cells of their bodies. Through his work with a group of persons who have supported one another in reclaiming painful memories and seeking healing through bringing such memories into the sunlight of acceptance, grace, and

125

truth, Dan is finding ways to reconstruct his life and experience healing. He is committed to ending the cycle of sexual and other forms of abuse that made his family of origin an incubator for toxic shame.

Alice Miller has written:

> The greatest cruelty that can be inflicted on children is to refuse to let them express their anger and suffering except at the risk of losing their parents' love and affection. The anger stemming from early childhood is stored up in the unconscious, and since it basically represents a healthy, vital source of energy, an equal amount of energy must be expended to repress it. An upbringing that succeeds in sparing the parents at the expense of the child's vitality sometimes leads to suicide or extreme drug addiction, which is a form of suicide. (Miller 1981)

Miller's comment serves as a useful transition to the final and most serious level of distorted shame we will consider. This we can properly call "shamelessness."

5. *Shamelessness.* At the extreme opposite end of our continuum from healthy shame, we find the form of distortion that can be called shamelessness. The roots of this position seem often to lie in severe disruptions of childhood relations of intimacy and reciprocal love with parents or caregivers. Remember that Erik Erikson points to the first challenge of the infant's life—for both the baby and those in the caregiving environment—as that of building a relationship of mutual emotional attunement and reliance that he calls "Basic Trust." Other students of early child development point to the role of parental "mirroring" in the child's building a coherent and responsive sense of being a self. By mirroring they mean the ways caregivers, through their attending to the child and their emotional responding to her, provide a kind of focal reflection through which she comes to feel known and loved, and to shape an experience of unity in a selfhood that is of cherished worth. Stern and other interpreters of early childhood emotional development speak of "affective attunement" in which the baby of ten to twelve months initiates emotional communication through facial expressions and body movements and experiences caregivers' recognizing and responding, also through facial expressions and

vocalizations, with both experiencing a shared sense of "I see you, I feel with you, I read your signals and meanings and share them." Infants vary widely in their interests and needs for these kinds of interchange, as do adults. But there seems to be a minimal threshold of need that, if not met, permanently cripples the person's capacities for empathetic feeling and knowing with others. When this kind of lack is combined with abuse, neglect, and disvaluing treatment, the child's lack of empathy can be combined with a deep going anger and rage. Such children can develop "hardened hearts"; they can lack *conscience* (*con*, meaning "with"; *scientia*, meaning "ways of knowing"; *conscience*, a "feeling or knowing with others"). In its hardened and extreme forms we are speaking here of the sociopathic personality. This is the person who so lacks empathy and compassion, who has such measureless rage that he can injure or destroy others with little or no feelings of remorse, guilt, or shame.

At the time of the outbreak of the war in the Middle East in January 1991, I read a book on Saddam Hussein, which included a chapter on his boyhood and adolescence (J. Miller and L. Mylroie 1990). There I found that the childhood of the Iraqi leader has many things in common with those of Joseph Stalin and Adolf Hitler. There are suggestions of illegitimacy in each story. In each case there are violently abusive fathers or stepfathers, partnered with mothers who are either ruthlessly cold and ambitious or ineffectual. All three men experienced the absence in their childhoods of any adult who invested in them a sense of assured worth, significance, or of nonmanipulative love. They each endured abuse in public and private, leading to a total experience of shame and violation of the body. Not one of the three had any adult to recognize and certify the legitimacy of his pain and anger, or to provide an alliance for him in his suffering. Their similarities continue in their resulting stances of deep rage, the violently cunning approaches they employed in claiming absolute power, and in the ruthless determination they demonstrated to enforce control through gratuitous violence, toward both outgroups and their own people, if need be.

The shameless position represents a deep distortion—in fact, the failure and suppression—of both discretionary and disgrace shame. Here we refer to the nonbonded, conscienceless personality, fueled by a sense of violated outrage. Such persons endured as infants and young children the extinction of trust and primal mutuality through early abandonment, abuse, neglect, or arbitrary and inconsistent treatment, administered without love, respect, or regard. This stance results from failure in attachment or bonding, from aborted affect attunement, and from failure to learn either the nonverbal or the verbal language of love. Here we may properly speak of a void of conscience, based on a lack of empathetic "feeling" and "knowing" with others. Frequently referred to as sociopathic personalities, such persons will adopt either a pervasive, listless conformity or a pathological, often cunning and utterly ruthless capacity for conning and destroying others. Both these stances are fueled by a measureless rage (see Wooden 1976; Magid and McKelvey 1987; Shengold 1989).

When Charles Manson stood trial for the Tate-LaBianca murders he was thirty-five. He had spent more than twenty-two years of his life in more than a dozen different penal institutions. He was born to a sixteen-year-old mother named Kathleen Maddox, who allegedly had been raped by a Colonel Scott. His birth certificate read, "No Name Maddox." When he was two, his mother filed a bastard suit in Boyd County, Kentucky, and the father agreed to a judgment of twenty-five dollars and a five-dollar-a-month payment for the support of the child. This was in 1936. His mother then married a man named Manson and gave Charles his name. During the first years of his life Charles was bounced back and forth between the care of his grandmother and maternal aunt. His mother, saying she was going to leave the boy with one or the other for an hour, would be gone for days and weeks at a time. From the time he was five until he was eight, his mother served a prison sentence for a filling station robbery in which she and her brother knocked an attendant unconscious with a soft drink bottle. During this period he lived with an aunt and uncle in West Virginia, who, he later told prison authorities, had a "difficult marriage until they found religion . . . and became very extreme."[3]

---

3. The story of Charles Manson and the quotation I will include in this section are dependent upon the account of Kenneth Wooden in his book *Weeping in the Playtime of Others: America's Incarcerated Children* (Wooden 1976). Manson's story is in chap. 4, pp. 47-57.

Manson never got very far in school. He lived with a foster family in Indiana for a year, but when his mother got out of prison, she moved to Indianapolis and sent for him. She lived with a long succession of men-friends, and the boy received little attention from her or them. In 1947 (when he was thirteen) she tried to place him with a foster family. None being available, Manson became a ward of the county and was sent to the Gibault Home for Boys in Terre Haute, Indiana. His record there revealed: "Poor institutional adjustment . . . his attitude toward schooling was at best only fair . . . during the short lapses when Charles was pleasant and feeling happy, he presented a likable boy . . . a tendency towards moodiness and a persecution complex." Running away from Gibault after ten months, Manson returned to his mother, who turned him away. He drifted into a life of crime and a succession of imprisonments and escapes. In the institutions where Manson was confined, he was regularly beaten. Between the ages of thirteen and sixteen he was confined at the Indiana Boys School at Plainfield. A volunteer at Plainfield reported that "he was very quiet, very shy, didn't want anything to do with anyone else." Teachers said, "He professed no trust in anyone." While in Plainfield he was attacked and raped by a man. Thereafter he too engaged in sexual activity with men. On his nineteenth attempt, he escaped from Plainfield. Stealing cars and robbing stores, he and a companion crossed the country, but were stopped at a roadblock set up for another robbery suspect. Because crossing state lines with a stolen car is a federal offense, sixteen-year-old Manson now entered the federal prison system.

At the National Training School for Boys in Washington, D.C., his records indicate that he was illiterate, though he had had four years of schooling, and had an IQ of 109. His caseworker described him as a "sixteen year old boy who has had an unfavorable family life, if it can be called a family life at all" and "aggressively antisocial. . . . It appears that this boy is a very emotionally upset youth who is definitely in need of some psychiatric orientation." A psychiatrist who assessed Manson when Manson was sixteen said: "Because of a marked degree of rejection, instability and psychic trauma—because his sense of inferiority in relationship to his mother was so pronounced, he constantly felt it necessary to suppress any thoughts about her. However, because of his diminutive stature, his illegitimacy, and the lack of parental love, he is constantly striving for status with the other boys . . . has developed certain facile techniques for dealing with people. . . . [O]ne is left with the feeling that behind all this lies an extremely sensitive boy who has not yet given up in terms of securing some kind of love and affection from the world."

The rest of his story is repetitious and dreary. On the verge of release on parole to the custody of an aunt who promised him a job, he pressed a razor blade to the neck of a fellow prisoner and sodomized him, resulting in his being reclassified as dangerous and reincarcerated. He married in 1954 at age nineteen, between stints in prison, but continued to steal cars and commit petty crimes, leading to reincarceration. In April of 1957 his young wife ceased to visit him, and he learned that she had begun to live with another man. He never saw her or their son again. At the time of his release from a ten-year sentence in 1967—his last before the Tate-LaBianca murders—Charles Manson begged his jailers to let him remain in prison: "Prison has become my home," he said; he doubted he could "adjust to the world outside."

In a statement to the court just before being sentenced for the Tate-LaBianca murders he said:

> I haven't decided yet what I am or who I am. . . . I stayed in that jail and I have stayed stupid, and I have stayed a child while I have watched your world grow up. . . . I'm already dead, have been dead all my life. . . . When you were out riding your bicycle, I was sitting in your cell looking out the window and looking at pictures in magazines and wishing I could go to high school and go to the proms, wishing I could go to the things you could do, but oh so glad, oh so glad, brothers and sisters, that I am what I am.

Manson's statement, no doubt, aimed to evoke sympathy from the court and to place much of the blame for his life's outcome on society. His statement expresses a denial of shame about what he has been and done. His final self-affirmation seems meant to convey an accusation of hypocrisy and false self-righteousness on the part of his accusers and those charged with trying and sentencing him for his crimes.

Not all persons who could be described as shameless spend most of their childhood and youth in prisons, as did Charles Manson. Some of them mask their shamelessness from others and from themselves by the achievement of positions of respectability and power, from which they can use and manipulate others through legal and financial (or spiritual) stratagems. Persons in the position of shamelessness, like those best described by perfectionist, toxic, and enforced minority shame, have defenses that protect them from much of the pain that conscious awareness of their feelings of shame would bring. *The "feathers" we grow to hide from others the vulnerabilities and wounds that make us shameful serve to hide them from ourselves as well.*

We have looked at five positions on a spectrum of shame experiences, from healthy shame to shamelessness. Healthy shame can be designated that way because it involves a minimum of suppression or denial of the painful awareness of personal flaw, deficiency, or defect of which it makes us aware. Healthy shame is embarrassing to acknowledge, and we must exercise prudence and discretion when choosing those persons to whom we may, in trust and confidence, disclose our sense of shame and deficiency. Nonetheless, it is shame we can face. It can motivate us to change, to grow, to repent, to improve. Or else it motivates us to undertake a process of accepting and learning to live with those aspects of our being that are shameful. As we move beyond healthy shame across the spectrum, however, it becomes clear that increasing amounts of our energy become tied up in defenses, denial, and deception—both of ourselves and of others. Though to some degree in each of these positions we are conscious and aware of our dis-ease and its sources, in each position on the spectrum a fair amount of our sense of shameful vulnerability is masked and hidden from others and from ourselves. Now we must try to understand and explain how it is that we suppress and cover the deficits, wounds, and fallibilities that give rise to our shame, and the maneuvers by which we hide our shame from ourselves and others.

CHAPTER EIGHT

SHAME AND GRACE: GENESIS, NIETZSCHE, AND JESUS

The second creation story in Genesis provides the setting for what the New Revised Standard Version of the Bible calls "The First Sin and Its Punishment" (Genesis 3:1-24). Traditionally this passage has been cited as the prototype for understanding the biblical account of the origins of sin and guilt. Looked at from the standpoint of our interest in shame, however, the story makes a different kind of sense. Let us examine some of the pertinent parts of the narrative with a hermeneutics sensitive to the dynamics of shame. We turn to that part of the text that constitutes its core as regards our interest in shame as painful self-consciousness, alienation, and inner self-division.

> Now the serpent was more crafty than any other wild animal that the LORD God had made. He said to the woman, "Did God say, 'You shall not eat from any tree in the garden'?" The woman said to the serpent, "We may eat of the fruit of the trees in the garden; but God said, 'You shall not eat of the fruit of the tree that is in the middle of the garden, nor shall you touch it, or you shall die.' " But the serpent said to the woman, "You will not die; for God knows that when you eat of it your eyes will be opened, and you will be like God, knowing good and evil." So when the woman saw that the tree was good for food, and that it was a delight to the eyes, and that the tree was to be desired to make one wise, she took of its fruit and ate; and she also gave some to her husband who was with her, and he ate. Then the eyes of both were opened, and they knew that they were naked; and they sewed fig leaves together and made loincloths for themselves.
>
> They heard the sound of the LORD God walking in the garden at the time of the evening breeze, and the man and his wife hid

132

themselves from the presence of the LORD God among the trees of the garden. But the LORD God called to the man, and said to him, "Where are you?" He said, "I heard the sound of you in the garden, and I was afraid, because I was naked; and I hid myself." He said, "Who told you that you were naked? Have you eaten from the tree of which I commanded you not to eat?" The man said, "The woman whom you gave to be with me, she gave me fruit from the tree, and I ate." Then the LORD God said to the woman, "What is this that you have done?" The woman said, "The serpent tricked me, and I ate." (Genesis 3:1-13 NRSV)

Earlier in Genesis we are given the setting of the story: a paradisal garden, replete with beauty for the eye to behold and bounteous food to answer hunger. The man and woman enjoy harmonious relations with each other and beneficent relations with the animals in the garden. They participate in a relation marked by obedience and presumably awe and gratitude to the Creator.

Erik Erikson was not the first observer, I suspect, to find in the account of Eden echoes of our personal and collective body memories of the time of flowing milk, loving and understanding eyes, responsive care, and unconflicted cherishing that mark our utopias of preweaning infantile experience. He suggested that the biting of the fruit, represented as the occasion for expulsions from paradisal gardens in myths from many cultures, likely symbolizes the species' collective memory of being separated from the provision of maternal breasts, which comes simultaneously—and seemingly punitively—with the exploding pain of emerging teeth. It can also represent the species memory of the loving, benign gaze of caretakers becoming "strange" with the imposition of necessary limits upon children and the responses they make to the violation of limits and the failure to meet expectations and standards.

Structurally and dynamically I find it difficult to avoid reading this passage from Genesis as a mythic depiction of that time of misty memory in each of our lives when we began to encounter parental limits and directives, their prohibitions, and their expressions of disapproval and discipline. Mingled with awareness of our separation from access to now-forbidden fruit, we see represented in this story the shudder of recognition brought about by the first experiences of seeing our mirrored images and of recognizing ourselves with painful self-consciousness as our own and others' objects of awareness and evaluation.

Augustine claims that it is with pride that Eve and Adam looked upon the fruit of the tree of the knowledge of good and evil (Augustine 1950, Book XIV, p. 13). For him it was pride and desire—both for the fruit and for the serpent's promise of acquisition of instant maturity—that led to the act of disobedience. Augustine's understanding of pride, built on the Christian tradition beginning with Paul, imputed a more adult and corrupted willfulness to the original couple than our interpretation of Genesis 3 would warrant. In the view taken here, our forebears were coming to first self-consciousness in the garden: They experienced "standing on their own two feet," accompanied with its first hints of autonomy and anxiety. They experienced seeing themselves mirrored in their mutual gazes of admiration and enjoyment. They are deeply curious about not only the forbidden and enticing fruit, but also their previously unreflective relation to their mysterious and powerful companion and limit-setting source of taboos, the one called God in the story. They felt rising interest-excitement in the new possibilities of god-like (adult) authority and power. Little wonder they found irresistible the promises and rationalizations that the tempter-serpent offered them as symbolized in the forbidden fruit.

In disobedience, they ate the fruit. Based on what we have learned about shame as a basic and innate affect, it is interesting to observe that already, even before any external chastisement for their transgression can be applied, the mutual mirroring in which the couple tasting the fruit had been participating changed in its quality. As Silvan Tomkins might say, the affect *shame-humiliation* did its work of interrupting their engagement in *interest-excitement* and *enjoyment-joy*. Reflexively, shame turned their awareness from each other and their mutual bliss back upon their individual selves. In their strained faces, downcast eyes, lowered heads, and hunched necks and shoulders, they each felt separately the flood of shame. Framed in their separate experiences of diminishment and the involuntary covering of their genitals, their mutual mirroring now disclosed them, each to each, and to themselves, as "strange," as pitiable, as vulnerable, and as exposed in their disobedience—to each other and to the Other.

The hiding, the covering, the confusion, the blaming—all these features bear the marks of shame. Theirs is an experience that includes at least the following consequences of coming to shameful self-awareness: (1) painful self-consciousness; (2) the experience of self and others as separate and as "strangers"; (3) alienation from a former nonreflective bond of interpersonal harmony; (4) a disturbing sense of their otherness and estrangement from God; (5) darkened shadows across their world, suggesting dangers and restricted abundance; and (6) introverted self-consciousness, coupled with a sense of personal stain or fault, in relation to the now more distant and remote authority.

In this enumeration of the consequences of Adam and Eve's disobedience we see the dimensions of their alienation, their estrangement. In German, the term for "sin" is *Sünde*. It is derived from the verb *sondern*, meaning "to separate," "to sever," or "to sunder." In the story, it is pride and desire that amplify the will's attachment to the possibility of eating the fruit and to the status of instant maturity it symbolized: "you will be like God." The objective fact of their sin is the *sundering* of their wills from obedience to God and their attachment instead to the deceiver-serpent's guileful promise, which leads to the consequent acts of taking and eating the fruit. It is their shame which interrupts and overrides the will's action, precipitating the couple's decathection from the fruit and their turn to painful self-reflection. Shame sets in motion the *subjective* experiences in Adam and Eve of their exposure before each other and God and precipitates their multidimensional sense of alienation.

In its irreversibility, this story strikes us as tragic. It is a "fall" into consciousness and painful self-consciousness. There can be no return to the former garden of innocent potential and un-self-conscious enjoyment of each other and the environment. For centuries interpreters of this narrative have sought to counter its tragic quality. Some have tried to turn the shame experienced by our foreparents into guilt: If they are truly filled with lust or prideful self-assertion, and if they willfully and knowingly overstep the prescribed boundaries as a result of corrupted and cunning wills to be free to claim God-like knowledge and prerogatives, then they are rightly punished and the Lord God is just. Moreover, guilt is easier to deal with than shame. At least in guilt the perpetrators are conscious agents, acting on motives and desires they can avow. Other interpreters, resenting the Creator and the situation as portrayed, have cried "Foul!" and "Set up!" and have sought to place the rap for evil's entry into the world upon a Creator who thus makes sport of those said to be created in his image.

I contend that this story, with its account of our foreparents' sin, depicts with psychodynamic and theological faithfulness some of the true contours of our personal and collective transition into the painful aspects of our own first encounters with the limits and expectations of our relational world and the first stages of conscious self-awareness. This story is about shame. Here we have the representation of a universal experience of becoming divided selves. Here we see the portrayal of our responding to shame by seeking to hide from ourselves and others, as well as the Other, that in ourselves that constitutes our defect, our fault. The story depicts how our will and our desire become awakened and begin to search and long for something that promises to fill the void left by our sundering from that which grounds our being in Being. If these claims are plausible, then this story has special contributions to make to our further work with shame.

Shame, in the approach we are pursuing, is viewed as evolving in our species as an innately given and culturally formed mechanism that functions to preserve a sense of the worthiness of the self and to avoid the severing of relations with others in which the self would be disvalued and experience itself as unworthy. Shame, in this sense, should be the result of any breach of relation involving violation of covenant relatedness to others or to God. Notice that Tomkins's characterization of shame, given earlier, described it as "the incomplete reduction of interest or joy." Shame does not sever us from the experience and hope of restored joy. *Shame is not the act of sin. Rather, it is the subjective amplification of the objective fact of the potential for separation or destruction of relation involved in the sinful act.* Shame provisionally interrupts the pursuit of sin in order to provide a time for self-aware evaluation for the sake of avoiding a more serious breach. Shame, in its undistorted and discretionary mode, keeps us sensitive, modest, respectful, and properly attentive to the reactions and responses of others. It keeps us suitably aware of conditions in the relations between us and others. This includes our relations with other persons and groups and, as our Genesis story reminds us, with the source of our lives as well. Dietrich Bonhoeffer, one of the few theologians in the twentieth century to focus seriously on shame, wrote that "in shame, man is reminded of his disunion with God and with other men; conscience is the sign of man's disunion with himself" (Bonhoeffer 1965, 24).

When experiences of shame flood over us—due either to appropriate responses by valued others to some pattern of our action and being or to distorting excesses in their reactions—there are other mechanisms than shame that step in to prevent our being overwhelmed or becoming abject.[1] When shame threatens to overcome us, the self, the ego, or the *proprium,* as Gordon Allport called our core sense of self (Allport 1955, 41-42), generates defenses that establish barriers or filters to keep the self intact. Even at the expense of truth, the defenses of the self switch on in order to screen from consciousness sudden or continual signals of shame that are more than the psyche can stand.[2] The splitting involved in what I described as the "false self," the "heartbroken self," and the "shameless self" can be attributed to defensive patterns constructed to screen out varying degrees and intensities of distorting shame. Each of these positions characterizes a significant degree of defendedness due to excessive shame. Each of them, in turn, denotes a significant degree of alienation from self, from others, as well as alienation, at least subjectively, from a gracious God.

To the degree that the Genesis story is psychodynamically and theologically true we cannot maintain more than a theoretical distinction between distorting shame and what might be called "normal" or "healthy" shame. None of us, the story affirms, will escape distorting shame. To be sure, thoughtful and balanced par-

---

1. The term "abject" comes from the Latin *abjectus,* from *abjicio,* "to throw away." It means "sunk to a low condition; worthless, mean, despicable; low, groveling" (*The New Webster Encyclopedia Dictionary of the English Language* [Chicago: Consolidated Book Publishers, 1980]).

2. For developments of this idea in greater richness see the discussions of "bypassed shame" in therapeutic settings (Lewis 1972, chaps. 7 and 10) and in social relations (Scheff and Retzinger 1991, chap. 1).

enting can reduce violence of all kinds in the process of nurturing children through their earliest years. The expulsion from the garden of infancy need not be punitive and demeaning. Nonetheless, I believe it to be inevitable that our kind will experience, in the months in which we "fall" into first conscious self-awareness, the shudder of awareness of ourselves as objects—both to ourselves and to others. In the period in which we begin to attend to standards and see ourselves evaluatively in relation to our partial and global apprehensions of them, we will experience some significant measure of lack, insufficiency, or defectiveness. And as the child collides with the structure of limits, demands, expectations and disciplines—and with competing others in the new world of conscious, optional choices—he or she will have murderous thoughts and feelings toward parents and siblings. Consequently he or she will experience the shame-humiliation affect and come to populate the feelings it brings with self-judgments, interpretations, and meanings, some of which will require the construction of defenses.

To bring insights on the dynamics of shame into the interpretation of the Genesis 3 story of Eve, Adam, and "the Fall" is to see our kinship with our forebears in new ways. To couch the story in terms of the issues of "autonomy versus shame and doubt" rather than those of "initiative versus guilt" (Erikson) places the encounter with the serpent, the forbidden fruit, and the awakening to nakedness and shame in a different frame. It alters the meaning of disobedience and changes the valence of any charge of excessive pride.

We are given a story that recalls the first era of a person's (or our species') consciousness and awareness of being seen and evaluated by others. We are invited to recall the emergence of a division in us between *willfulness* and *willingness* (May 1982, chap. 1), a division between our living up to standards of which we are becoming aware and a resistance to the standards coupled with the experience of being exposed before we are ready. In short, the Genesis 3 narrative recalls for us our earliest months of consciousness and self-awareness brought about by the loss of an innocence that could not last—an innocence born of lack of reflective self-consciousness, limited mobility, inability to articulate our meanings and experiences, and a mutuality of dependence. Coming to stand on our own two feet and to begin to form boundaries for the self—"me, my, mine, yes, no"—means to encounter the clash of our wills with others'. It means coming to terms with expectations and limits imposed by others. It means taking on the burdens of self-consciousness and self-aware evaluation. It means embracing the risk of alienation from those we love most and of alienation from the deepest place of truth in our own souls. These developmental experiences and risks are universal. The story depicts the irreversible step toward self-responsibility and an elemental sense of costly liberation from the provisional paradise of our experience before language and before accountability.

How different the course of Western history might have been had Irenaeus's doctrine of sin and the fall played as strong a role in the theology of the church as has that of Augustine. Irenaeus saw our forebears as exhibiting immaturity and as falling into awkward and painful first self-consciousness. He saw the Fall as a transition in our collective lives, opening the way to a difficult and ongoing process of "growing up" into the fullness of the image of God. Accordingly, Irenaeus's account of our redemption did not stress the sacrificial atonement made by God's requiring the crucifixion of an innocent Christ. Rather, he offered the assurance of God's solidarity and support for us through the doctrine of Christ's *recapitulation* of our journey from immaturity to the fullness of maturity in the image of God, but *getting it right*. Thereby, God, through the Christ, opens a path for us and provides a vicarious completion and the grace of empowering example for the journey to which we are called.[3]

SOME REFLECTIONS ON NIETZSCHE
AND THE JESUS OF THE GOSPELS

Friedrich Nietzsche admired the moral courage and the heroic self-donation of Jesus the Christ. He found ways to make Jesus an exemplar of his image of the *Übermensch,* the superior man, the noble spirit who has the strength and genius to press his own terms

---

3. On this contrast between Augustine and Irenaeus, see Hick 1966, especially parts II and III.

onto life. At whatever cost, the *Übermensch* stands apart through resolute adherence to the realization of his own greatness, claiming the honor and exerting the impact of fulfilling his destiny. Nietzsche admired the nobility of Jesus' chosen path—calling his followers to claim the full dignity and honor of their potential as children of God and laying down his life willingly, on his own terms, to make that realization possible. But he despised how, in his view, the church had twisted the notion of discipleship, shaping it into a path of self-denying humility and self-abnegation. He saw the church's doctrine of sin and redemption as endorsing human weakness and baptizing a perpetual immaturity. In short, Nietzsche accused the church of turning the robust heroism of Christ's self-donation into a required, cramping posture of abject self-denial and immaturity. Nietzsche indicted the church and Christianity with the charge that it called people to embrace a posture of shame in following a Christ whom it had reinterpreted as an innocent and passive victim of the world's power.

Alice Miller, in a book titled *The Untouched Key,* offers the following perspectives on Friedrich Nietzsche's early childhood: Born to a Protestant pastor and his young second wife, little Friedrich spent his first months in a household dominated by his disciplined, scholarly father, his paternal grandmother, and two rigidly pious maiden grandaunts. When he was two and three, if he would remain quiet and still, Nietzsche was allowed to sit in the study while his father worked. Nietzsche's happiest moments were when his father, taking a break from his scholarship, would sit at the piano and play, often allowing Friedrich to sit on the bench with him while he improvised. By late in his third year, Nietzsche's father began to suffer from a rapidly deteriorating condition, possibly a brain tumor. Within eleven months the incapacitated father died, subjecting the four-year-old Friedrich to the domination of the grandmother and grandaunts, for whom his young mother was no match. Soon his younger brother, the only other male in the household, followed his father in death. Miller, a psychoanalytically trained psychiatrist, observes that the Christianity that Nietzsche so roundly excoriated seems identical in its spirit of oppressiveness to that which he experienced in the household left by his dead pastor-father. Miller writes, "The many passages in which Nietzsche characterizes Christianity are a key to how he felt about his relatives. We need only substitute 'my aunts' or 'my family' for the word 'Christianity' for his vehement attacks suddenly to make sense." She quotes Nietzsche:

In Christianity the instincts of the subjugated and oppressed come to the fore: here the lowest classes seek their salvation. The casuistry of sin, self-criticism, the inquisition of the conscience, are pursued as a *pastime*, as a remedy for boredom; the emotional reaction to one who has *power*, called "God," is constantly sustained (by means of prayer); and what is highest is considered unattainable, a gift, "grace." Public acts are precluded; the hiding place, the darkened room, is Christian. The body is despised, hygiene repudiated as sensuality; the church even opposes cleanliness (the first Christian measure after the expulsion of the Moors was the closing of the public baths, of which there were two hundred and seventy in Cordova alone). Christian too is a certain sense of cruelty against oneself and against others; hatred of all who think differently; the will to persecute. Gloomy and exciting conceptions predominate; the most highly desired states, designated with the highest names, are epileptoid; the diet is so chosen as to favor morbid phenomena and overstimulate the nerves. Christian too is mortal enmity against the lords of the earth, against the "noble"—along with a sly, secret rivalry (one leaves the "body," one wants *only* the "soul"). Christian, finally, is the hatred of the *spirit*, of pride, courage, freedom, liberty of the spirit; Christian is the hatred of the *senses*, of joy in the senses, of joy itself. (Miller 1990, 111-12; quoted from *The Antichrist*, sect. 21, pp. 588-89 in *The Portable Nietzsche* [Nietzsche 1959])

One must read the whole of Alice Miller's long section on Nietzsche to feel the full force of her thesis. My purpose in introducing Nietzsche and Miller's commentary is not to settle the validity of her claims but to frame the question of the stance of Jesus, as portrayed in the narratives of the Gospels, toward the question of shame and discipleship. I find it refreshing to look at the stories of Jesus' encounter with persons where the dynamics of shame are palpably present and to see how he is portrayed as relating to them. It is striking how many of the stories in which shame is a dynamic feature involve Jesus' interactions with women.

We can start with the story of the woman caught in adultery (John 7:53–8:11). For my purposes it does not matter that this story has a disputed place in the Gospels based upon historical critical scrutiny. The fact that it is included in the canon—and that it has contributed decisively to the shaping of our image of Jesus for nineteen hundred years and that it seems utterly consistent with the other portrayals I will share—makes it reliable for present purposes.

In this story Jesus is accosted in public by a group of Temple leaders bringing a woman whom they allege to have been "caught in the very act of committing adultery." They point to the place in the law where stoning is required for such women. They attribute this requirement to the authority of Moses. They demand that Jesus say what should be done. (There was a double trap in this situation. The Romans had prohibited the Sanhedrin from imposing capital punishment for any violation of religious codes; therefore, for Jesus to assent to stoning would be to place himself at odds with Roman policies; on the other hand, to treat the woman's alleged offense lightly would reveal Jesus as being "soft" on the law. Their question to him was meant to be a source of consternation and embarrassment to him, leading to a public affirmation of the charges that he set aside important aspects of the law.) In this story we see the portrayal of a double shaming: Jesus is being shamed by potential exposure of his "softness" and his "laxness" with regard to the law; the woman is being shamed by the public exposure of her alleged sexual misconduct, and perhaps by the exposure of her body.

Jesus' response initially reflects his shame *for* the accusers and *for* the woman. He averts his eyes, looks and bends downward where he begins to write with his fingers on the ground, refusing to credit their questions. When they persist in demanding a response, he "straightens up" meets their gaze, and says to them, "Let anyone among you who is without sin be the first to throw a stone at her." Eye to eye, straightforwardly, he throws the shame, directed at her and at himself, back upon them. Then he kneels down again, resuming his writing on the ground. The crowd melts away, led by the elders, leaving him alone with the woman. When they have gone he stands again, looking at her, and asks, "Woman, where are they? Has no one condemned you?" She says, "No one, sir." And he says, "Neither do I condemn you. Go your way, and from now on do not sin again." He does not dismiss the question of her guilt ("from now on do not sin again"), but he subordinates it to the matter of dealing with her shame and her misuse at the hands of those who would have entrapped them both.

Another of the most vivid narratives about Jesus and his dealing with people involved in shameful conditions is found in Mark 5: 1-20, wherein Jesus heals the Gerasene demoniac. Jesus had crossed the Sea of Galilee to the region of the Gerasenes, where lived a man "with an unclean spirit," well known in the region for his madness. Efforts to restrain this man had failed: "the chains he wrenched apart, and the shackles he broke in pieces; and no one had the strength to subdue him." When this man sees Jesus coming, he runs out to him and bows before him. When Jesus says to him, "Come out of the man, you unclean spirit," the man shouts, "What have you to do with me, Jesus, Son of the Most High God? I adjure you by God, do not torment me." Jesus asks him his name, and he answers, "My name is Legion; for we are many." Jesus orders the unclean spirits out of the man, and they enter a herd of swine, who run into the sea.

Today it is well known that multiple personality disorder generally results from severe and protracted early childhood abuse, often including sexual abuse. Apparently Jesus conveyed such authority and such acceptance of this man (and of others like him) that his soul, split and shattered like a broken crystal, could find healing and reintegration. Grace is the most powerful antidote to shame. This man must have felt a grace of such acceptance and of value as to make possible the opening of his repressed memories and the reunification and integration of his divided selves.

There are many other stories in the Gospels that portray Jesus' interactions with people in positions of personal or social shame. Among these one can point to the woman with an issue of blood (Luke 8:43-48), the story of the Pharisee and the tax collector praying (Luke 18:9-14), Jesus and the Samaritan woman at the well (John 4:7-42), and the story of Jesus' gracious initiation of relationship with the tax collector Zacchaeus when he invites himself to the little man's home and, by eating with him, conveys a profound acceptance that opens the way for his seeking forgiveness and a new life (Luke 19:1-10). In every case Jesus breaks through ethnic or religious taboos that govern relations and build barriers between persons and groups. In every case, Jesus offers a quality of really *seeing* each of these persons and conveying such acceptance and regard that they find a new relation to him, to God, and to the communities of which they are part. Even when Jesus speaks harshly about and toward his religious enemies, the Pharisees, he never falls into *ad hominem* attacks in which he assaults them with global condemnation. In each case, he indicts specific practices and attitudes that are unjust, inviting the Pharisees themselves to repentance and a new quality of life. He is careful to appeal to their capacity for an appropriate recognition of *guilt,* which could lead to repentance. He does not fall into global labeling and characterization of them as persons as though he were trying to evoke a sense of shame (Luke 11:37-52).

It may be that Nietzsche, whose perfectionist shame and deep woundedness were transmuted into fierce anger against Christianity, sensed in Jesus and his movement a grace that might have required and enabled him to embrace his own weakness and open himself to the grace of others. This would have been particularly threatening to him. Early in life he had learned to expect no one to see and affirm him with acceptance and delight simply for being the person he was. Indeed, Nietzsche, like his more recent soul brother, Jean Paul Sartre, expressed a deep resentment at the idea—and the shame—of being known to the core by the deity (Schneider 1992, 135-36). Carl Schneider sees both Sartre and Nietzsche as "trapped in their doctrine of the solitary and self-sufficient self" in which the self is seen as an "ultimate loneliness." Intuiting the possibility of such a grace, Nietzsche's instinct, learned early and practiced all his days, would have been to distrust it radically and to reject it with ridicule and contempt. Yet had such a grace become real for him—taken on flesh—he might have relinquished the *resentiment* that fueled the energy and passion that flowed with such acerbic brilliance in his writing. While that would have involved loss, who can know what so fertile a mind and so sensitive a soul might have offered in its stead?

PART III

FAITH AND THE CHALLENGES OF POSTMODERN LIFE

T*he final chapters of* Faithful Change *explore the implications for Christian life and education of the claim that ours is a hinge time in human history, every bit as significant and far-reaching as the Enlightenment of the eighteenth century. Future historians will have to evaluate this claim and propose names for this period of transition and the emergence of new forms of thought and consciousness it brings. At present people who talk about these matters refer to our era as "late modernity" or as "postmodern."*

Returning to our work with theory and research in faith development in part I, in chapters 9 and 10 we will reexamine descriptions of the faith stages that correspond to the patterns of belief typical of educated adults in modern societies. Using these stage descriptions, we will try to model and contrast the forms of consciousness and practice that emerged as normative during the Enlightenment of the eighteenth century, and those that may be emerging as normative in our time. The comparisons we make should illumine some of the deep going tensions over beliefs and the grounding for ethical values we face in this time of "culture wars." These chapters close with a call for the kind of Christian leadership that combines deep faithfulness to Christ with a readiness to work with people from other religious or secular traditions on the agenda of an increasingly complex, pluralistic, and systematically interdependent world.

Chapters 11 and 12 offer an entry into the challenge of rethinking Christian theological and ethical foundations for postmodern faithfulness. How shall we discern, trust, and give ourselves in vocational faithfulness to the work of God in this hinge time in consciousness and practice? How is God present and active in this transitional era? Reviewing several options in contemporary theology, our constructive proposal draws on biblical imagery of covenant and vocation, and of God's creative, governing, and

145

liberating-redemptive work, to give direction and norms for our partnership with God.

We conclude the book with proposals for faithfulness in the tasks of creating environments and communities where the children and youth of our common responsibility can be nurtured toward wholeness and faithfulness. Addressing the challenges of violence and corrosive incivility in our societies, chapter 13 calls for initiatives from churches and other communities of faith to work for the renewal of family life and the reclaiming of our inner cities from violent and crippling influences. Using the theological framework of the preceding chapters, and giving attention to the relations between shame, violence, and this society's fixation on firearms, it calls us to practical theological engagement with the creation of new community centers of intergenerational education, and to seriousness about making our growing coterie of prisons and jails places of redemption and genuine rehabilitation.

Chapter 14, with a special focus on schools that stand in religious traditions, points the way toward approaches in Christian education that prepare children and youth for lives of personal and public commitment to faithful change. Its closing section shares a vision for a kind of Christian formation that combines discipleship to Christ with passionate commitment to the common good in our pluralistic society and world. It envisions the preparation of Christian youth and their generations for leadership in "public churches."

CHAPTER NINE

AWAKENING TO MODERNITY: THE ENLIGHTENMENT AND LIBERATING FAITH

Many acute observers suggest that presently we are in the midst of a watershed time of cultural and intellectual change that equals or exceeds the eighteenth-century Enlightenment in depth and significance. They see us as deeply engaged in an era of radical transformation that involves our fundamental modes of thought, the patterns of organization of our societies, our technologies, our structures of consciousness, and our efforts to deal with the nonconscious. This chapter and the next seek to explore parallels between the transitions in structures of consciousness identified in the stages of faith and the larger movements from premodern to modern consciousness in the Enlightenment of the eighteenth century. Does the transition from the Synthetic-Conventional stage of faith to the Individuative-Reflective stage in individual lives offer a model for better understanding the transition in cultural consciousness that we call the Enlightenment? If so, might the transition from the Individuative-Reflective stage to the Conjunctive stage provide a useful model for grasping some of the aspects of the transition in the structures of consciousness we seem to be undergoing at present?

As we pursue these issues, two subsidiary questions may be addressed: (1) To what degree is the faith development research and theory itself an outgrowth of Enlightenment impulses, and thereby caught up in both its strengths and its limits? (2) If we find parallels between the transition to the Conjunctive stage of faith and what appears to be a culture-wide struggle toward post-Enlightenment modes of consciousness in the present era, how do we account for widespread evidences of *regression*—the avoidance of

change, both at societal and personal levels—to pre-Enlightenment and pre-Individuative modes of faith and consciousness? We
will make a beginning in dealing with these questions in this
chapter and continue the discussion in the one following.

THE ENLIGHTENMENT AND CHANGE

The Enlightenment as a revolution in Western consciousness is
primarily associated with the eighteenth century. Though the
creation of its decisive breakthroughs was primarily limited in that
century to an intellectual elite, in the two centuries since its taking
form it has transformed European and North American societies.
The thinkers of the Enlightenment left virtually no dimension of
human activity and self-understanding unchanged. In politics and
government they left a powerful legacy to democratic theory, with
their doctrines of human equality and human rights and their
legitimation of governments through a variety of versions of social
contract theory. In science and technology they built upon the
great achievements of the seventeenth century to establish empirical and analytic methods. They completed the severance of physics
and cosmology from theology and initiated the scientific study of
psychology and sociology. In religion, thinkers of the Enlightenment turned the tools of analytic reason onto the record of biblical
faith. Neither doctrinal traditions, priestly hierarchies, nor the
Bible itself could withstand the relativizing impact of critical historical study. The Enlightenment pressed for formal and universal
criteria for morality and faith and established rational standpoints
from which the particular claims of revealed religions could be held
accountable.

In offering his "model" of the Enlightenment, historian Craine
Brinton proposes three major components: (1) a passionate commitment to *reason* as the instrument of knowledge and emancipation; (2) a turn toward *nature* and the *natural* (including human
nature) as the central object of scientific study and as the source of
true insight and norms; and (3) a confidence in *progress,* from the
achievement of peace through international law, to the reform of
religion and the conquest of disease in human societies (Brinton

1967). Though we will need to add some elements to Brinton's framework, it will serve to organize this brief overview. Immanuel Kant begins his 1784 essay, "What Is Enlightenment?" with the following words:

> Enlightenment is Man's leaving his self-caused immaturity. Immaturity is the incapacity to use one's intelligence without the guidance of another. Such immaturity is self-caused if it is not caused by lack of intelligence, but by lack of determination and courage to use one's intelligence without being guided by another. *Sapere Aude!* Have the courage to use your own intelligence! is therefore the motto of the enlightenment. (Friedrich 1949, 132)

The instrument of liberation and model of intelligence that the eighteenth century so celebrated was, of course, reason. Ernst Cassirer writes: "The age senses that a new force is at work within it. . . . When the eighteenth century wants to characterize this power in a single word, it calls it 'reason.' 'Reason' becomes the unifying and central point of this century, expressing all that it longs and strives for, and all that it achieves" (Cassirer 1951, 5). Through reason, through the disciplined and confident use of rational methods, Enlightenment thinkers anticipated the emancipation of persons and culture from their embeddedness in superstition and unexamined traditions. They intended their liberation from docile obedience to unaccountable forms of governance. And they intended to open the "ripe" secrets of nature, which had waited so long for penetration and disclosure, through the instruments of empirical rationality. Cassirer captures the Enlightenment's grasp of reason, as a semidivine, dynamic force and as an instrument of revelatory power, in the following passage:

> Reason is now looked upon rather as an acquisition than as a heritage. It is not the treasury of the mind in which the truth like a minted coin lies stored; it is rather the original intellectual force which guides the discovery and determination of truth. This determination is the seed and the indispensable presupposition of all real certainty. The whole eighteenth century understands reason in this sense; not as a sound body of knowledge, principles, and truths, but as a kind of energy, a force which is fully comprehensible only in its

agency and effects. What reason is, and what it can do, can never be known by its results but only by its function. And its most important function consists in its power to bind and to dissolve. It dissolves everything merely factual, all simple data of experience, and everything believed on the evidence of revelation, tradition and authority; and it does not rest content until it has analyzed all these things into their simplest component parts and into their last elements of belief and opinion. Following this work of dissolution begins the work of construction. Reason cannot stop with the dispersed parts; it has to build from them a new structure, a true whole. But since reason creates this whole and fits the parts together according to its own rule, it gains complete knowledge of the structure of its product. (Cassirer 1951, 13-14)

The Enlightenment, building on the astronomy, physics and mathematics of Kepler, Galilei, Newton, and others, dissolved classical views of nature. "The clear-cut form of the classical and medieval conception of the world crumbles, and the world ceases to be a 'cosmos' in the sense of an immediately accessible order of things. . . . One world and one Being are replaced by an infinity of worlds constantly springing from the womb of becoming, each one of which embodies but a single transitory phase of the inexhaustible vital process of the universe" (Cassirer 1951, 37). It is the glory of human reason that it can endure—yes, even execute—this dissolution of its inherited world images and, at the same time, assume a stance from which, through probing inquiry and patient synthesis, it can disclose the implicit lawfulness and intricate interrelatedness that are to be found in nature. In reflecting upon this exhilarating capacity, Enlightenment thinkers became aware of a new intensity and concentration that is fundamental in the nature of the mind: "The highest energy and deepest truth of the mind do not consist in going out into the infinite, but in the mind's maintaining itself against the infinite and proving in its pure unity equal to the infinity of being." In its capacity for maintaining itself against the infinite, the mind is capable of enabling us to "place it [the infinite] within measure and bound, not in order to limit its realm but in order to know it in its all-comprehensive and all-pervasive law. Universal law, which is discovered and formulated in thought, forms the necessary correlate of the intuitively experienced boundlessness of the universe" (Cassirer 1951, 38).

In its reconstruction and rebinding of the world of knowledge, the Enlightenment constituted nature and the natural as its horizon. To the realm of nature belongs everything in the sphere accessible by "natural light" *(lumen naturale)*. This includes everything that can be investigated and understood with no other aid than the natural forces of reason. The realm of nature was thus established apart from the realm of grace, where truth is accessible only through the power of revelation. But for the Enlightenment there need not be conflict or opposition between belief and knowledge, between revelation and reason. The truth of nature is revealed:

> not in God's word but in his work; it is not based on the testimony of Scripture or tradition but is visible to us at all times. But it is understandable only to those who know nature's handwriting and can decipher her text. The truth of nature cannot be expressed in mere words; the only suitable expression lies in mathematical constructions, figures and numbers. And in these symbols nature presents itself in perfect form and clarity. . . . In nature . . . the whole plan of the universe lies before us in its undivided and inviolable unity, evidently waiting for the human mind to recognize and express it. (Cassirer 1951, 43)

Brinton reminds us that not until the seventeenth century does a confidence begin to emerge that the present might be better than the past, and that the future can bring consistent and continuing progress for humankind. The French reformer and philosopher Turgot gave a speech at the Sorbonne in 1750 entitled "On the Successive Advances of the Human Mind," which outlined a complete doctrine of progress. His friend and disciple Condorcet recast these ideas in his *Sketch for a Historical Picture of the Human Mind*. This offered an extraordinarily optimistic vision of a utopia of unending progress, leading ultimately to the attainment by all humans of immortality in the flesh on this earth (cited in Brinton 1967, 521). Most Enlightenment thinkers avoided these excesses and, in fact, had realistic conceptions of the ways in which reason can be subordinated to the service of egocen-

151

tric and selfish passions.[1] Nonetheless, the fundamental spirit of emancipation, coupled with confidence in the potency of education to form persons capable of rationality, gave rise to a great energy of optimism in the age. Not until the bitter excesses of the French Revolution would fundamental questions about the fragility of reason and the power of deeper sources of distortion and perversion in human nature emerge.

CHARACTERISTICS OF THE INDIVIDUATIVE-REFLECTIVE STAGE OF FAITH

The hard-won structures of rational autonomous consciousness, shaped and claimed on behalf of all humans for the first time in the Enlightenment, still must be constructed and claimed by persons in contemporary societies. Though there now exist cultural models and templates and educational supports for developing post-conventional, critical consciousness, this revolution still requires of individuals something of the courage and determination of which Kant spoke. And it may also require more sponsorship and support than he acknowledged. The civil rights, feminist, racial, ethnic, gay, and other liberation movements that have emerged with special force in the last three decades have in large measure been efforts, collectively, to create political, economic, and social space for these groups to claim the full maturity of rational autonomy and its public usage.[2]

I gave this description of the Individuative-Reflective stage of faith in *Faith Development and Pastoral Care:*

---

1. See Cassirer 1951, pp. 103-4: "Voltaire says in his *Treatise on Metaphysics* that without the passions, without the desire for fame, without ambition and vanity, no progress of humanity, no refinement of taste and improvement of the arts and sciences is thinkable: It is with this motivating force that God, whom Plato called the eternal geometer, and whom I call the eternal machinist, has animated and embellished nature: the passions are the wheels which make all these machines go"

2. It is interesting that Kant, in the essay I cited earlier, said, "All that is required for this enlightenment is *freedom;* and particularly the least harmful of all that may be called freedom, namely, the freedom for man to make *public use* of his reason in all matters" (Friedrich 1949, 134.) Though his essay turns out to be more about academic freedom than freedom of speech generally, he articulates well what contemporary liberation movements have been about: the claiming of space in which previously subordinated groups can make *public* use of their freedom and rationality, be the guardians of their own lives and welfare, and be agential participants in shaping the conditions of our common life.

> This stage we find emerging only in young adulthood or beyond.
> . . . Specifically, two important movements must occur, together or
> in sequence. First, the previous stage's tacit system of beliefs, values,
> and commitments must be critically examined. This means that
> persons must undergo a sometimes painful disruption of their
> deeply held but unexamined world view or belief system. The
> familiar and taken-for-granted must be [objectified and] made
> strange. The assumptive configuration of meanings assembled to
> support their selfhood in its roles and relations must now be allowed
> to become problematic. Evocative symbols and stories by which lives
> have been oriented will now be critically questioned and inter-
> preted. So the first movement involves disembedding from the
> previous stage's assumptive and tacitly held system of beliefs and
> values. (Fowler 1987, 68)

We see here an effort to describe the awakening of analytic reasoning and the effort to focus it reflectively upon the previously
implicit body of opinions, beliefs, and values that have constituted
and oriented the self. It marks the beginning of a process of
assessing the validity of the assumptive foundations and elements
of one's worldview in the critical light of one's reflected-upon
experience. Structurally this move shows parallels with the Enlightenment's critical dismantling of received systems in theology, philosophy, and cosmology.

Like the Enlightenment, the Individuative-Reflective stage is
paralleled by a second movement in which the knowing subject
makes the self, its capacities and constitution, the object of critical
inquiry and reflection:

> Second, the self, previously constituted and sustained by its roles
> and relationships, must struggle with the question of identity and
> worth apart from its previously defining connections. This does not
> mean that the relations *have* to be broken. Nor does it mean that
> the roles *must* be relinquished. Rather, it means that persons must
> take into themselves much of the authority they previously invested
> in others for determining and sanctioning their goals and values. It
> means that definitions of the self dependent upon roles and rela-
> tionships with others must now be regrounded in terms of a new
> quality of responsibility that the self takes for defining itself and
> orchestrating its roles and relations. (Fowler 1987, 68; italics added)

153

Just as the Enlightenment's emancipatory thrust derived from a new apprehension of reason, so also the groundwork for the double movement in critical reflection characteristic of the Individuative-Reflective stage of faith depends upon new cognitive capacities. In the first place, it requires the full development of what Piaget called "formal operational" thinking. This means constructing the operations necessary for formulating and manipulating abstract concepts. It means being capable of "thinking about our thinking." It means being able to understand and construct mental models of systems of interaction to represent the interrelations of interacting phenomena (Piaget and Inhelder 1969).

As an intermediate and crucial step toward full formal operational thinking, especially as it can be used in reflecting upon the self and one's implicit system of values and beliefs, one must develop a new level of social perspective taking. We call this level, after Selman (1974, 1976), "third-person" perspective taking. The Synthetic-Conventional stage of faith, the one typically arising in early adolescence and just prior to the Individuative-Reflective stage, is marked by its embeddedness in "mutual interpersonal" perspective taking.

> In the acute attunement to the expectations and evaluations of significant others that marks . . . the Synthetic-Conventional stage . . . persons depend at first upon external relations for confirmation and support of the self. Gradually, in that stage the expectations and conforming judgments of valued others become an internalized part of one's personality. These internalized "voices" of significant others provide guidance and constraint for the interpersonal self. When external or internalized authorities conflict, however, or when their tutelage becomes cramping or constrictive for a developing person, the self must construct a perspective from which both self and the relations with others can be seen from beyond the embeddedness in interpersonal relations. The third-person perspective provides an angle of vision from which evaluations of the expectations of others can be made and from which conflicting claims or expectations can be adjudicated. The use of the third-person perspective provides a basis from which assessments and choices can be made in relation to the beliefs, values, and elements of life style one has evolved. (Fowler 1987, 68-69)

The third-person perspective opens the way for the use of formal operational abilities to analyze the contents of one's worldview and value system and to see their interrelated elements as part of a system. It may be seen as the epistemological basis for the "transcendental ego." It makes possible the movement from being embedded in one's ideology to an at least partial realization of that status of critical self-awareness that we could describe as *having* one's ideology (see Kegan 1982). The third-person perspective also makes possible the construction of self-other relations seen as located in and constrained by the context of systems. This includes the possibility of the awareness of economic and political as well as familial and religious systems.

As a summary for this exploration of structural and functional parallels between the Enlightenment and the transition to Individuative-Reflective faith, consider another quotation from *Faith Development and Pastoral Care:*

> The Enlightenment represented a movement in cultural evolution where inherited symbols, beliefs, and traditions were subjected to the scrutiny and evaluation of critical reasoning. Similarly, the development of the Individuative-Reflective stage of faith involves the critical examination and exercise of choice regarding a person or community's previous faith perspectives. In many respects this is a "demythologizing" stage. Creeds, symbols, stories, and myths from religious traditions are likely to be subjected to analysis and to translation to conceptual formulations. . . . Paul Tillich pointed out that a symbol that is recognized as a symbol no longer has the power of a symbol. The powerful participation of a symbol in that which it symbolizes, which makes it possible for the symbol to mediate relationship with its reality, is now broken. While the conceptual analysis and translation of the symbol makes its meaning explicit, we may fail to notice that in the process of communicating meanings the initiative has shifted from the symbol to the analyst of the symbol. (Fowler 1987, 70)

The last line of this quotation points gently toward the massive overconfidence and blind undersides of the Enlightenment as a movement. In its exhilaration at the emancipatory and critically clarifying power of reason, it failed to anticipate the consequences of enthroning reason without bringing forward the forming and constraining influences of human wisdom in religious and cultural traditions. In its confidence regarding the possibility of dissolving and reconstructing knowledge of reality, and thereby of controlling the complexities of nature, it remained blissfully ignorant of both the social and the psychic unconscious. In its overconfidence in its hard-won self-consciousness and rational clarity, it could not measure the degree to which the human soul resents its finitude and strives to ground and defend itself in myopic and self-serving ideologies.

But balance and the wisdom of hindsight are not easy to come by in the midst of a revolution. We need to celebrate the courage and genius of the Enlightenment. We need to celebrate the courage and determination of those who in each generation recapitulate, with their own risky struggles, the Enlightenment's path toward self-conscious possession and public use of their rational autonomy, no matter how much developmental self-deception it necessarily involves.

BEYOND ENLIGHTENMENT: TOWARD POSTMODERN CONSCIOUSNESS

In conclusion let us briefly address the two questions identified at the end of our introductory section. First, to what degree is the faith development theory and research itself an expression of Enlightenment impulses, and thereby a participant in both its strengths and limits? Cassirer reminds us that at its core the Enlightenment was not basically irreligious or inimical to religion.

> The strongest intellectual forces of the Enlightenment do not lie in its rejection of belief but rather in the new form of faith which it proclaims, and in the new form of religion which it embodies. . . . This era is permeated by genuine creative feeling and an unquestionable faith in the reformation of the world. And just such a reformation is now expected of religion. . . . [E]specially among the thinkers of the German Enlightenment, the fundamental objective is not the dissolution of religion but its "transcendental" justification and foundation. (Cassirer 1951, 135-36)

The conception of faith with which faith development theory works is both made necessary by the Enlightenment and is part of the fruit of the Enlightenment's effort to "reform" religion. This theory and research makes an Enlightenment move when it seeks to provide formal definitions of faith and formal characterizations of "structuralist" stages. Not until the Enlightenment did this kind of separation of the "structuring" and the "content" of ideological perspectives come into play. Though less confident than the Enlightenment about the establishment of rational and ethical bases from which all particular religious traditions can be evaluated, faith development theory does provide a criteriology for assessing the adequacy of a given person's or group's appropriation of its religious content tradition, and the adequacy of the tradition itself. In contrast to the Enlightenment, however, and in ways that show its indebtedness to post-Enlightenment hermeneutics, faith development theory knows that the structural features of faith are at best half the picture and that any adequate study of lived religious faith must balance the initiative of the interpreter and inquirer with the hermeneutic initiatives of classic traditions. Moreover, faith development theory seeks to acknowledge and systematically account for the important shaping role of the emotions and of the unconscious—personal and social—in the life of faith (Fowler 1984, chap. 4).

Second, do we find parallels between the transition to the Conjunctive stage of faith and what appears to be a culture-wide struggle toward post-Enlightenment modes of consciousness in the present era? This is a question we will explore more fully in the next chapter. We will see if it is fruitful to parallel the discussion of the Enlightenment and the Individuative-Reflective stage with a similar consideration of the Conjunctive stage in relation to a variety of contemporary post-Enlightenment approaches to hermeneutics and the philosophy of science.

Since the Second World War we have been formulating the ground lines of philosophical approaches that may help us to grasp and express the structural features of another revolution in process in Western consciousness—one that will likely prove to be as significant a watershed as did the Enlightenment (this movement was anticipated earlier by such thinkers as Einstein, Wittgenstein,

Heidegger, Whitehead, and Gadamer). Formulations of this new consciousness will have to incorporate the crucially important contributions of the nineteenth century: a full orbed doctrine of evolution and development (biological, cultural, ontological); the critique of ideology and a full grasping of the role of overt as well as covert interests in shaping scientific and philosophical thought and behavior; an accounting of the "will to power" and the dynamics of *resentiment* as forces in human behavior; the social sources of religion, language, and the fundamental categories of thought; and the tremendous cunning of defenses and the repressed unconscious in affecting our knowing, valuing and interpreting as well as acting.

But such philosophical perspectives will also have to incorporate the great contributions of twentieth-century reflective experience: the awareness of the fundamental participation of everything in *process*; the relativity to each other, and to what they observe, of all perspectives on the universe and experience; the intrusion into and involvement of any investigator within phenomena being scientifically studied; the ecological interdependence of all systems, including systems of thought and consciousness; the maintenance of the cosmos through the counterpoising pull and force of tensional vectors, giving rise to a unity of such variegated and pluralistic inclusiveness as to challenge the human capacity to fathom, even using a panoply of the infinitely fast computers now available to us for synchronous knowing. Thinkers such as Paul Ricoeur, Michael Polanyi, Jürgen Habermas, David Bohm, and, in theology, David Tracy and Gordon Kaufman are pointing the way toward such formulations. In the examination of their work, and that of their coworkers and correspondents, we find characteristics that call for the "second naiveté" and the dialectical, multiperspectival structures of knowing and valuing that descriptions of the Conjunctive stage of faith have tried to capture. Extensive work in these philosophical sources, combined with fresh empirical investigations of the faith structuring of late-stage respondents, promises to lead toward enriched and more precise characterizations of the Conjunctive stage.

Times of cultural revolution in consciousness are un-nerving and frightening as well as exhilarating. It seems clear that in the face of the complexity and newness of the ways we are being called to think and be, many groups from all over the globe are retreating toward the hope of authoritative grounding in the resurgence of pre-Enlightenment religious commitments or the heedlessness of hedonist ideologies. In our next chapter we will examine the political, religious, and cultural struggles that attend the shift in cultural consciousness beyond the Enlightenment we have explored in this chapter. Perhaps theory and research in faith development, which provides a language and a conceptual system for ordering and speaking intelligibly about the clash of cultural levels of development, have contributions to make to understanding these tensions and struggles. This effort to find models that help clarify these struggles is important for those who, in our time, want to bring as much courage and clear-eyed thought to the challenges of our era as the thinkers of the Enlightenment brought to theirs.

CHAPTER TEN

BEYOND CULTURE WARS

Times of transition in cultures and societies mean ferment, social tension, and conflict. They bring widespread experiences of dislocation. Established institutions and practices undergo changes and loss of coherence. Assumptions that have guided public and private patterns of life without much examination become problematic and suffer questions of legitimation. My writing about the Enlightenment of the eighteenth century in the preceding chapter may have made it seem, in retrospect, far more orderly and unidirectional than those who experienced it would have recognized. Political revolutions, regicide and civil war, religious conflict and sharp intellectual debate, coupled with widespread movements of populations, made the eighteenth century tumultuous. It seems likely that presently we are undergoing an epoch of such deep going change in the structures of cultural consciousness and social practices that it may make the Enlightenment seem mild indeed by comparison.

Building on the previous chapter, here we explore how later faith development stages, understood as models of adult faith consciousness, may help to illumine some of the tensions that threaten civility and create seemingly irreconcilable differences in politics and society in the United States. Drawing on the work of James Davison Hunter, a sociologist of religion, we identify two disparate sociomoral "tempers" he sees as vocally present in American cultural and political struggles at present. Faith development stages will serve to expand and flesh out these tempers of cultural consciousness, sharpening the contrasts of their respective approaches to religion, politics, and organizational life. I will argue that one set of reasons for deep going political differences and incivility results from the inability of either of the two struggling tempers—Hunter calls them "Orthodox" and "Progressive"—to

160

help us maintain orientation and moral leverage in this time of rapid change. Whether people have a theory of postmodern experience or not, I will argue, we all are living in the midst of postmodern experience. Using the structural characteristics of the Conjunctive stage of faith, we will consider a provisional model for the kind of *practical postmodern consciousness* that seems to be taking form in contemporary societies. In the conclusion we will explore some implications of this analysis for the shape and missions of religious, political, and organizational life in this transitional time.

For purposes of this discussion our attention will focus on the three most frequently encountered stages among educated adults in American society, the *Synthetic-Conventional,* the *Individuative-Reflective,* and the *Conjunctive* stages of faith. Let me review, in brief, some of the claims made in the preceding chapter. There I suggested that the *Synthetic-Conventional* form of faith consciousness can be seen as having rootage in and preserving important elements of *pre-Enlightenment forms of cultural consciousness.* The *Individuative-Reflective* stage, I argued, corresponds to *forms of cultural consciousness* introduced by the *Enlightenment.* At a later point, I will explore further whether the *Conjunctive* stage of faith provides a paradigm by which to make explicit some features of a structural model for *postmodern forms of cultural consciousness.* Before we take those turns, however, let us examine some recent work on forms of cultural and faith consciousness in the United States by James Davison Hunter (Hunter 1991).

CULTURE WARS

For at least a decade and a half broad coalitions of religious and political groups in the United States have polarized into moral and value stances that reveal deep going and seemingly irreconcilable differences. Some of the issues around which this polarization has occurred include the abortion debate ("Pro-Life" vs. "Pro-Choice"); the struggle over distinguishing between art and pornography; the cultural neutrality of the public schools versus (Christian) prayer as a part of classroom routines; and conflicting views about the rights guaranteed to homosexual men and women.

Particularly divisive are debates over the reform of social welfare programs and efforts to widen access to affordable healthcare in the society. Though such terms as "liberal" and "conservative" (or "new right") are often used to distinguish these perspectives, these labels, suggesting traditional political alignments, can be deceptive if we fail to attend to certain easily overlooked features of these debates.

The polarized alignments of these two oppositional groups cut across the lines of traditional religious and political boundaries. Defining pluralism in terms of the differences between Protestants, Catholics, and Jews is no longer descriptive of where the real battles are occurring in the culture wars in United States society. Nor do racial or ethnic divisions prove particularly meaningful in this emerging pattern of cultural conflict. The oppositional coalitions that have emerged in these struggles cut across such traditional divisions.

James Davison Hunter has proposed the names "orthodox" and "progressive" to characterize the two broad coalitions that oppose each other in the conflicts over the values, lifestyle options, and public policy that are to be determinative in the country. We may use the term "temper" to describe the combination of emotional, moral, and ideological dispositions that constitute the unifying characteristics of members of each of these two orientations. We can speak of the *orthodox temper* and the *progressive temper.* These tempers are faith orientations, both in *content* and in *process.* They adhere to deeply differing convictions about the locus of authority in morality and religion; they espouse contrasting "myths of origin" and interpretations regarding the normative story of the nation's founding and its meanings; they each claim ownership of the ideals of justice and freedom, but they nuance the meanings of these terms in virtually mutually exclusive ways.

In matters of belief and morality, orthodox groups honor sources of authority that are external to the self. Located in holy scriptures, in received traditions, and in the authorized interpreters of such sources, authority has a lawful quality. Authority is a fixed and unchanging reality. Appealing to "laws of nature" or "laws of God," adherents of the orthodox temper express a readiness to claim a universally binding validity for the moral rules and religious beliefs established in their traditions. In the North American context, groups that hold to the orthodox temper are prepared to see the founding of the nation in biblical terms, as a "city set on the hill," and to interpret the constitutive political documents—the Declaration of Independence and the Constitution—as permeated with and validated by biblical ideals.

One can readily see how the temperaments of fundamentalist and some evangelical Christians can find mutual respect and alliance with some orthodox Jews and conservative Catholic groups, not to mention both traditional Muslims and members of the Nation of Islam. For the orthodox, freedom tends to be understood in economic terms. Freedom means commitment to "free enterprise," the freedom to pursue one's economic interests without governmental interference or political constraint. In economics, orthodox speakers express trust in a "free market system" and see economic competition as grounded in biblical principles. For the orthodox, economic and spiritual freedom go hand in hand. Neither is possible, they hold, without the other. Justice, for the orthodox, is usually understood in terms of Judeo-Christian standards of moral righteousness. Justice means personal and social adherence to the laws of God. As Hunter says, "A just society . . . is a morally conscientious and lawful society. When its people abide by these standards it is also an ordered society" (Hunter 1991, 112).

Progressives, on the other hand, tend to reject orthodox appeals to particular traditions as sources of authority. Instead they espouse ethical principles derived, in part, from the nation's religious and humanist traditions. For them the founding documents of the country do not reflect absolutes either given by God or rooted in nature. Rather, "the founders gave us a 'living Constitution,' one that cannot be straightjacketed, forever attached to the culture of an agrarian, preindustrialized society, but one that grows and changes with a changing society" (Hunter 1991, 113-14). Law, one of the highest expressions of human reason, must evolve as a society develops and matures.

The progressives' appeals to freedom and justice contrast significantly in focus from those of the orthodox. Here freedom focuses primarily on protection of the social and political rights of individuals. Freedom in this sense means the guarantee of immunity from interference by others in one's life, whether from state, church, or others. Similarly, justice, in the progressives' frame, focuses on the assurance of equality for all persons and groups and the ending of oppression in the social world. Adherents of the progressive temper are prepared to hold the United States accountable for economic inequities and political oppression, both within the society and in other parts of the world, that result from the country's national practices and policies. As Hunter sums it, "Where *cultural conservatives* tend to *define freedom economically* (as individual economic initiative) and *justice socially* (as righteous living), *progressives* tend to *define freedom socially* (as individual rights) and *justice economically* (as equity)" (Hunter 1991, 115).

This brief synopsis of Hunter's study of the two dominant tempers involved in cultural struggle in the United States confirms the claim that they represent competing and conflicting faith orientations. Both tempers are grounded in *convictional emotion;* both tend to *resist or bypass rational argumentation* with the other. These two coalitions appeal to their own cultural canons; each confines its discourse largely to the community of its own adherents. Engagements with representatives of the other temper tend to be conducted in terms of debate rather than of dialogue; their representations of each other occur primarily in caricatures and stereotypes.

ADULT FAITH STAGES AS MODELS OF THE "TEMPERS" OF CULTURAL CONSCIOUSNESS

Now our task involves elaborating two of the adult stages of faith development as models of cultural consciousness that parallel the orthodox and progressive positions. Structural features of the *Synthetic-Conventional* stage can be used to build the paradigm of *orthodox* consciousness. We will employ structural features of the *Individuative-Reflective* stage to model the paradigm of *progressive* consciousness. Each of these paradigms will be elaborated to suggest its approach to religion, politics, and organizational life, as well as to faith consciousness. After examining the juxtaposition of these two tempers, we will consider a paradigm of cultural consciousness that suggests the structural features of a third "temper" struggling for voice and mediating influence in this present time of transition. Consider the following table, which provides the categories of our analysis of these first two tempers. In subsequent pages we will flesh out the models and their tensions.

Faith Stage/ Temper	Faith Consciousness	Religion	Politics	Organization
Synthetic-Conventional; rooted in pre-Enlightenment; *orthodox*	Tacit; inter-personal; non-critical; external locus of authority	"Some of my best friends are . . . "; assumed superiority; *mystery-mastery*	Reduced to personal qual-ities of leaders or ref-erence groups; *organic society*	Hierarchical authority; information control
Individuative-Reflective; rooted in Enlightenment; *progressive*	Explicit; autonomous; critical-reflective; internal locus of authority	Dichotomous; competing truth claims; either exclu-sive truth or relativism; *demythologizing*	Ideological; claim chosen political and economic philosophy as defining self; *social contract*	Specialization; differentiation of function; rational-bureaucratic organization

SYNTHETIC-CONVENTIONAL FAITH AND THE ORTHODOX TEMPER

The *orthodox temper* exhibits many of the structural features of the *Synthetic-Conventional* stage of faith. It preserves many dimensions of consciousness that resemble pre-Enlightenment modes of thinking and experiencing. In terms of faith consciousness the orthodox temper adheres to an implicit, tacitly held ideology. To be sure, there are explicit formulas and slogans that express deep going value options. Orthodox adherents, however, likely do not have a critically reflective, conceptual grasp on the worldview they espouse taken as a whole. Emotion-laden images and symbols provide cues for reactions and judgments that have the power of instincts or the voice of conscience within. Authority for the for-mulation and defense of this largely tacit value system is left, for

165

the orthodox, to the recognized leaders of religious or political groups, interpreters of sacred scriptures or tradition, or political leaders certified as being congruent with the canons of their orthodox group or tradition. Authority, therefore, is located external to the person, and is located in sacred texts, in the group, in the tradition, or in the group's authorized representatives. Reliance upon such authorities tends to be justified in *personal* terms: trust is grounded in personal qualities of authoritative persons. Although ideological compatibility is a part of what makes a given leader acceptable as an authority, the overall reasons for the investment of trust likely include an amalgam of personal qualities, charisma, approval by like-minded friends, and the personal salience of the issues they (the authorities) represent.

For those persons and groups of the orthodox temper who are explicitly religious, the locus of authority most likely rests in concrete and literal readings of sacred scriptures, the indisputable teachings of tradition, and the dictums of authorized interpreters. Relations with persons of other religious traditions, ethnic groups, or races tend to be personalized. Persons of the orthodox temper are likely to say of persons of other racial, ethnic, or religious groups than their own, "Some of my best friends are . . . " (naming the particular out-group to which they are referring). The unexamined assumption seems to be that "because I enjoy personal and friendly relations with one or a few representatives of that group, I understand, accept, and could get along with *all* such persons." Such a position makes examining the question of whether one holds personal or group prejudices unnecessary. It allows one to ignore issues of deep going differences regarding symbols, beliefs, worldview, and institutional culture between religious traditions. It also allows the generalization of negative stereotypes for entire groups, based upon difficult relationships with one or a few representatives of those groups. Because orthodox adherents base their emotive loyalties on unquestioned external sources of authority, they allow themselves to live and act out of a largely unexamined sense of the superiority of their religious tradition over those of others. This may lead to consistent pressures to "convert" representatives of other religious traditions. It certainly gives sanction for political initiatives to legislate their groups' moral and religious standards of behavior, seeking to impose them on the larger, religiously pluralistic society. For instance, to orthodox adherents who understand justice in society in terms of Judeo-Christian standards of moral righteousness, religious and cultural pluralism represents a condition that must be made to give way, through moral teaching as well as through legislative and judicial procedures, to a cultural homogeneity based on their own traditions and teachings.

In approaches to politics, the tendency to personalization and avoidance of explicit ideological analysis, which we noted with regard to religion, carries over into the broader field. In fact, for politically committed orthodox adherents, the lines between religion and politics tend to be blurred. Along with that, there tends to be a blurring of the lines between the public and the private lives of persons. Under the pressures of personalist politics, the conduct of family life, the patterns of friendship and sexual relations, and the forms of piety and religious belonging all represent factors by which the public lives and leadership of politicians must be evaluated. This makes for frequent employment of *ad hominem* approaches in political discourse and debate.

Underlying the political approaches of orthodox persons and groups one finds an organic metaphor for society. In the terms of Ferdinand Toennies' classic analysis, orthodox adherents envision and long for a *gemeinschaftlich* society—one in which deeply shared values and beliefs make for consensual unity, where there is congruence between all members' personal and private lives, and where social conflict is avoided through the leadership of a morally aristocratic leadership class (Toennies 1963). In the vision of an organic society, in both religion and politics there are assigned roles and statuses for men, women, and children. In families and in religious communities, patriarchal models receive most favored authorization and support. These commitments carry over into the main political preoccupations of the orthodox.

The implicit reliance upon organic metaphors for society and politics also carries over into orthodox approaches to organizational life. Organic societies give rise to hierarchical patterns of authority—often with leadership elites enjoying the implicit sanction of natural or divinely ordained authorization. In such organizations, leadership utilizes control of information as a means of power, with the controlled flow of information coming from the top down. Personal initiatives and independent responsibility by subordinates must be carefully exercised, so as not to threaten the authority of the hierarchy. Leadership in organizations, in the orthodox persuasion, tends to operate on the basis of a *mystery-mastery* approach to authority. By this phrase, taken from David Bakan, I refer to the pattern in which leaders, on the basis of presumed superior experience, knowledge, preparation, and wisdom, make decisions for their constituents on the basis of one-way consultation and communication, without making the procedures and data on which their decisions are based accessible to their followers. By keeping mysterious the character and sources of their judgment and knowledge, they enhance the aura of power that surrounds them and heighten the felt legitimacy of their followers' sense of dependence upon them (Bakan 1966).

In order that we may feel the depth of differences between the orthodox and the progressive alignments in the culture wars of present-day American society, let us carry out a parallel analysis of the progressive temper.

INDIVIDUATIVE-REFLECTIVE FAITH AND THE PROGRESSIVE TEMPER

The *progressive temper* honors and preserves many of the procedural ideals introduced into Western societies through the impact of the Enlightenment of the eighteenth century. They keep alive the Enlightenment's suspicion of received traditions and its spirit of knowing by analytically breaking down the subject matter to be known into its constituent parts. Correlatively, the persons and groups best described as progressive exhibit many of the structural features of the *Individuative-Reflective* stage of faith. They tend to place authority for making choices on matters of personal and political concern upon the experience, reflective judgment, and personal conscience of presumably rational individuals. Prizing the powers of objectivity made possible by the disciplined use of reason, they tend to give a kind of sovereign privilege to the critical and reflective deliberations of the individual.

In terms of faith consciousness, progressives employ critical and reflective procedures for analyzing and making explicit the contents of ideological perspectives or particular theological positions. Though there can be respect for authoritative creedal or traditional teachings, progressive religionists reserve the right of individual review and personal revision of received traditions, based upon experience, reason, and coming to terms with new circumstances and continually changing conditions. In faith consciousness, progressives tend to be resistant to appeals to authority based upon unexamined traditional doctrine or to claims dependent primarily upon ecclesial authority for their validity. Progressives locate authority *within* the self.

In their approaches to religion, progressives favor approaches to scripture and tradition that employ strategies such as *demythologization*. In such approaches, myths, parables, symbols, and allegory in scriptures or tradition are analyzed from the standpoint of the assumptions, experiences, and knowledge of educated moderns for the *meanings* they conserve and express. These meanings may be restated in *conceptual* formulations, thus yielding their existential wisdom in terms that are acceptable to modern consciousness, while stripping off the "husks" of premodern worldviews and prescientific superstitions. Progressives demand explicit formulations of truth claims and their justifications. They incline toward dichotomous decisions for or against given positions or truth claims. Ambiguity and paradox often tend to be looked at as obfuscation and as the products of fuzzy thinking. The combination of their allegiance to personal judgment—based on experience, reason, and personal conscience—with their discounting of received religious and moral traditions means that progressives frequently turn out to be cultural and moral relativists in matters of faith.

Underlying the political approaches of progressives one finds a reliance upon the metaphor of the *social contract*. As in classical liberal political theory, the rational, autonomous, self-interested self constitutes the basic unit from which societies are built. Social membership is seen as voluntary, and the contractual basis for political society rests on the mutual agreement to respect equally the rights and freedoms requisite for the exercise of personal conscience and the pursuit of personal conceptions of the good. In the progressive vision, persons define *themselves,* not through ascriptive membership in a conventional society, but through explicit choices of moral and political values, and through voluntary alignment with self-selected associations and ideologically defined groupings. For progressives there must be a firm line between the public and private spheres of the self. With varying degrees of intensity, progressives assert that each person or group has freedom to pursue their own notions of the good in society, including their choices of lifestyle, and the exercise or nonexercise of religion. From the progressive standpoint, what adults do in the private spheres of their lives, as long as they do not injure others or infringe upon their rights, should be a matter of no interest to the government or to one's neighbors.

Voluntarist and social contract principles inform progressives' ways of approaching organizational life. Constitutions, bylaws, charters, and explicit delineation of powers and responsibilities mark the utopias of organizational life favored by progressives. Meritocracy, rather than aristocracy, should govern the choice of incumbents of leadership roles. These should be frequently rotated, so as to avoid oligarchical pretensions. Rational bureaucratic forms of organization, honoring specialization and differentiation of function, fit nicely with progressives' predilection for contracts. Progressives tend to regard organizations, which they see as volitional and contractual creations of cooperating persons, as individuals writ large. Each institution or corporation functions as a rational, autonomous self-interested *corporate* persona. Like persons, corporate entities also have rights to pursue their own particular conceptions of the good, constrained only by the equal rights of other such bodies, and by the commitment to cooperate in the maintenance of common social conditions required for their flourishing.

Prizing—and often overprizing—the rational capacities of individuals, progressives, in theory, espouse open debate and assert confidence in the robustness of reason and truth, which if untrammeled can lead contending parties to agreement and advancement. In practice, overconfidence in their own conscious rationality, coupled with obliviousness to unconsciously distorting factors, can give organizations run along progressive lines great difficulties. This particular form of self-deception often gives progressives a tone of self-righteous moral superiority fully as pretentious as the moral self-righteousness sometimes exhibited in public by the orthodox.

THE INCOMMENSURABILITY OF THE ORTHODOX AND PROGRESSIVE TEMPERS

The juxtaposition and comparison of the structural differences of the orthodox and progressive tempers, by way of adult stages of faith, demonstrate how monumental are the differences between them. Not only do they have *substantive* differences—differences regarding the *contents* of their worldviews and value systems; we have seen that they also differ profoundly as regards the underlying operations of their knowing and valuing. Consider the following:

Orthodox		*Progressive*
External locus of authority	v.	Internal locus of authority
Literal or symbolic interpretation of teachings	v.	Demythologizing interpretations
Organismic political metaphors	v.	Social contract metaphors
Implicit, tacit ideology	v.	Explicit, conceptual ideology
Freedom in economic terms	v.	Freedom in terms of human rights
Justice as moral righteousness	v.	Justice as equality and fairness
Blurring line between public and private lives	v.	Clear line between public and private lives

When we recognize these procedural and operational differences, it becomes clear why members of these two tempers have such difficulty communicating with each other, let alone convincing each other to change. Further, debates between representatives

171

of these two tempers, when they occur, tend to be carried on from the extreme ends of the continuum. There are several reasons for this. Frequently the debates are carried out in the streets and are covered by press and television reporters who too often present polarizing perspectives. Such accounts may include angry persons in opposing picket lines in front of abortion clinics. They may present opposing groups at a state prison clashing over the morality of capital punishment as they await the execution of a prisoner. Representatives of these tempers usually clash on *Firing Line* and similar television programs, where the format is confrontational, and where the rationale is at least in part the provision of entertainment and commercial profit. During political campaigns their clashes take place through fifteen- and thirty-second sound bytes on television and radio. On those media, the aim is primarily that of eroding the image of the opponent and all the values he or she represents.

The particular virulence of the struggles between these two tempers may be partially understood by recognizing that both these ways of seeing and being in the world are presently under threat. Though this sense of threat may be only partially conscious in both camps, it seems growingly clear that we are in a time of pervasive transition in the structures of cultural and social consciousness. The shrillness of representatives of both the orthodox and the progressive alignments may result from their sense of the loss of familiar certainties in the face of a revolution in consciousness so powerful that it likely will dwarf the impact of the eighteenth-century Enlightenment.

POSTMODERN CONSCIOUSNESS: BEYOND ORTHODOX AND PROGRESSIVE

I believe the present time is a watershed in the evolution of cultural consciousness. As I indicated in the introduction, there is talk across many disciplines in the universities about "postmodern" modes of thought. My sense of and argument for the point I want to make now, however, does not rest on the presence or influence of theories of postmodern thought in the academy. Whether persons or groups have academic theories of postmodernism at hand or not, we are all involved today—reflectively or not—in postmodern experience. Consider some of the elements of this experience:

- Instantaneous global communications, surrounding ordinary citizens, as well as leaders, with the daily experience of an overwhelming range of images and reports concerning the crises and struggles of humans and nature.
- Experience of global systems of economic interdependence and mobility, their impacts on financial markets and interest rates, the closing of local industries or corporations, and the shifting of jobs from one continent to another.
- Resurgence of interest in and claiming of particular cultural traditions, coupled with the unprecedented availability of information and access to one another's traditions and histories. These factors are paradoxically juxtaposed with the widening proliferation and intensification of bloody ethnic, racial, religious, and national conflicts.
- Growing realization of ecological interdependence and the fragility of the earth's biosphere. Our mobility, our attending to the world more and more through the mediation of telecommunications technology and electronic screens flashing information, separates us ever further from the rhythms of nature. Those rhythms—the predictability of the seasons, the primal confidence in nature's capacity for self-renewal and adaptation—are being deeply disturbed by the consequences of our technological development in the modern world.
- The end of the "modern world"—the world of heavy industry, of assembly lines employing semiskilled labor, the world interpreted by print media, augmented by radio and television, the world driven at ever accelerating paces by our expanding use of fossil fuels.
- The end of the world of Cartesian epistemology and of positivism in science, now supplanted by revolutionary uses of computer technologies that power paradigms built upon theories of relativity, indeterminacy, quantum mechanics, chaos, and emerging new cosmologies.

173

While many academic analyses of the postmodern fix their attention on the deconstruction of concepts and patterns of thought that have characterized modernity, I am aware of few efforts to characterize the emerging shape of postmodern modes of thought and understanding as forms of *practical thought and consciousness.* From our research and theory in the study of faith development I have found it informative to shape a preliminary model for the structuring of postmodern consciousness using the categories of our analyses of the orthodox and progressive tempers. The following continuation of our chart presents some elements of a *practical postmodern temper,* based on the *Conjunctive* stage of faith:

Faith Stage/ Temper	Faith Consciousness	Religion	Politics	Organization
Conjunctive; emerging post-Enlighten- ment outlook; practical postmodern	Multiple perspectives and systems; second naiveté; commitment in embraced pluralism	All reality outlooks are constructed; God's reality exceeds our constructs; integrate con- scious and unconscious	Multiple realities; multiple sys- tems; beyond ideology; ecological inter- dependence; covenant	Ecological networks; multi-related project orien- tation; infor- mation-driven; flexibility

Postmodern consciousness, explicitly and implicitly, is a consciousness populated with *systems* and *systems awareness.* I am suggesting that structurally postmodern consciousness parallels the *Conjunctive* pattern of faith consciousness. The term *conjunctive* derives from Carl Jung's appropriation of Nicholas of Cusa's concept of the *coincidentia oppositorum,* the conjunction, the holding together in one frame, of opposites. In the case of postmodern consciousness there is the juxtaposition—the holding in one complex range of models—of multiple systems and, indeed, of systems of systems. My claim is that the construction of these postmodern, multiple systemic forms of consciousness represents a practical necessity for reflective persons in our era and is happening, willy-nilly, whether we have adequate theories or awareness to account for these constructs or not.

In postmodern faith consciousness there is a recognition that there are no "naked" facts, truths, or events. All knowing involves interpretation; interpretations contrast and overlap due to the differing perspectives of those who construct meanings from different vantage points in a system or systems. Multiple perspectives must be taken into account and coordinated—including paradoxical or opposing perspectives—if anything deserving the complex name "truth" is to be modeled and understood. Recognizing that myths and symbols from classic traditions often "hold" and bring into view this sort of truthful richness, postmodern consciousness in faith manifests a *second* or *willed naiveté* (Ricoeur 1967). Persons and groups in the postmodern pattern may well hold allegiances to particular religious traditions. They recognize that we have no alternative to embracing interpretations and traditions of interpretation and that the complexity of our situations and demands for knowing commend stances of epistemological humility toward the richness of classic traditions that have perennially been accorded revealed status. From this practical postmodern standpoint it makes sense to eschew *relativism,* while acknowledging *relativity,* and with it the necessity of commitment in the midst of an embraced pluralism of such perspectives.

Epistemological humility correlates with the recognition that all reality outlooks involve the constructive activity of human spirit and imagination. God, imaged in relation to cosmic and microcosmic systems, can readily be acknowledged as exceeding our imaginative and epistemological constructs. Further, practical postmodern faith requires attention and practices that enable persons to work at the integration of the internal systems of the conscious and unconscious dimensions of psyche and spirit.

The shape of a practical postmodern politics defies adequate treatment in this space or by this author. Nonetheless, it seems clear that many of the features hinted at with regard to faith and religion will mark the political processes we will need. We are already beginning to come to terms with the ways financial and economic systems, along with communication systems, are relativizing the role of national governments and economic autonomy. Moreover, the ending of the cold war and the dismantling of states that had lived under a coerced ideological unity suggest that the politics of a practical postmodern approach will require attention to realities of interdependence, which have already made sweeping ideologies—of the right or the left—obsolete and increasingly distorting.

In organizational life, practical postmodern approaches point toward ecologies of project oriented teams, connected in interactive communication nets. Geographical centralization, no longer a necessity, gives way to connections through phones, fax machines, the Internet, and teleconferencing. The increasing use of consultants and temporary experts changes corporate ethos and values environments, while information driven flexibility puts a premium on corporate responsiveness to market possibilities, personnel adaptiveness, and continual technical enhancement.

The economic implications of these changes in organizational life have been impacting the social and economic conditions of postindustrial societies for nearly two decades. For those who flourish under the new organizational patterns there are both economic rewards and the possibility of enriched leisure activities, involving similar features of mobility, variety, and freedom from encumbering connections to particular locales. Among the increasing numbers of persons displaced from more traditional "modern" roles in production and bureaucratic activities, large-scale unemployment, the shrinking of middle classes, and the formation in the United States of a permanent economic "underclass" have been extremely dislocating and disruptive experiences.

CONCLUSION: PUBLIC CHURCHES, LEADERSHIP, AND FAITHFUL CHANGE

I have argued that the present struggle between coalitions representing the orthodox and the progressive tempers in the United States today cannot be understood unless we take the faith dimensions of those tempers seriously. By comparing and contrasting the structural features of these tempers through the use of adult faith stages, I have tried to show how deep going and incommensurable are their respective values and worldviews and their ways of holding to them. I have suggested that the growing impasses in communication and cooperation between representatives of the two tempers result in significant measure from the partially recognized loss of resonance and power those who embrace both of these tempers feel in the face of the everyday experiences I have summed up under the rubric of *postmodern* conditions.

Religious communities, political leaders, and leaders in the professions and institutions of our society face at least three challenges of great importance with regard to the analysis offered in this writing. First, I believe that we are called upon in this period to work consciously and effectively at nurturing and supporting a substantial minority, a *political and cultural leadership group,* who embrace their faith in terms of the structures of the *practical postmodern* stance of faith in this time of transition in cultural consciousness. This first task, to put it bluntly, is that of nurturing and supporting political and cultural leaders prepared to *claim and model Conjunctive faith* in American society. The nineteenth- and twentieth-century jurist Oliver Wendell Holmes once said, "For the simplicity on *this* side of complexity, I would not give you a fig. But for the simplicity on the *other* side of complexity, for that I would give you anything I have."

Conjunctive faith and practical postmodern approaches call for the simplicity on the other side of complexity. In addition, they call for leadership groups who stand firmly yet flexibly enough in their own faith traditions that they can affirm plurality and diversity in faith in the larger society as sources of strength to be celebrated. In the United States, such leadership groups need to forcefully affirm the Constitution's First Amendment in terms of the guarantee of the nonestablishment and free exercise of religious faith. This is in contrast to the paralyzing emphasis upon the "wall between church and state." We need such communities to lead in the creation of models for *commending,* not *imposing* or *privatizing* faith. Such leadership groups can provide lay and pastoral leadership for *public churches and synagogues*—congregations that combine deep, particular faith commitments with a principled and specific openness to the stranger and a devotion to active care for the common good (see Fowler 1991).

Second, we need political and cultural leaders to help *alter the environments of debate and dialogue* about the relations between our differing faiths and our common life. We need to find alternatives

177

to our crippling reliance upon methods of publicity that define our debates in terms of the extremes. We need to change the media environments that polarize persons and groups by encouraging and exploiting social and moral conflict in its most dysfunctional forms and by demonizing their opponents, thereby distracting attention from the *real* issues that need address. Further, we should encourage contexts for dialogue and debate where nuanced exploration of issues is modeled and taught. We must remember that a *campus* was originally a field of struggle where people could engage in combat without resort to arms. Public churches and political leaders are called to create and maintain campuses where civility in exchange and depth in debate can be modeled and learned. In the United States we would be well advised to alter the patterns by which we avoid or abort public debate of sensitive issues by prematurely turning to the judiciary—to the courts—for legal resolutions of moral and political problems.

Finally, we need leaders in religious communities and in politics to help us, as a society, *acknowledge and work constructively with the dimensions of ultimacy* in our political, economic, and moral value systems. Faith is part of the *essential human* in both its personal and its collective expressions. With the courage of a practical postmodern approach, we can open the way for offering the richness and wisdom of our particular traditions as resources for guidance and courage in facing the collective challenges of a new millennium. In this emerging postmodern era, the churches are called to move from perceiving themselves as gatekeepers of heaven to being leaders in establishing God's commonwealth of justice and love on earth. We are called to lead the movement in public life from concentration on "saving" faith to the unifying and empowering possibilities of "ordering" faith (Marty 1981).

CHAPTER ELEVEN

THEOLOGY AND POSTMODERN EXPERIENCE: FOUR RESPONSES

In light of claims that we are in the midst of a transition in cultural consciousness, it is commonplace today to assert that we are in a time "between the times" in the work of theology. A recently published collection of essays in the United States has the title *Theology at the End of Modernity*. There are many signs of efforts to shape theological reflection in dialogue with postmodern patterns of thought and emerging postmodern consciousness.

Intellectually, the emergence of postmodern thinking means a loss of confidence in the foundational features of thought established by the Enlightenment. Three such threatened features are particularly important for theology: (1) the commitment to an epistemological ideal of rational, disinterested, objective, ahistorical, and universal knowledge; (2) the elevation of science and the rationality it embodied to the status of arbiter of truth; and (3) the relegation of religion to the realm of the private, the subjective, and the self-validating experience of the divine (see Fowler 1991; Placher 1989).

In a succinct paragraph that captures much of the contemporary academic discussion of postmodernism, theologian Linell Cady writes:

> The movement of postmodernism clearly involves the abandonment of the Enlightenment project and its animating vision of reason as an ahistorical, disinterested capacity to apprehend objective reality. Far from transcending the particularity of its location, rationality is understood to be fundamentally shaped by its historical context. We think in and through traditions of interpretation, whose symbols, biases, and interests inevitably shape the reasoning process. To the extent that modernity is equated with the early modern

Enlightenment project, this historicist turn is a move toward a postmodern orientation. (Cady 1991, 86)

In addition to stressing the radical historicizing of thought upon which Cady focuses, we need to see postmodern thought and theory as taking account of the following contributions of twentieth-century reflective experience:

- the awareness of the fundamental participation of everything in *process;*
- the relativity to each other, and to what they observe, of all perspectives on the universe and experience;
- the intrusion into and involvement of any investigator within phenomena being scientifically studied;
- the ecological interdependence of all systems, including systems of thought and consciousness; and
- the constructed character of all symbolic and meaning systems, cultural, religious, and scientific, and the metaphorical quality of the language and models they employ (Fowler 1991).

At the heart of theology's challenge at the end of modernity is the practical theological task of evoking and shaping a depiction of the *praxis* of God. Related to that task is the challenge to help postmodern persons and cultures claim the possibility of shaping their lives and institutional systems in response to and in partnership with the praxis of God.

This chapter and the next point in the direction of a theology of the praxis of God for postmodern times. This chapter provides an overview of four theological strategies that hold promise for addressing postmodern conditions and consciousness. Chapter 12 sketches the outlines of a constructive practical theological approach that tries to evoke a credible depiction of God's praxis for our time. It will incorporate aspects of each of the four strategies surveyed in this chapter. It will suggest one way we may address the question of God's presence and influence in nature and history as directly as possible. In this effort we will acknowledge the necessity—as well as the difficulty—of shaping a theology that can speak publicly.

FOUR THEOLOGICAL STRATEGIES ADDRESSING
POSTMODERN EXPERIENCE

I turn now to a brief overview of four clusters of theological responses to the range of postmodern experience and to the intellectual reflections upon that experience. In my descriptions of these approaches I do not intend to be comprehensive or detailed; rather, I want to sketch them as types. I will focus on two issues in dealing with each cluster: (1) its particular strategy for engaging and providing theological illumination for postmodern experience and (2) its characterization of the praxis of God and of the human calling to respond.

The intent of this overview is *constructive*. Part of the challenge and invitation of postmodern experience is to maintain the illuminative aspects of a multiplicity of perspectives, holding them in tension with one another. These tensions, however illuminative and mutually critical we may find them, arise out of genuine and deep going differences. Many of them cannot be reconciled at the level of thought or theory. My proposal will be that many of these tensions can and must be reconciled, not in thought, but in praxis. I believe that theology that can be effective in the situated, historical, relative, yet radically open conditions of postmodernity always arises from and returns to praxis.

Liberation and Political Theology Approaches

The experiences of radical pluralism and relativity have been central among factors breaking down confidence in the modernist consciousness in North America. For Europeans, in contrast, it is my sense that the most powerful factor undermining the possibility of theology in the modern paradigm has been the experience of the holocausts of the twentieth century. It seems that for European theologies these searing, profoundly disruptive and destructive events have made *theodicy* the fundamental issue with which any public theology must begin. They have made *suffering* the place of engagement with postmodern experience. Johannes Metz has said, "I could never again do theology with my back to Auschwitz" (Metz in Schüssler Fiorenza and Tracy 1984, 26-33).

Political theology in Germany (e.g., Moltmann 1967, 1973; Metz 1979; Soelle 1975), liberation theology in Latin America (e.g., Gutiérrez 1973; Segundo 1976; Bonino 1976; Sobrino 1978), and theology among African Americans in the United States (e.g., Cone 1970; Washington 1967; Jones 1973) have made the questions of massive suffering and the maldistribution of life chances in our world the starting points for reinterpreting Christian faith and the calling of the churches in our time. No one has understood the challenge to modern theology represented by liberation and political theologies more clearly than my colleague Rebecca Chopp in her book *The Praxis of Suffering*. Let me quote from Chopp:

> Bringing suffering into the midst of reflection, liberation theology rethinks human existence, Christian tradition, and present Christian experience. What can theology say to the problems of human suffering? Who is the human subject created by God and destroyed by humanity? Who is God and where is God when history is marked more by suffering than by caretaking? . . .
>
> Such questions acknowledge the nature of liberation theology, that the knowledge of God is today discerned in the midst of suffering. . . . [S]uffering and its quest for freedom is the fundamental reality of human experience as well as the location of God, Christ, and the church in history. Liberation theology urges action, strategy, and change in human existence; it demands justice, equality, and freedom in Christian witness. Consequently liberation theology is a new language of God, seeking, in the present historical situation, to be the voice of those who suffer.
>
> As a new language of God, liberation theology is formulated in opposition to modern, progressive theology. Modern theology, in attempting to be a language of God in its historical situation, found its focal center in a quest for the authenticity of the subject. . . . In liberation theology the bourgeois individual is no longer the primary subject, and authenticity and meaning no longer the central crisis for theology. Now the focus of theology is the nonsubjects of history, those who have been denied any voice or identity in history by their fellow humans. Through this focus Christianity converts, becoming a praxis of solidarity with those who suffer and working for the transformation of human agency and social structures. Through this focal center the sacrament of God's grace makes

visible the identification of suffering and hope, while the service of God's love opens faith toward a future. (Chopp 1986, 3-4)

Note that liberation and political theologies are eminently *practical* theologies. They arise out of a praxis of identification and solidarity with victims, and they return to that praxis. They live from the conviction that suffering is the locus where Christ is to be found in the world. Liberation and political theologies engage postmodern experience directly at the point of suffering and theodicy. They seek to exorcise the solipsistic despair of existentialism and the suspect neutrality of phenomenology. They question the emancipatory power of hermeneutical work apart from stances of solidarity with the dispossessed. They look for the praxis of God in relation to the empowerment of the subjected to become subjects (i.e., actors and agents in history), and in human praxis leading to the breaking down of structures of domination based on class, race, gender, or economic privilege.

Cosmological Approaches: Creation and the New Common Story

A second promising theological strategy addressing postmodern experience is that made possible by the broad emerging consensus regarding the scientific accounts of the creation and evolution of the universe. These approaches are made possible by postmodern biology, astro- and theoretical physics, and biochemistry. Identified by Thomas Berry as "the new common story," the fresh scientific concern with a unified cosmology calls for—and makes possible— new theological approaches grounded in the doctrine of creation. At present many thinkers are articulating a shared framework for rethinking the ongoing role of God in creation. Some of them are developing theological anthropologies that give normative characterizations for the direction and limits of human responsibility in an expanding, ever-changing universe.

To characterize this approach I shall draw from an essay by Sallie McFague. She sketches the picture of cosmic reality emerging in the accounts of postmodern science:

The picture it provides of reality is organic, dynamic, and open, one in which relations are more central than individuals and internal relations pertain among all its constituent parts. The universe is a whole: it has a common history dating back fifteen billion years, gradually emerging through transformations of enormous complexity into the billions of galaxies of the present observable universe, including our own tiny planet Earth. All that make up our planet, from bacteria to coal, robins, water, iron, wildflowers, oak trees, deer, and human beings, have a common origin and are, at some stage, related. (McFague 1991, 25)

McFague points to five features that affect our appropriation of the new cosmic story for theological work: (1) The scales of space and time in this story are immense. It jars humans out of a too easy anthropocentrism. (2) It is a *story*—a narrative—with a beginning, a middle, and, presumably, an end. It calls upon us to revise our customary ways of seeing our separate human histories in the light of this vastly longer and more inclusive cosmic story of a dynamic and unfinished universe. (3) The common story is precisely that— a unified story of the becoming of all that is or will be. All things have a common origin and hence are interrelated and interdependent. Yet, says McFague, this commonality reflects no lack of individuation: "No two things, whether they be two exploding stars or the veins on two maple leaves, are the same; individuality is not just a human phenomenon, it is a cosmic one" (McFague 1991, 32). (4) This common story discloses the multileveled, hierarchical character of the universe—from the flow of energy in subatomic reality to the incredibly complex sets of levels that comprise a human being. This means, says McFague, "that there is no absolute distinction between living and nonliving things, because life is a type of organization, not an entity or substance" (McFague 1991, 33). Making the same point, Ian Barbour says, "The chemical elements in your hand and in your brain were forged in the furnaces of the stars" (Barbour 1989, 147). (5) In contrast to the creation stories of particular religious traditions, the emerging common creation story is a *public* one, available to all who wish to learn about it. It is available to be remythologized by any and every religious tradition, and therefore can be a constructive and unifying meeting place for our diverse and often conflicting religious traditions.

Theologies that address postmodern experience from the framework of the "new common story" engage us by inviting us to reconstrue our lives, institutions, and traditions in the light of this vastly enlarged, unified, and breathtaking picture. God's praxis is disclosed as the creative source and pattern within the cosmic process, enriching, differentiating, and bringing more complex freedom and consciousness to expression in reality. While operating at a distance from the experience of individual human beings, or even of large collectivities, this perspective evokes powerful, inclusive images of the unified processes of nature and history within the creative faithfulness of God.

Hermeneutical Approaches: The Christian Faith as "Classic"

Catholic theologian David Tracy, reworking the correlational approach of Paul Tillich, has made hermeneutical method the principal tool for reasserting the integrity and normative claims of Christian faith, while acknowledging and clarifying the postmodern experience of radical relativity. To do this, Tracy has appropriated Hans Georg Gadamer's idea of the "classic," using it to honor the depth and richness of religious traditions. He has coupled the notion of the religious classic with a hermeneutical understanding of the human sciences. Empowering his approach is a set of convictions about the power of the "texts" that constitute classical religious traditions. Tracy trusts such "texts" to be sources of present revelation when properly and respectfully approached. Let me explain.

A "classic" in any literature is an expression of the human spirit, born of a particular context and time. The classic opens up and focuses some dimension of experience with such engaging power and depth that persons from other times and contexts find themselves addressed, expanded, and informed by it. Classics evoke, in Paul Ricoeur's words, a "surplus of meanings." They give rise to conflicts of interpretation.

The religious classic, in David Tracy's usage, is a special instance of the larger idea of the classic. Like a literary classic, a religious classic is an expression of the human spirit. But the religious classic has the additional, special quality that it conserves and makes powerfully accessible moments that may be called "disclosure-concealment events." A religious tradition is constituted by a series of mutually interpreting events of disclosure-concealment of the kind we call revelation. Revelation, says Tracy, is the disclosure of the Whole by the power of the Whole. These moments of disclosure are also moments of concealment. God's self-disclosure never exhausts God's being, and our apprehensions and expression of disclosure events are never fully adequate to appropriate what is offered. Through engagement with a religious classic the events of disclosure-concealment it brings to expression become accessible to us. Those moments can become for us moments of present revelation.

For Tracy the work of practical theology is to bring interpretations of the Christian classic into mutually critical correlation with interpretations of present situations that require address and action. Through the mutual interpretative dialectic of classic texts with present contexts we can experience the emergence of intellectual and spiritual clarification and a sense of direction formed in synergy with God.

Tracy's correlational and hermeneutical approach addresses the postmodern experience of religious and ideological pluralism and relativity. It does so by reasserting the integrity of particular religious traditions as mediating relatedness to the Ultimate. His accounting for the praxis of God rests upon the conviction that the hermeneutical opening of access to the disclosive power of the text, in relation to the interpreted shape of present, situated issues, allows present revelation to occur.

Narrative-Linguistic Approaches: Christian Faith, the Church's Story

The fourth theological strategy I want to describe takes as its starting point the postmodern critique of modern theology's identification of God with the supposedly universal object of subjective religious experience. Cultural-linguistic approaches embrace that dimension of the postmodern mood that rejects all universals and celebrates the locus of truth in particular, situated traditions. With a temper deeply indebted to the Karl Barth of *Church Dogmatics*, its advocates hold that the task of theology is to so reform the church that, by contrast, the secular, postmodern world will recognize its own secularity. At the heart of this movement, which is called "Postliberalism" in the United States, is the work of Yale theologian George Lindbeck.

A brief review of some central themes of Lindbeck's book *The Nature of Doctrine* will serve to clarify this approach. Lindbeck distinguishes three understandings of doctrine. The first he calls the *propositional* understanding. Here doctrine is taken to be the precise formulation, as in creeds and confessions, of the truth of God revealed in Scripture and experience and conserved in propositional statements. Orthodox faith, in this context, means giving intellectual, emotional, and behavioral assent to revealed truths as so stated and conserved. In its most literal forms, this approach holds that the very language and terms in which the received creedal statements are expressed are themselves part of what constitutes their normative claims.

Lindbeck names the second understanding of doctrine *experiential-expressive*. Associating this approach with "liberal" theologies of the nineteenth and twentieth centuries, Lindbeck uses this term to refer to positions that assume that there is a capacity for and quality of religious experience that is universal among human beings. Each religious and faith tradition awakens and forms a variant of this universal religious experience with its particular narrative, symbol, and ritual traditions. Doctrine, in this view, serves as the key to the expression and symbolization of each tradition's particular shaping of this more universal experience. From this perspective, Lindbeck argues, the question of "truth" gets located among functional considerations, particularly around the values of moral responsibility and personal integration. In this perspective, Lindbeck asserts, doctrine loses its normative status; "orthodoxy" becomes parochial and negotiable; and religious traditions come to serve primarily instrumental interests.

Lindbeck refers to a third understanding of doctrine as the *cultural-linguistic* approach. Here doctrine serves as the source of both regulative and generative creativity in communities of faith. From this standpoint, personal faith arises in communities of faith through the proclamation of the Word of God and the administration of and participation in the sacraments. The rituals, gestures, language and narratives of faith precipitate in members a deep structural "grammar" of faith. In using this language Lindbeck is relying on the analogy of how one learns to be a competent speaker of one's native language. One learns to speak grammatically long before one gives any attention to the rules of grammar. The rules of grammar become important later as persons become generative in their use and extension of the language they have received. Explicit statements of doctrine serve the church in ways that are analogous to the ways the rules of grammar guide us in extending language to name and express new realities and dimensions of truth. As faith communities shape their missions and responses to ever-changing contexts, they need the guidance of the grammatical rules of orthodoxy *(regulae fidei)*. These are not literal formulations that must be slavishly repeated, but generative and regulative sources to guide the fresh minting of metaphors and images that can awaken, nurture, and guide faith truthfully. (It should be acknowledged, in passing, that this stress on "generative creativity" in relation to doctrine is more the position of this author than that of Lindbeck or his followers.)

Lindbeck has stressed the formative power of the language and liturgy of the church for its identity, and has clarified the regulative and generative role of doctrine. His students—professors Stanley Hauerwas, George Stroup, and others—have emphasized the power of Christian faith as *narrative* for grounding the identity of the church and shaping it for discipleship. Echoing the Barthian theme "Let the church be the church," theologians in the cultural-linguistic approach argue for the public impact of sectarian faithfulness on the part of the church. At the same time, it must be pointed out, they tend to decry public commendation or argument for faith.[1]

THE QUESTION OF A POSTMODERN THEOLOGY OF THE PRAXIS OF GOD

Each of the theological approaches I have sketched here offers something that is essential for anyone concerned with trying to

---

1. A biblical theologian, Walter Brueggemann, who brings a Reformed background over against Lindbeck's Lutheranism, supplies an important corrective at this point. In an exegetical study of 2 Kings 18–19, Brueggemann has forcefully argued that the church must speak two languages: the language to be employed behind the city wall, based upon the stories and memories of Yahweh's promises and faithfulness; and the language to be employed upon the wall, through which the witness, proposals and protests of a story-grounded people can address public life (Brueggemann 1989, 3-34).

shape a theology of God's praxis for this late modern or postmodern era. The theologies of liberation and political theologies, represented here by the voice of Rebecca Chopp, remind us forcefully that in a century where upwards of 100 million people have died from wars, and at a time when more than one-third of the world's people live in severe poverty, we dare not speak glibly about God's presence and effective influence in the processes of nature and history. In making the theme of suffering central and in pressing the question of whether God stands in solidarity with human and natural suffering, these theologies rule out all theologies of a remote, detached, utterly transcendent God. They press toward an imaging of God in terms of participation, passion for justice and liberation, and one whose spirit means liberation and redemption in this world as well as the next.

Theologians who draw upon the possibilities of the new cosmologies and new biologies for imaging God's authorship and involvement in the "common creation story" urge us away from theologies that separate nature and history, body and spirit, matter and soul, structure and process. They urge caution in too quickly assimilating the new metaphors and models of an expanding universe to the mythic narratives of creation offered by our religious traditions. But after giving that caution, they provide richly suggestive examples of how a mysticism sufficient for our time of recognized global interdependence can find its partner in a robust theology of creation that offers illumination regarding how the human species—in all its diversity—is called to be part of God's ongoing work of creation and a balanced ordering of human and the rest of natural life.

The challenges of coming to terms with the diversity of religious traditions and faith claims in this postmodern era receive impetus from theologians who invite us to the paradoxical affirmation that religious traditions, approached as classics, can affirm the integrity and revelatory power of other traditions than their own, without falling into a fatal stance of relativism. Interreligious dialogue, in the deep sense, involves experienced and deeply grounded religious peoples inviting persons formed in the faith stances of other traditions to enter into their classic traditions.

Implicit in this kind of invitation, when it is authentic, is the commitment to replace proselytization with commitment to in-depth conversation. It offers the equally important commitment to accept the invitation—and the disciplines of study—required to enter the classics of others. To make these transits into the depths of the faiths of other persons and traditions is to return to one's own tradition enriched, deepened, and more aware of important aspects of one's own revelatory classic.

The stern voices of those in the fourth group, who warn us against looking too quickly for commonalities between religious traditions, also press us to recognize that the claims of religious traditions often have a quality of mutual exclusiveness. They want us fully to recognize that the practices of faith—its language, its disciplines of community, its music, its motions and emotions—shape us far more deeply than just the contents of our conscious beliefs and notional assent. They call for us to honor difference with regard to religious traditions. They would have us feel the imperatives of our particular traditions. And, taking their stances in biblical faith, they are more concerned that the world should recognize that it is *not* the kingdom of God than that it (or adherents of Christian faith) should be overly concerned to make connections that avoid offense between the truths of Christian faith and the world's wisdom.

Can these four groups of voices make a choir? Is it possible to offer a Christian theology of God's praxis and human partnership that has integrity while addressing the concerns these four approaches have put before us? The next chapter offers the outline for one such approach.

CHAPTER TWELVE

TOWARD A POSTMODERN
THEOLOGY OF THE PRAXIS OF GOD

It is easier to characterize the preceding chapter's four types of theological strategies in relation to their engagement with postmodern thought and experience than it is to account for their address to the issues of the *praxis* of God. For reasons that are understandable and not easily overcome, each of these theological strategies has difficulty bringing into focus an adequate account of God's *praxis*. By this provocative term I mean "the characteristic patterns of God's involvement in and providential guidance of the processes of our evolving universe, including God's interaction with humankind" (Fowler 1991, 31).

At the end of the modern period, the doctrine of God's providence has become virtually absent in reflective theology. There are reasons for this having to do with intellectual traditions stemming from the Enlightenment. Among others, the following are some of these factors: the post-Kantian bifurcation of nature and history; positivism and the eclipse of cosmology in the natural sciences; the commitment to value-free inquiry in the social sciences; the radical challenges to theism from the projectionist theories of Feuerbach and Freud; the dismantling of conventional notions of God by Nietzsche and his deconstructionist successors; reductionistic strategies of demythologization in biblical studies; the dominance in Protestant theology of Barth's confessional approach; the linguistic analytic turn in philosophy; and the collapse of the philosophy of history.

Equally if not more important in undermining coherent thought about God's providence in our time, however, have been the collective experiences that have thrust us into the postmodern era. Perhaps it is enough to say that for millions of people the God of modern theology began to die in the gas-filled trenches and bloody battlefields of World War I and was radically called into question by the Holocaust. As Dietrich Bonhoeffer put it, "God has been edged out of the world and onto a cross."

It is important to ask, "Who is the God who is dying in late modernity?" What visions of God's presence and activity in history no longer seem credible or important? This is a highly complex question, and one we cannot begin to address adequately here. But it seems clear that for many the dying God includes at least the following:

- the God who symbolized the hope and assurance of inevitable human progress;
- the impassable, sovereign God of classical theism, with *His* omnipotence, omniscience, and omnipresence;
- the God tied to a shaming doctrine of the Fall, in which humans are destined to inevitable sin, due to the disobedience of Adam and Eve, and yet held responsible for that sin;
- the moralistic God whose chief role lay in the reinforcement of the commands of parental superegos;
- the God who legitimated the collusion between thrones and altars and blessed the accompanying patterns of economic power and social class systems, in the variety of monarchical, socialist-democratic, or capitalist-democratic forms;
- the God with the "invisible hand" who could be counted on to manage everything benignly, from the "free market economy" and the avoidance of nuclear war, to the preservation and healing of nature;
- the God of nationalist doctrines of "manifest destiny" and world imperialism;
- the God of the gospel of wealth; and
- the male-gendered God.

Given the death, at least among some segments of populations in late modernity, of traditional images of God, how shall we depict the praxis of God in postmodern terms? What language and metaphors shall we call upon to represent the presence and action of God in our multisystemic, culturally plural, and ecologically threatened world? While postmodernity marks the ending of the viability of one range of representations of God, it may provide us with the possibility of others.

In trying to form a theological response to these questions, I find help from a theologian who approaches the task through the image of praxis. I cite Peter Hodgson in his 1989 book, *God in History*. Let me quote a key passage from Hodgson's book:

> My thesis is that God is efficaciously present in the world, not as an individual agent performing observable acts, nor as a uniform inspiration or lure, nor as an abstract ideal, nor in the metaphorical role of companion or friend. Rather, God is present in specific shapes or patterns of praxis that have a configuring, transformative power within historical process, moving the process in a determinate direction, that of the creative unification of multiplicities of elements into new wholes, into creative syntheses that build human solidarity, enhance freedom, break systemic oppression, heal the injured and broken, and care for the natural. A shape or gestalt is not as impersonal and generalized as an influence or a presence, since it connotes something dynamic, specific, and structuring, but it avoids potentially misleading personifications of God's action. What God "does" in history is not simply to "be there" as God, or to "call us forward," or to assume a personal "role," but to "shape"—to shape a multifaceted transfigurative praxis. God does this by giving, disclosing, in some sense *being*, the normative shape, the paradigm of such a praxis. This is what I mean by the divine gestalt. (Hodgson 1989, 205)

A *gestalt* is a pattern, a shaping, a forming and transforming pattern of action and being. Do you catch what Hodgson is trying to say in those abstract terms? He is suggesting that behind the events that represent breakthroughs in the history of people and nations, a discerning observer can detect long lines of convergent providence. Whether we are speaking of the civil rights movement in the United States or of the final breakthrough to putting the scourge of apartheid behind the unifying people of South Africa, there are lines of faithfulness, not always visibly connected, that converge to make the breakthroughs possible. Even the visible, human leaders of these movements have themselves been influenced and nurtured by communities of faithful people whose names the world will never know. These are the kinds of things Peter Hodgson is trying to help us see.

Hodgson is telling us that God animates and is present in specific shapes and patterns of praxis that have a configuring, transformative power within history. These gestalts of divine praxis he proposes, move history in determinate directions. The gestalts of God's praxis move toward

- a *unity* of being that does not compromise or negate diversity, but results in new synergy;
- the formation of creative syntheses that build human solidarity with other humans and with nature;
- the enhancing of freedom and the shaping of just communities;
- the breaking of systemic oppression and the reconstitution of institutions;
- the healing of the injured and broken and the deep equalization of life chances;
- care for nature and for our reconciliation in mutuality with earth, sky, water, and our brother and sister humans and animals.[1]

Sanctioned by the notion of the "classic" as developed by Tracy, and by the postmodern emphasis upon the *traditioned* character of all thought, it is legitimate to begin our public rethinking of God's praxis with the normative imaginal resources of the Bible. Biblical faith proposes the foundational metaphor of covenant to symbolize God's praxis and faithfulness in relation to the universe. Here our use of the term "covenant" is not limited to God's special relation

---

1. While claiming Hodgson's image of the gestalts of divine praxis active in nature and history, it is important to point out that there are also gestalts of evil that capture human hearts and exert palpable destructive influences in history. To acknowledge the reality and influence of gestalts of evil and the anti-divine is not to give way to dualism, or to grant the forces of evil ontological status. It is to recognize, however, that such influences do take on institutional and culturally pervasive forms. They require naming, unmasking, and opposition. They must be met with profound trust in and commitment to the governing, as well as the liberating and redeeming praxis of God. In this regard, the writings of Walter Wink, especially *Engaging the Powers: Discernment and Resistance in a World of Domination* (Minneapolis: Fortress Press, 1992), are indispensable.

with Israel. Rather, as in the covenant with Noah (Genesis 9:8-17), it refers to a universal pledge of faithfulness to creation and all humanity. It conveys the conviction that the unity and dynamism of the expanding universe are given coherence and symmetry by the force field of God's covenantal care. Within the holding power of covenant, God's praxis may be seen, biblically, in terms of three great comprehensive patterns: (1) *God Creating*—God's origination and continuing nurture of the evolving universe; (2) *God Governing*—God's structuring, ordering, and sustaining of relations at every systemic level, honoring forms of freedom, and aimed at right relatedness and flourishing in creation; (3) *God Liberating and Redeeming*—God's ongoing, costly praxis of reclaiming and restoring relations with and between those entities in opposition to life and creation, absorbing in suffering the consequences of oppositional freedom and of enmity to God's purposes and shaping novel alternate possibilities for fulfilling the divine hopes. (For earlier developments of these ideas, see Fowler 1985, 1987; Niebuhr 1960.) Let us look more closely at each of these patterns of the divine praxis.

1. *God's Creating Praxis.* Postmodern reflection on the praxis of God creating receives great impetus from the "new common story." Theoretical physicists are at work on "grand unified theories" that promise mathematical models showing the interplay of gravity, the weak and strong forces, and the electromagnetic force—the four forces that, taken together, maintain balance and symmetry in our expanding universe. The "Big Bang" theory offers accounts of the beginnings of the universe—literally *creatio ex nihilo* (Davies 1984, 1988). The wedding of the most recent biological work on evolution with the perspectives of process philosophy discloses patterns in which species emerge, evolve, and often disappear. But overall, each emerging stage of species life contributes to increasing complexity and internal differentiation, which lead toward qualitative increases in consciousness and the continual enrichment of experience (Birch and Cobb 1981). Both biologists and astrophysicists point to anomalous moments of freedom in the creative process. There are leaps in evolution; genuine novelties appear, without apparent precedents or causal explanations. Efforts to account for these patterns based upon randomness and chance have sharply

declined. Methodological atheism among scientists of the first order has diminished significantly. There is emerging among them an honoring of the beauty, the intricate ordering, the purposefulness, and the astonishing anomalies present in "nature" at every systemic level.

Theologians of God's praxis must resist the temptation to make too easy identifications of traditional theological and biblical images with the often poetic metaphors of scientists and cosmologists. With careful work, however, scientists and theologians sharing postmodern starting points can lay the groundlines of public theologies of God's praxis in creation with the power to show the complex unity of this dynamic universe. Such work can provide the intellectual bases for the reintegrating of our now disparate and fragmented disciplines. Moreover, such work nurtures a holistic spirituality—a reborn mysticism—that may enable us to reverse patterns of the degradation of nature and learn collectively to live in ecologically just relations to creation.

2. *God's Governing Praxis.* How might we begin to shape a postmodern depiction of God's presence and praxis in the processes of nature and history as a structuring that intends right relatedness in the created and social orders? Building on our discussion of creation, we may begin by suggesting that such a structuring can be detected in the lawfulness constituted by the forces that maintain symmetry and orbital integrity in our expanding universe. It can be detected in the laws governing the combining of elements in biochemical processes. Such structuring can be discerned in the operations of the complex coding that guides cell reproduction and that determines the genetic integrity of organisms.

But now let us make a leap to human life and society. Such structuring can be discerned in the fundamental conditions of trust and loyalty, mutual regard and ethical sensitivity required for human communities to flourish. Such a structuring that intends justice and right relatedness can be seen at work when corrupt regimes collapse as much from internal patterns of injustice and deceit as from external opposition and correction. I am pointing here to the possibility of a postmodern exploration and imaging of a deep *logos*—a structuring of reason and lawfulness that intends justice and right relatedness—in creation and the evolutionary process, that cannot be flouted or violated without self-injury and destruction (Fowler 1987, 1991).

Postmodern thinking challenges the Enlightenment's too easy undermining of the authority of religious, moral, and cultural traditions. To be sure, we do not expect to find universal ethical principles encoded in every set of regional mores or in the customary morality of small town or tribal cultures. Nonetheless, work on the ordering praxis of God should insist on a practical theological reappropriation of traditioned moral wisdom. It should reclaim the relevance of the Decalogue and reflect upon the ethical truth and imperativeness of the love commandment of Jesus. In many ways and in many centuries, the world's religious traditions have included in their classics expressions of a moral *logos*. The *Tao,* understood as *Way*; *Torah,* understood as *Law* or *Way*; the *Eightfold Path* of Buddhism; *Dharma* in Hinduism; the idea of *Natural Law* or *Justice* as taught in Stoicism—all these symbols represent efforts to formulate and make visible a structuring that intends right relatedness in the processes of human life.

Modernity has made us deeply mindful of the oppressive potentials of a too easy identification of the morality of particular groups or classes with the will of God or the dictates of Natural Law. In its affirmation of the worth and dignity of each individual and its insistence upon the rights of individuals to pursue their own conceptions of the good, modernity alerted us to the need for continuing vigilance against moralistic oppression. But postmodernity calls for a restoration of balance: The traditioned, situated, contextual formulations of the bases of moral living should be attended to. The virtues that enable persons to contribute to the common good are indispensable. They may help us discern and align ourselves with the shape of God's ordering praxis.

3. *God's Praxis of Liberation and Redemption.* Within the processes of the divine creative and ordering praxis, human beings have evolved into an ontological vocation—a specific calling and role in creation. Again, following the biblical imagery of *covenant,* we have evolved (or God's praxis has evolved us) for partnership with God. We are the species that has developed with capacities for reflective consciousness and with potentials for being part of (or in opposition to) the creative, governing, and liberative-redemptive action

197

of God. Through this evolving vocation we have claimed our deepest identity—that of *imago dei*—creatures evolving in the image and likeness of God. We are evolving for purposes of spiritual communion with God, for creating and maintaining community with our fellow humans, and for living in dynamic mutual respect with nature. God has called us to be part of God's purposes of caring for and fulfilling creation. We are called and evolved for the ontological vocation of partnership in the creative, governing, and liberative-redemptive work of God.

At the same time, however, individually and collectively we are creatures at full stretch. We have evolved forms of consciousness and technology that render our old modes of thought and action—and their regulation—obsolete. Our widened horizons of consciousness serve to deepen our sense of our finitude and limits. We are a combustible combination: Creatures with varying degrees of reflective self-transcendence, we live enmeshed in systems at multiple levels, yet we have a sense of free will and responsibility. This tension can lead us into self-deception and excessive pride, on the one hand, or into resignation and despair, on the other. Our capacities for moral restraint and love of our neighbors are fragile. Deprive us of adequate care when we are infants, abuse us consistently as children, and we may use our intelligence and cunning, for the rest of our lives, to inflict our rage on innocent others. Place us in authoritative roles defined by large corporate structures or systems and we can utilize our power to act out the hidden wounds and repressed shame of early childhood experiences in our families. Regularly we will substitute values oriented to the economic bottom line for commitments to distributive justice. We have at our disposal an extraordinary and dangerous array of technologies. Our ethical sense cannot keep pace with their range of application. All of this is intermixed with a defensive awareness of our mortality and a resistant sense of our finite limitedness. Apart from groundedness in the reality and spirit of God, this combination can make for moments of happiness; but more frequently it makes for an undercurrent of profound *anxiety*. This anxiety is the basis for our *sin*.

As we speak about God's praxis of liberation and redemption and the human call to partnership in it, we come to the most difficult place for a theology that would be public. With the "common story" of creation, credible claims for human responsibility and involvement can be made. We can see how in science, medicine, and public health humans can be part of care for creation. We can see how in art, architecture, and aesthetics, generally, we can be cocreators with God. We can see how in parenting and in education we can participate in and enhance creation.

Similarly, we can see publicly comprehensible dimensions of the human calling to participation in the divine praxis of ordering and maintenance of right relatedness. The ongoing struggle for adequate law to achieve and maintain justice and good order in societies is at the core of the public meaning of God's ordering praxis. Likewise, the work of maintaining peace between nations and, increasingly, the regulation of international economic relationships toward the common good constitute high challenges in our co-governance with God. The effort to keep punishment in the service of rehabilitation in the criminal justice systems, and the effort to shape new governments for liberated peoples are all aspects of our cooperating responsibility in God's governing work.

But how shall we speak, in publicly comprehensible ways, of God's praxis of liberation and redemption? Here, finally, Christians who want to speak of God's praxis in public ways cannot avoid speaking of a suffering participation of God in the processes of nature and history. As liberation theologies make most clear, God's praxis enters into solidarity with suffering and oppressed persons. This is true of those whose suffering is directly physical and political; it is also true in patterns of judgment and hard love for those whose suffering is due to their or our hardness of heart, to their or our corrupted wills, and to their or our opposition to God's purposes. Here a Christian theology of God's praxis must point to the long-forming gestalt of God's grace that came to focus in Jesus of Nazareth. Here a theology of God's praxis must point to the pattern of a praxis of liberation and redemption that has issued from Jesus' announcement and enactment of a divine commonwealth of love and justice. Here a theology of God's praxis must point to the faithful death of Jesus as the Christ. That death and subsequent resurrection are the constitutive paradigms for a participating and transforming involvement of God in history. This paradigm alerts us to see and trust—and nerves us to join—this pattern of redeeming and transforming praxis in the historical processes of our time.

CONCLUSION

The perspective offered here, sketched in the barest of outlines, points in the direction of a Christian and biblical imaging of the praxis of God and of the covenantal vocation of humankind. This account does not point toward a theology of *Christian* vocation alone. Rather, it points to a *Christian understanding of the human vocation.* Similarly, it is not limited to a theology of the praxis of God seen as confined to the mission, public presence, and influence of the churches. Rather, it aims to characterize a Christian understanding of the much broader praxis of God in the processes of nature and history. The praxis of God is by no means limited to the praxis of the church.

It is the special calling of the Christian churches and our theologies at the end of modernity to offer images by which the praxis of God can be discerned and trusted. We do not assume that our images will be accepted as offered, nor do we make their acceptance a condition of our claiming solidarity with others. Postmodernity needs convictional images that mediate hope and courage. We need communities that model justice and engage in liberating praxis and understand it as part of the praxis of God. It is the calling of the churches in the postmodern world to witness, with lives of covenant faithfulness, to the human possibility of embracing our ontological vocations in the work of God. Offering such public witness and public presence, while trusting in the presence and power of God's spirit, lies at the heart of our calling as we enter a new millennium.

*   *   *

I wrote the first draft of this chapter in Advent, in the midst of anticipation of the coming of Jesus as the Christ. On Christmas Eve I witnessed the reenacted drama of Jesus' birth—the incredibly rich and layered portrayal of God becoming flesh. Children and adults and a five-week-old baby, backed by a choir and an organ in a crowded church, together reasserted the most extraordinary theological claim I can imagine: to reground our being in our Source; to replace our anxiety with assured connectedness to God; to empower us to give up our hatred and love each other; to dissolve our shame and to reconfirm our worth to God; to release us from our sin and restore us to our vocations; *the Word—the Logos—became a human being, full of grace and truth.*

Can postmodern thought go far enough in its reopening of the apertures of our minds and hearts to embrace this anomaly of incarnation? Can a postmodern reworking of a theology of the praxis of God not falter at this dramatic event upon which our healing and restoration depend? Can we hold in one universe of meanings the "new common story" of creation and this situated, historically delimited story of salvation? These are questions each of us must answer.

I must tell you this in closing: As I watched the drama and sang the carols and pondered these questions myself, *I had the sense that the story has much more public power and truth than we who live in Christian ghettos usually realize.* Of this much I am morally certain: The praxis of God is far larger than the praxis of our churches. The biblical theme of covenant and the correlated theme of our vocation to partnership with God do not issue in just an understanding of *Christian* vocation. Publicly offering this story, this classic, this liberating and redeeming narrative and helping to shape the communities of faith that it keeps re-forming constitute what the work of Christian practical theologians in postmodernity is all about.

CHAPTER THIRTEEN

KEEPING FAITH WITH GOD AND OUR CHILDREN

The test of a practical theological vision such as that presented in the preceding chapter comes when we bring its perspectives to bear on situations of challenge in the social and political contexts where we live and work. This chapter and the next represent tests of that sort for this theology of the praxis of God and the call to human partnership in the work of God. This chapter addresses the calling of the churches and other religious communities to offer effective leadership in addressing the challenges of violence—especially the violence that threatens to engulf a generation of children and youth in our inner cities. The book's concluding chapter will bring these perspectives to bear on the role of churches and church-related schools in providing leadership in moral and faith formation in this pluralistic, growingly postmodern society. Here the faith to change and lead depends directly upon attending to and aligning ourselves with the praxis of God.

CRISIS/APOCALYPSE NOW

At this writing, The Honorable Glenda Johnson is Chief Presiding Judge of the Fulton County Juvenile Courts in the state of Georgia. Hers is the largest and most urban juvenile jurisdiction in the state where I reside. Her county includes much of the center of the Atlanta Metro Area. In a recent speech, Judge Johnson spoke with a sense of heartsickness and outrage on the topic "Violence in Youth." Drawing on figures compiled by the National Council of Juvenile Court Judges, she reported the following findings:

- Last year in the United States over one million children and youth were referred to juvenile courts on instances of juvenile delinquent criminal behavior.
- Last year almost one-quarter million children were involved in the court systems due to incidents of abuse and/or neglect.
- Nearly one-half million children were involved in our systems for providing temporary protective custody. These numbers have tripled over the last three decades.

Judge Johnson pointed to the year 1985, the year that crack cocaine hit the streets and spread in epidemic proportions, as marking the turn toward radical increases in juvenile crime and violence. Nationally, between 1987 and 1991 there was an increase of 85 percent in the number of juveniles arrested for murder across the country. Then she turned to her own jurisdiction in Fulton County. In approximately the same time period (1986–91) Fulton County saw a staggering 1,700 percent increase in drug-related crimes. She stressed the correlation between the sudden wide availability of crack cocaine and these exploding statistics. This period marked a 300 percent increase in serious crimes committed by juveniles in the county. And, most chillingly, in that same period the number of children in juvenile court charged with first degree murder increased by 600 percent.

To give these statistics human faces, Judge Johnson recounted a recent Monday morning when she was greeted by her clerk with the news that her docket that week would include five teenagers under eighteen whom the police had arrested over the weekend on capital felony charges: two on aggravated assault, two on murder charges, and one on a charge of rape. Then, before she could take her seat on the bench, one of her fellow judges informed her about a particularly alarming bind-over hearing he had from the end of the previous week. This involved a fifteen-year-old boy who had confronted a homeless, mentally retarded man and demanded that he empty his pockets. Impatient when the man stalled or did not understand him, the youth shot him in the leg. While the man rocked in pain on the ground, the boy searched him for anything valuable to steal. Finding nothing but a battered cigarette lighter, he expressed his rage and frustration by blowing out the man's brains at point-blank range. "What is it about out society, our communities, our families, our schools in America," Judge Johnson asked, "that we would be dealing with a fifteen-year-old boy who would take the only thing a homeless, retarded man had—his life—in an effort at petty robbery?"

Judge Johnson's talk made graphically clear the interrelation of several factors that I believe we are all already aware of: the permeative presence of violence in and accepted by the adult society in this country. This includes violence mediated by film and television as "reality"; violence enacted through abuse and brutality in too many homes; violence ruthlessly engaged in by enforcers, pimps, and drug traffickers in our city streets; the brutality and hostility of many police toward children and youth (especially those of Hispanic backgrounds and those of color); and all this violence facilitated by the easy availability of both legal and illegal firearms—pistols, shotguns, semi-automatic weapons, and lethal assault rifles. Most of all, however, this violence of children upon children reflects their sense that we, as a society, have given up on them. In our inner cities young Black boys are tempted to become involved in selling drugs early. Fred Smith, who works on a task force on violence from the Carter Center in Atlanta, tells me about the talk among such youth who rationalize their fast and dangerously risky life choices with the image of the "pretty corpse." In their perspective, it is better to have lived recklessly as a high roller, to die in the prime of one's youth, and to be mourned by the community in a highly publicized funeral, than to grow to adulthood in prison or be maimed for life by lack of education and opportunity. Judge Johnson captures this attitude when she says, "Our children are giving up on this society, because they believe we are giving up on them."

Judge Johnson, speaking from the Christian faith, formed in her family and in the bosom of the Black church, ended her talk with the voice of determination. She declared, "There will be no eulogy for this generation: We will not concede, as some seem all too willing to do, that this generation cannot be redeemed. We will not give these precious children over to the dehumanizing violence and life shattering seductions of drugs, crimes, and futile educational systems. We cannot build a future without them; we cannot afford to give up on them. There will be no eulogy for this generation."

Can we, along with Judge Johnson and leaders like her, find the faith and framework to commit our determination, alongside many others who are so committed, that today's children and youth shall not end up as members of a lost generation in this society?

OUR CALLINGS AND GOD'S PRAXIS: A PRACTICAL THEOLOGICAL FRAMEWORK

As I wrestled with questions like these, I found that my mind tended to run to partial solutions of one sort or another. I seemed unable to grasp the larger picture and find a way to pursue what I felt called to say until it became clear to me that our approach needs to be grounded in a practical theological perspective. I want draw on the theological perspectives of the preceding chapter to sketch such an approach here. I hope that it will help focus both our courage and the ground of our trust for this task, and that it may deepen our sense of the imperatives and the hope that results from seeing our callings in relation to the praxis of God.

From a biblical and Christian point of view, we human beings have been called into being—we have evolved in God's creation—toward callings to partnership with God. The term we use for this fact of our calling is *vocation* (in Greek, *klesis*, "calling or summons" [noun], and *kaleo*, "I call, I summon" [verb]; in Latin, *vocatio* [noun] and *vocare* [verb]). From a Christian standpoint, at the heart of what it means to be a human being is the conviction that we are called into being by God for covenant partnership with God. We have an *ontological call*—a call that constitutes our very being—to be part of the purposes of God. This is not just a teaching about *Christian* vocation—as important as that is. Rather, it is a Christian conviction about the *human* vocation.

Viewed this way, vocation is a bigger matter than our job or occupation. Vocation is both more basic and more comprehensive than profession or career. In my own terms, *vocation* is the response a person makes with his or her total life to the call of God to partnership. This means that children have vocation; it means that retired persons have vocation; it means that those who serve through volunteering have vocation; it means that the unemployed have vocation. Vocation is the response one makes to God's constituting call to each of us to partnership in the purposes and service of God. Augustine said, "Thou hast made us for thyself, and our hearts are restless until they find their rest in Thee." From the standpoint of vocation we might say, "Thou hast created us for partnership with Thee, and our hearts are restless until we find purposes for our lives that are part of Thy purposes."

God does not call us to our vocations in individualist isolation. God calls us into covenanted relations in community with others. Those of us who are members of particular churches or synagogues are likely to understand our covenanted relation to God to pertain in a special way to those communities. Our most intimate covenant ties are to other precious human beings whom we count as our friends, our lovers, our wives or husbands, our parents, our children. But there is a deeper and broader sense in which we are called by God into covenant solidarity with all God's children and, more radically, with all of God's creation. This, I believe, is the deepest meaning of God's calling of Adam and Eve into a relation of stewardship in the care of God's "garden." We are to be in covenant solidarity with God's creatures and to be accountable to God in the care and tending of the garden.

Let us draw upon the three biblically grounded metaphors we employed in the preceding chapter for depicting the *caring and praxis* of God: *God creating, God governing,* and *God liberating and redeeming.* Think with me a moment about some of what might be included in each of these dimensions of God's praxis—God's providential patterns of care and action.

God Creating

Here we think first of the ongoing creation of a universe 15 billion light-years in extent and still evolving. Contemporary astrophysicists tell us that right now there are regions in the expanding universe where, at tremendous temperatures and under incomprehensible pressures, new stars and planets are being formed. Under the impact of science's investigative and often reverent eyes, we are increasingly aware of the mysteries of God's creating action at both the microcosmic, subatomic levels and the macrocosmic, intergalactic levels. In the midst of all this, on a pygmy planet wondrously blue, green, and white, with water, foliage, clouds, and precious air, we find myriad species of living things. And among them we find one species gifted with self-reflective consciousness and remarkable powers of communication, a species—humankind—called and evolved in the image of its Creator. What incredible risks the Creator has taken in the evolving and calling of humankind. As the psalmist says, "You have made us a little less than God . . . given us stewardship over the works of thy hands" (Psalm 8:5-6, author's paraphrase). God creating has evolved this species with capacities for partnership in such ways as to give us a vital part in shaping the ongoing processes of creation. Our creativity has been allowed, in ways both wonderful and supremely dangerous, to extend and modify—even to threaten with destruction—the ongoing work of the creation on this our planet home.

God Governing

We detect a lawfulness in the processes of creation. Elements can combine with each other, but only in lawful or predictable ways. There are four forces that seem to hold the stars and galaxies in their orbits—gravity, the electromagnetic force, the strong force, and the weak force. These forces are not arbitrary and inconsistent, but dependable and certain. Though there is a texture of freedom in the processes of nature, one is overwhelmingly impressed with a deep lawfulness in the patterns of creation. Analogously, there seems to be a deep lawfulness at work in the processes of human history. In the preceding chapter we pointed to the fact that each of the great world religions has testified to its presence: The Eightfold Path in Buddhism; the idea of Dharma in Hindu traditions; the Torah or Way in Judaism; the Tao or Way in Taoism. For Christians, the law of love of God and neighbor, as articulated from Hebrew Scriptures and lived by Jesus, captures most comprehensively and economically this deep structure of moral law. God's governing pattern, we may say, is a structuring that intends right

207

relatedness, a structuring that intends justice, in the processes of history.

In accordance with this deep structuring that intends justice, corrupt and unjust communities bring about their own destruction through internal moral collapse as much as through opposition from beyond their bounds. But opposition is essential, for morally rotting collectivities can impose terrible suffering on innocent people before they are brought down. There is a true and tragic sense in which the sins of the fathers (and mothers) *are* visited upon their children to the third and fourth generations. As theologian James Cone has said, the other side of the love of God is the wrath of God.

God Liberating and Redeeming

For Christian faith, the personal dimensions and depth of God creating and God governing are disclosed and revealed as love in the liberating and redeeming action of God in Jesus the Christ. God not only shares the risks of grafting humanity's finite freedom and creativity into the divine creative process, but God also participates in the innocent suffering that results from our misuses of our freedom. There is a suffering love of God that comes close to us in our captivity to forms of human oppression and exploitation, nerving us for liberation and fullness of personhood. There is a suffering love of God that takes upon God's self the suffering that we are due, offering us the possibility of redemption, restoration to wholeness, and reconciliation to God and to our estranged neighbors. This is the liberating and redeeming praxis of God.

The cross of Christ is a direct parable of this liberating and redemptive work of God. In the cross we see mirrored the grim realities of all in our personal and collective lives that stands stubbornly in resistance toward God. The brutality of the cross, tearing the body of the innocent Christ, discloses the oppositional evil that even now seizes and shreds the human potential and seduces the souls of millions of the children of our common trust. On the other hand, the cross of Christ offers a vivid disclosure of the great loving heart of God and of the extent God's love will go to reclaim, redeem, and reconcile us in our lostness and our enmity to God. The cross is a true symbol of God's participating pain in solidarity with victims of human brutality and of our rebellion against our vocations.

We have set forth, in review and with enrichment, three inter-penetrating dimensions of the praxis of God. We have evoked the imaging of God creating, God governing, and God liberating and redeeming. Now let us look further at humankind's co-related callings to partnership in God's praxis, with special reference to our partnership in care for the children of our common trust.

Partnership with God Creating

One of the most blessed gifts of God's creative action is the wondrous possibility of our being biological parents. Partnership in God's creative work in relation to children, however, does not end with the question of our caring for the children that may be our personal biological offspring. Our partnership with God in co-creation involves the development of culture and, within it, the nurture, formation, and education of *all* of the young in each generation. These are the children and youth of our *common* trust.

I find it tremendously ironic that while we now know more about early childhood development, in its various dimensions, than ever before in recorded history, at the same time, we tend to invest less and less of our quality time and resources in creating the environments and supports to provide the kind of nurture and care our knowledge calls for. This has rightly been called the century of the child: from John Dewey to Jean Piaget, from Sigmund Freud to Erik Erikson, from Maria Montessori to David Elkind—then more recently we mark the contributions of persons such as Jerome Kagan, Robert Emde, Judy Dunn, Daniel Stern, Bettye Caldwell, and hosts of others. We have constructed minutely detailed maps of the tasks and potentials of human development. We have bundles of clear indications regarding the kinds of experiences, support, and stimulation that evoke the full realization of children's potentials. Yet we have approached the education of our children with that peculiar blend of private individualism and tight-fisted capitalism that affirms that each child is the possession—and responsibility—of its particular parent or parents. We seem to be reasserting that schooling for the public should be a no-frills, back-to-basics enterprise. At the same time, we provide little or nothing—at any level of education—that would prepare boys and girls for what is potentially the most important work of their lives, namely, being parents.

We know, for example, that there are ontic needs that children need to have met, first in family life, and then built upon in nursery, preschool, "head start" programs, kindergarten, and later schooling. By ontic needs, I mean needs that must be met in some fashion for a child to flourish, to experience being and well-being. These ontic needs include *experiences of belonging*—being in relationships of mutual trust and love; the experience of being seen, known, and cherished for the unique person one is; the experience of being irreplaceable, of being delighted in by persons who matter.

Among these ontic needs, second, are *experiences and contexts of safe autonomy and agency*. As children emerge onto the stage of language and self-consciousness, healthy development requires the assertion of initiatives and freedom of response in terms of their own feelings and experience. This autonomy must, of course, be explored in the context of safe limits and boundaries, and of the emerging bonding of conscience and values.

Third, children have ontic needs for *shared rituals and meanings*. From "peekaboo" in infancy, to the more serious rituals of saying good-bye (with trust that departing parents can be depended upon to return), to the life-enhancing routines of well-run child-care centers, to the sharing of stories that depict the character of good and evil, young children depend upon rituals and meanings to form images that make sense and give them orientation within a large and confusing world. Ritual and meanings, shared with others, give them powerful identifications and buffers of stability in the face of the fears of powerlessness, loss, and change.

Fourth, children have ontic needs for *shelter, bodily well-being, and opportunities for gender identification*. This brings us to questions of adequate housing and nutrition and to primary healthcare. It also brings us to the need for role models and confirming interaction with persons who can meet the child's needs for gender identification. For boys, between the ages of twenty-two and thirty-six months there is both a physiological and an emotional need for consistent interaction with an adult male. "Father Hunger," the psychiatrists call it. Robert Bly identifies it as the boy's need to learn the frequencies at which the adult male body vibrates. Similarly, girls need safe and consistent relations with adults of both sexes to widen the ranges of their cognitive and emotional repertoires and to test their initiatives and emerging skills.

How these clusters of ontic needs are met has tremendous implications for the formation of conscience and of a moral sense. Excessive shaming and demands for perfection as conditions of worth can lead to the creation of a false self or, worse, the strictures of a shame-bound personality. On the other hand, severe abuse and neglect, not offset by someone in the child's world who gives consistent love and effective care, can give rise to the shamelessness and the cunning rage of the sociopath.

Ours is a society where, increasingly, children who have had little or no parenting are begetting and birthing children. Many of their offspring are surrounded from birth with violence, abuse, and vivid experiences of human exploitation and deprivation. If we would be in partnership with God's creating work, we need to expand the role of child-care centers and schools in many areas of our cities and states. In extreme cases, we must separate some children from settings where they are continually violated and subject to abuse and neglect. For the coming decade or more, churches and synagogues need to take the lead in providing kibbutz-like centers where children who have these needs will receive care, combined with schooling. For the young parents of these children, there should be required evening sessions for training in parenting coupled with education for real economic viability in a twenty-first-century economy. It will take the equivalent of a Marshall Plan for cities and counties in most of our states if we are to finally break the cycle of poverty and ill-prepared parenting and end the neglect of medical and basic educational care. We must develop extraordinary approaches to help both young parents and their children get educational groundings to prepare them for roles in the economies and the other challenges of the twenty-first century.

Partnership with God Governing

Working within the practical theological framework we have developed, we must consider economy, politics, moral education, and law enforcement in relation to our callings to partnership with God governing. First, some attention to economics: It seems clear that close to the roots of many of the problems that breed the forms of violence that surround our children in this society there lie the consequences of profound changes in our technologies and in the economy. The disappearance of technologies that employed un-skilled and semiskilled laborers in the face of computer driven technologies has occurred so rapidly that we have had little time to adjust. At the same time, political stances have been taken that have rationalized, for the sake of short-term profits, a rapidity of techno-logical change pursued without much concern for creating alter-nate sources of jobs and incomes for the dislocated. For persons at all levels, from laborers to middle and upper management, this has been extremely disruptive. For those at the bottom of the economic structure, it has been devastating. We have become accustomed to referring to those who have learned to live on the street and on street economies, and those who have come to depend upon welfare payments and Aid to Families with Dependent Children, as a permanent underclass. Apart from the condition of structural and social shame this status entails, it also brings conditions of greatest hardship for children.

These are the conditions that make the appeal of drugs and other substances irresistible to many youth. The economic hope-lessness and sense of having no future in legitimate pursuits lead many to become involved in selling drugs, in prostitution, in criminal activities, and in depending upon gang membership for peer group belonging and for protection. The multibillion-dollar illegal drug industry recruits many of our brightest youngsters with its promises of economic rewards that make the fruits of their parents' week-by-week toil seem utterly meaningless. With drug money, or with the one to two thousand dollars dealers pay sixteen- or seventeen-year-olds to become assassins in the protection of their turf, comes the purchase of easily available weapons, placing firepower—often superior to that of the police—in the hands of the very, very young and of the very, very angry.

Changing these terrible conditions requires at least a triple strategy. The ecology of kibbutz-like child development centers I spoke of earlier, allied with parenting and economic skills development for teen parents, will help to lay foundations both of self-esteem and educational-economic viability for the children. Coupled with meaningful approaches to job creation for their parents, the appeal of absorption in the drug economy can be relativized and offset. At the same time, children with self-esteem and with rebuilt families will generate different horizons of hopefulness for their futures, thus being less susceptible to the wiles of the pushers and the pimps.

Further, for partnership with God governing, there must be new, serious cooperation between churches, citizens' groups, and law enforcement agencies. The corruption of police and public officials afforded by the drug cartels, we have reasons to believe, is so extensive as to require unprecedented pressure, from citizens and political action committees, for elected and appointed officials to free themselves from this bondage. We must turn our most courageous and brilliant law enforcement teams toward the economic tracking and political disruption of the paths of illegal importation and distribution of street drugs. We must make the cost of doing business so high, and the laundering of illegal money so costly, that their operations will be impaired and closed. This suggests again that our partnership with God—here in God's governing praxis— calls for a decade or more of extraordinary action on behalf of those who are the *victims-who-become-perpetrators* in our cities and towns.

We must believe deeply that in mounting the public and governmental resolve to take on the lords of drugs and the princes of exploitation in this society we will be aligning ourselves with a structuring that intends right relatedness and justice in the processes of nature and history. We will be aligning ourselves with the wrath and judgment of a God who does not countenance the waste of young lives and the suffering of the old in our cities and towns. The consequences of our failure to act are just as graphically clear: Nations that allow corruption to permeate their economies, nations that harden their hearts toward the suffering of children and the poor, are like those cities that the prophets charged with selling the needy for a pair of shoes. The judgment and destruction of a God who intends justice on such a society is *still* certain and sure.

Partnership in God's Liberating and Redeeming Action

There is a love manifest in God's claiming human form and entering human history in Jesus Christ that goes far beyond the grace expressed in creation, far beyond the righteousness expressed in judgment and the call to renewed societies. God goes to the most extravagant extreme imaginable to identify with us in our finitude and vulnerability, in our suffering and our estrangement. God's participation in the conditions of our finite lives discloses a love that will not let us go—a love that will not give up on restoring us to the fullness of the image of God. This is a love that simply will not consent to our loss without the most costly effort to reclaim and redeem us. We are called to partnership in this liberating and redeeming love of God.

We are learning, through the work of Twelve Step programs and through our growing understandings of the role of shame in addictions, that there is no healing for shame and alienation without *grace*. We know that education, no matter how technically well grounded and competently offered, if given without love and care, lacks the power to motivate and transform the learner. We know that teens need the fearless eyes and caring hearts of those who can see through their bravado to their hungers for affirmation and need for adult sponsorship and support. In the absence of such care they must turn to peers and gangs in the desperate effort to nurture each other toward adulthood. We know that those whose worth and survival depend upon giving their bodies for use by others emerge with numbed psyches and deep feelings of worthlessness and violation. In short, we know that there is no redemption and liberation from the personal and social bondage to which children of violence and poverty are often subject, apart from the presence and commitments of persons and groups who have aligned themselves—sacrificially and wholeheartedly—in partnership with God's liberating and redeeming action.

If we would be partners in God's liberating and redeeming action in this era, among the most crucially important places for ministry are the shining, high-tech, low-warmth corridors of our burgeoning system of jails and prisons. In the decades of the eighties and nineties we have spent far more of our precious resources, per capita, on prisoners and the building of new prisons than on students in our schools and colleges or in the support of schooling at all levels. Custodial at best, breeding grounds for resentment and places of initiation to lives as hardened criminals at worst, our prisons have become the sealed-off environments where we confine the young people our society has failed and given up on.

From the standpoint of Christian education and ministries of liberation and redemption, there may be no more important arena at present than our prison system. As the Nation of Islam has shown us, these are environments where evangelical and fundamentalist faiths have special contributions to make. They lead persons to decisive conversion experiences, offer clear behavioral guidelines, and model specific approaches to prayer and the reshaping of lives. We will not convert prison life from punitive confinement to rehabilitative transformation without serious attention to the spiritual core of incarcerated men and women—and their "keepers." It is not by accident that the liberating Spirit of God came so powerfully to the apostles in prison, or to Malcolm X in the Charles Street Prison. Time in prison can bring the rock-bottom experience of facing oneself and one's condition. It can be an incomparable time of receptivity to new horizons of repentance, forgiveness, and the making of new beginnings. As part of our churches' alignment with the liberating and redeeming love of God, we should give the development of comprehensive prison ministries serious and high priority.

SHAME AND OUR ADDICTION TO AND IDOLATRY OF GUNS

As I wrote this chapter, Congress struggled over a $30 billion "crime bill." Finally passed, it managed to retain a banning of the sale of nineteen types of assault weapons. Despite the fact that the

215

well-publicized discussion of this possible ban created for gun merchants a boom market of persons who wanted to get supplies of these weapons and ammunition before the new law took effect, the ban on their sales is actually and symbolically important. The Brady Bill, the first successful legislative defeat of the National Rifle Association's powerful gun lobby, began to crystallize a public recognition of the irrationality of our firearms policies. Why do firearms and their possession hold such fetishistic power over American males (and a growing segment of females)? Why does having guns and, ever more frequently, using guns on others hold such power over the minds and imaginations of Americans?

There are answers that go back to the early colonial days in this nation's history: families on the ever-moving western frontiers needed rifles to protect themselves from the Native American tribes they displaced, as well as from unscrupulous folk of their own kind; the minutemen and other armed militia could resist and eventually wear out the British and their Hessian troops, only because they had their own weapons; the Constitution guarantees the right to each citizen to have and to bear arms. In fact, the National Rifle Association began as a kind of commercial memorial to Confederate marksmanship in the Civil War. Arms manufacturers, with markets suddenly diminished at the end of that war, encouraged civilians to form rifle clubs to strengthen familiarity, safety, and accuracy in shooting, so as to be better prepared against the possibility that war might come again. No one then, I suppose, foresaw the traffic, legal and illegal, in automatic and assault weapons that make our city streets vulnerable to pitched firefights.

Why this American fixation upon guns? I attribute the power of this fixation—and fascination—to three fundamental ingredients: (1) the American individualism myth; (2) the American tradition of personal and vigilante "justice"; and (3) the dynamics of unacknowledged shame. In the brief sketch of these ideas I can give here, I hope to show how these three factors relate to partially suppressed fears of weakness, of inadequacy, and of violation in this society; and how this, in turn, makes the possession and use of the gun the symbol of equalization, pride, and revenge. To offer this sketch means to bring into focus aspects of personal and social

216

alienation in this society, and suppressed or bypassed personal and social shame based on class, race, and other dividers.

1. *The American Individualism Myth.* Newcomers to North America from the beginnings in the seventeenth century have thought of this land as a place of individual opportunity and individual success. The covenant imagery of Federalist theology had so receded by the 1780s that the language of individual rights far overbalanced public articulation of shared goods and virtues in the nation's founding documents. Often overlooking the essential role of such factors as extended family, ethnic solidarity, and the support of communities of shared religious ideals, this nation gave rise to a mythology of the triumph of individual imagination, energy, determination, and drive. If a person succeeded under these circumstances, the success could be construed in individualistic terms—by him (or her) and by others. Failure to succeed and thrive in this paradise of entrepreneurship and the work ethic led to both internal and often external judgments about one's deficiencies.

As this myth of individualism became intertwined with theologies of God's favor, the idolization of successful individuals could be wrapped with divine blessing, just as failure or nonachievement could be marked with divine disfavor. The pride/shame axis, created by the distortions of the individualism myth, fueled deep going resentment and outrage, much of which had to be suppressed because of the ideological legitimation the myth provided. The resulting structure of social inequality could not be frankly named, because ostensibly there were to be no hereditary patterns of class privilege. Even today, 80 percent of Americans, when asked, claim to be "middle class." A poor man's property and home—his "castle"—symbolized both the base from which his striving might yet be successful and his autonomous dignity. Standing with a gun, at the door or gate, he was any man's equal. He had legitimate right, by custom and by law, to defend his home and dignity. Attachment to the gun rests upon both the conscious sense of entitlement to the safety of dignity and property and the suppressed sense of individual failure or victimization.

2. *The American Tradition of Personal and Vigilante "Justice."* Frontiers and boomtowns, by definition, bring persons into interaction without the mediation of established legal and police institutions,

217

or the moderating influences of religious or civic associations. Arming oneself and affiliating with gangs or associations for mutual protection and assertion of rights represent an inevitable stage of social development in those settings. In the settlement of what became the United States, such frontier and boomtown conditions kept developing: first with the westward movement of the establishment of permanent settlements, then with the successive waves of poor immigrants coming to the seacoast cities of the east, and later of the Gulf and the Pacific. Add to these factors ethnic and religious prejudices and competition, and you begin to see the tinder for violent clashes and the reliance upon weapons for personal or group protection and assertion. Violence *is* as American as apple pie. And the personal weapon—the handgun, sawed-off shotgun, or hunting gun—has been the instrument of intimidation, equalization, or revenge in frontier, boomtown, or, now, the urban wastelands of our core cities.

3. *The Dynamics of Unacknowledged Shame.* Shame is a largely hidden but deeply toxic reality in American society. The dark, shadowy side of the American myth of individual achievement and success, as I suggested earlier, is the suppressed sense of inferiority, inadequacy, and personal fault people feel for nonoptimal achievement. Nonoptimal achievement is a radically elastic concept. For the millionaire, it consists in not being a billionaire. For the reasonably secure upper middle-class manager or professional, it consists in not having a stock portfolio or savings to hedge against loss of job or reduced insurance for patient care. This unacknowledged sense of personal failure fuels the drivenness of our consumer society. For many in lower income brackets, Wal-Mart and Kmart and their equivalents are the temples for acquisitive assertions of equality and optimal achievement.

Those who have been pressed out of the ranks of competition for optimal achievement on *any* scale bear a deep stigma in this society. This stigma gets crystallized in the term "permanent underclass." Earlier in these pages I called attention to the relation between drugs and the mercurial increase of violence in our inner cities. I pointed out that the sense of exclusion from economic opportunity in this increasingly high-tech society makes young men and women in the underclass vulnerable to the attraction of drug-

and prostitution-related activities. In the face of stigmas of race, class, and ghettoized living areas, and lacking the emotional support of stable family, church, and neighborhood organizations, many young people are pushed beyond tolerable limits of social shame. To offset these massive indices of shame, they slip into an extreme form of denial and suppression and adopt stances of apparent *shamelessness*. Through the route of coercion and violence they say, "You will see me and take account of me; you will reflect my power and agency through your fear of me. I am powerful because I can and will blow you away. If I have no worth, then certainly your life is of no worth to me." The myths of the "pretty corpse" and of status through lethal power go together. Both reflect a deep hopelessness and a rage born of the suppression of deep and pervasive shame. Again the gun serves as symbol and instrument of desperate and destructive ways of dealing with suppressed shame.

Our efforts at reducing the attractiveness of guns and their use in this society will not succeed unless we begin to address the kind of factors I have sketched here through our work on education in society, schools, and religious communities.

CONCLUSION

Several years ago, former president Jimmy Carter articulated a challenge to my city, Atlanta, that in some important ways has inspired the practical theological vision I have begun to sketch here. Atlanta, expecting the Super Bowl in 1994 and the summer Olympics in 1996, was experiencing great excitement. We were learning to speak of ourselves as a "world-class city." President Carter—himself inspired by an Emory University doctor who works in Grady Hospital, our great city hospital in the heart of downtown Atlanta—laid down a grim challenge to all of us. He recalled how, in preparation for the coming of the Democratic National Convention in 1988, we had swept the streets of homeless persons, had bulldozed and removed the "hutvilles" and "shantytowns" of plywood and cardboard houses under our bridges and trestles, so that the eyes of television cameras and foreign correspondents would see "our alabaster city's gleam, undimmed by human tears." He pointed to statistics on school failure, the numbers of homeless men, women, and families in our streets, the pitiful shortfall in healthcare for our poorest citizens, and the rolling riptides of violence and drug-related crime in our housing projects. Then he challenged us to undertake the most comprehensive approach to community renewal to be mounted anywhere so far in the decade of the nineties—the Atlanta Project.

It should not be surprising that the man who proposed and has spearheaded the launching of the Atlanta Project is a man of faith. People and communities who have a deep trust in a praxis of God that both transcends and includes us may be empowered to take on the kind of comprehensive vision for the renewal of a city that Carter has proposed. If we see and embrace our callings to be part of God's creating, governing and redeeming providence, perhaps we will be given the nerve, the stamina, and the hope to sustain the reclaiming of the generation of children about whom Judge Glenda Johnson expressed such deep and anguished concern.

CHAPTER FOURTEEN

MORAL AND FAITH FORMATION
IN AN UNCIVIL SOCIETY

THE ECLIPSE OF CHILDHOOD

Paralleling the emergence of childhood and youth in modernity have been efforts to provide educational support toward moral and religious nurture and for citizenship. We need to be reminded of the tremendous role of churches in this country in shaping the initial colonial village schools, followed by the Sunday school movement, which began its educational efforts with the large numbers of eighteenth- and early nineteenth-century children involved in factory and farm work. The latter led directly to the passion for the so-called common schools that became the vehicles for this nation's commitment to universal education for morality and citizenship. Alongside the common schools there emerged the vital network of parochial schools, founded and directed by churches—Episcopal, Lutheran, Catholic, Presbyterian—as well as Hebrew schools and yeshivas of various sorts. Communities of religious faith have provided the central motivating thrusts for all of these movements.

It is becoming clearer that the period from the 1950s through the early 1980s may have marked the cresting of the recognition of childhood and youth as privileged eras in the life of this society. It is worth noting that these decades also marked the periods when our national policies and local mores were challenged to finally bring our social practices into congruence with our national ideals of equality, freedom, and a justice blind to color, ethnic origins, gender, and social class. As noted earlier, I find a paradox as I reflect on these recent decades. True, there has been a veritable explosion of research and theory providing us comprehensive and rich perspectives on child and adolescent development. This century—and especially the period from 1950 to the present—has rightly been called "The Century of the Child." Yet during this same period we have had to acknowledge the growing reality of child abuse, child neglect, and of a resentment and punitive control directed toward children in this society. We seem now to be involved in a dangerous loss of the protections, the supports, the nurture in morality and faith that have underpinned all that was hopeful for moral progress and the realization of social patterns of justice and compassion in this nation. This erosion threatens a serious *eclipse of childhood*. Consider the following.

For more than a decade, informed students of childhood and adolescence have been documenting the increased intensity and broadening of pressures and demands on children for precocious mastery of skills associated with schooling. This has been accompanied with the movement toward earlier and earlier placement of children in day care and nursery schools, resulting in a radical shrinkage of unstructured, non-goal-directed time for children. For middle and upper class children, the rigors of early instruction in music, reading, computer literacy, dance, and organized athletics have increased the demands for achievement and accomplishment, adding new layers of expectations and conditions of worth. We are just beginning to recognize the implications of such high and structured expectations on the souls of young children. New York educator Kay J. Hoffman says, "The trend to intellectualize early education is a dangerous one. I see more children with high anxiety levels and learning problems caused by the enormous pressure that is being put on them to think and speak like adults before they are ready" (quoted in Franks 1993, 32). Writer Lucinda Franks observes, "Highly verbal children will use words, without really understanding them, as coin of the adult realm." She quotes a doctor from her research who said, "They use [adult words] . . . to push away their own experience as children. One 4-year-old that I tested kept running out of the room saying he had to go get his 'concentration.' He couldn't just be a child and say, 'I don't want to do this test!' He had to parrot an adult concept that he hardly understood because he was afraid to disappoint me" (Franks 1993, 32).

As earlier parts of this book suggested, the fear of failure, the tremendous desire to meet successfully the expectations of parents, often leads children to create what D. W. Winnicott and Alice Miller have called "false selves." The price of success, or of the effort to achieve it on all fronts, can mean for our children loss of access to the place of truth in their own hearts, the loss of spontaneity, and the neglect of a natural development of imagination and fantasy. Even for children who "succeed" in such heavily programmed early childhood regimes, the price may be burnout and serious alienation from purpose and meaning by ages ten or eleven. For those who fail, or who are deprived of such opportunities, shame and self-doubt can be magnified in genuinely crippling ways.

For children of all classes a second major factor in what we may call *the eclipse of childhood* comes with the dominant technological mediators of images and information in our society—the television screen and the computer games explosion. The steady, often unsupervised, widening diet of daily and nightly television programming exposes "channel surfing" children and teens to powerfully pervasive and subliminally affecting images. Anecdotal evidence from long-term teachers suggests compellingly that attention deficit disorder is expanding markedly in our classrooms, as are hyperactivity and patterns of aggressive and violent acting out. Moreover, the content of playground activities seems to involve increasing reliance upon the "violence of total destruction" that is featured in such films as the *Rambo* and *Terminator* series and even in the *Teenage Mutant Ninja Turtles* programs. More and more the "good guys" and the "bad guys" are scarcely distinguishable as regards their ruthlessness and willingness to use strategies, weapons, and techniques of total wipe-out and destructiveness.[1]

Ours is a society that shows greater willingness to grant the status of "reality" to the expressions of human violence and hard-heartedness than to relationships of tenderness, fidelity, and empathetic understanding. Saturation in programming and newscasts with the steady diet of brutality and violence, by criminals and "defenders of society" alike, presses the young to embrace a combination of surface bravado and toughness, which likely masks subliminal

---

1. Personal correspondence from Montessori school director Karen R. Holt, Anderson, South Carolina.

states of anxious despair. The reality of playground massacres and of weapons smuggled into their schools ups the ante for altercations and conflict at school to levels of anxiety their parents' generation never had to deal with. Lucinda Franks's words may be applicable to many of the students in our schools:

> For decades now, children have been growing up faster and faster, each new generation emerging more precocious than the last. But today's crop of under-12's particularly in middle- and upper-middle-income families and particularly in urban America, seems to have reinvented—or even bypassed—childhood as we knew it. They are proud, independent and strong-willed; they are worldly-wise and morally serious. They are a generation that has been raised to challenge and doubt authority, to take little at face value—in short, to enter the world of maturity long before they are mature. . . . I think sometimes we cannot know how profound that fear [that they might disappoint us] runs in our children, especially since we have burdened them with such a sense of their own importance. At times, their officiousness seems to be bluff; they simply cannot afford to be wrong. . . . As we hover over their development as though we were tending orchids in a greenhouse, are we not also guilty of a kind of neglect? In integrating them into our daily lives, have we taken away their freedom to do childish things? . . . Will our independent children thank us for making them the center of the universe, or have we robbed them of a childhood they can never regain? (Franks 1993, 31, 32)

THE MORALLY CORROSIVE ENVIRONMENT OF AN UNCIVIL SOCIETY

On a recent Friday morning in Atlanta I was driving to the airport to pick up a friend. I turned on radio station AM 750 to check traffic in the metro area. Nine A.M. On came local talk show host Neal Boortz. I had heard him before; I knew that he had political commitments opposite to my own. But I left the radio on. Starting his morning program, he presented a truncated and slanted version of a story from the *Atlanta Constitution* involving the closing of a vending machine business, run by two blind persons, at the Chamblee, Georgia, office of the IRS—an installation with three thousand employees. Boortz spoke, he said, with the intention "to rile you listeners up!"

In referring to the blind people, he ridiculed calling them "visually impaired." "These people are *blind*," he said. "They stumble around over things and walk with canes: they are blind! Do you understand?"

In his "interpretation" of the situation at the IRS center, he scalded the Department of Education, which had set in place a policy for giving qualified disabled persons opportunities to develop businesses in federal offices. "What business does the Federal Government have using federal office complexes to give anybody a special break at taxpayers' expense?" he asked.

Then, coming to the point of the story, he reported that the IRS complex was throwing out the vending machine business because its cafeteria had lost $160,000 in the preceding fiscal year. The IRS blamed the vending machine concession for the loss because of its competition with the cafeteria. Here he stormed at the stupid IRS managers for penalizing the blind operators for their efficiency and success.

Indeed, it was hard to tell what he was for: He was against everyone and everything. He made everyone he talked about sound small-minded, stupid, perverse, and intent on ripping off the "honest citizens" of the country. Then, hoping that he had effectively "riled up" his listeners, he began to take callers.

His second caller was a well-spoken, African American woman, who barely began to raise a question regarding some teenagers who had broken into a school in the nearby suburb of Smyrna. Before she could finish asking her question, Boortz exploded in a hateful voice, "Katherine, you're calling in to ask me why I don't mention the names of these white kids in Smyrna, because I used the name of that Black kid on the air. I know what you're doing!" (The call came on the heels of a case in which an African American teen had appealed and won a repeal of a three-year sentence imposed on him for stealing twenty dollars worth of ice cream from a middle school icebox.) Mimicking old Southern Black patterns of speech, he continued, "Why doesn't you discuss de names o' doz white kids lak you did dat Black kid?" Then returning to his own hate-filled voice, he said, "I know what you're up to, Katherine! You are a *damned bigot, you dumb-ass!*"

I was shocked. This was a first for me. On the air, Boortz displayed an utter lack of respect for another human being; he engaged in a frank and vicious caricaturing of a racial group; he displayed a foul-mouthed contempt for the sense of fairness and regard—for the basic respect—we accord each other in a civil society. Listening to this man for the twenty-minute trip to the airport was like taking a bath in a polluting substance. His bitter and nasty discourse offered legitimation for every prejudice, every little and perverse form of smutty disregard for persons different from himself. His venom crossed over a line we cannot violate if we have any hope of a civil society, dedicated to justice and the peaceful resolution of deep going differences in perspectives and interests. Our children and teens listen to such programs. In their interactions with each other, and often with their parents or teachers, they adopt the tones, and often the language of abuse and scorn, modeled for them by such "cool" public personalities.

Talk show hosts of different political persuasions across our country regularly cross over the same line in propagating what passes for "debate" of the alleged issues that divide us. Rappers respond to such insults with intensely assaultive imagery, calling for and offering a kind of legitimacy for violence against authorities and what they take to be oppressors in this society.

We are a nation with the most remarkable capabilities for public communication in the world. At the same time, we are a nation that allows virtually all political debate to be reduced to the level of instrumental utilitarianism or personalist controversy: what will work, what will serve the best interests of those who compete for the benefits of a society of vast inequalities. Only rarely do we witness the operations of debate and discussion formats where genuine principles of equity, fairness, and justice can be employed to invite any of us beyond the lowest common denominators of our group or class interests. Little wonder the bypassed shame of our cities builds up until an event like the acquittal of the officers who beat Rodney King ignites a holocaust in Los Angeles. The message to our children and youth seems clear: Important adults interact with each other in petty and childish ways; there are no real rights or wrongs at stake, just cheap shots and emotional outbursts.

Almost daily, children and youth get vivid lessons in conflict resolution by use of lethal violence. Through newscasts they see images of private citizens being carried to morgues or hospitals because of shootings or stabbings resulting from disputes often between acquaintances or family members. Our children see the violence of abortion answered by the violence of the murder of doctors affiliated with abortion clinics.

In the economy of the wealthiest nation on earth, our children and youth are painfully aware of the growing numbers of homeless persons and families. They see the vast sums paid to professional athletes and are not blind to the immense disparities between the salaries and compensation of major corporate officials and workers in those same corporations in this country. Recent studies reported that the average Fortune 400 CEO makes two hundred times the annual wages of the average worker in those corporations. (In Japan, the comparable ratio is seventeen to twenty times.) At the same time, young people are increasingly likely to be sensitive to the amounts of waste materials we generate and the ecological damage that results from our national and global patterns of resource use.

My point is an obvious one: On many fronts, children and youth cannot escape being aware of the myriad ways in which we fail to maintain the standards of simple decency in our society—locally and nationally. Though they may hear and experience teachings and examples in their churches and schools that go counter to their broader experience, they hear and see a great deal that would encourage them to admire hard-heartedness and moral expediency and to emulate patterns of prejudice and the disvaluing of vulnerable persons and groups.

Finally, they are more likely to see public expressions of religious commitment directed toward the fueling of conflict over such issues as abortion, school prayer, the rights of homosexual persons, or the banning of artworks, literature, or the use of self-esteem building exercises in school, than they are to hear religious appeals for justice for the economically deprived, for interreligious tolerance, or for ecological responsibility. Mainstream churches—liberal and evangelical—have largely acceded to the privatization of religion. While we may support lobbyists and policy researchers in Washington, we rarely sponsor or participate in local and national public debates or causes that would model a religion devoted to work for peace and justice, or to appeals for civility.

FAITH AND MORAL EDUCATION IN AN UNCIVIL SOCIETY

Twelve years ago, Theodore Sizer wrote a searching book on public education, titled *Horace's Compromise: The Dilemma of the American High School* (Sizer 1984). In a chapter on character education, he made what then seemed to me to be a minimalist proposal. He said, "Any school of integrity should try to help its students become decent people. This is an appropriately limited objective." He continued, "Decency denotes satisfaction of a widely understood and accepted standard, and, as such, it is limited." Then he went on to spell out the kind of decency schools should promote:

> *Decency* in the American tradition (obviously the creation more of our Judeo-Christian than of our republican tradition) comprises fairness, generosity, and tolerance. Everyone should get a fair shake. People who are in trouble or who for whatever reason are weak deserve a special hand; the big guys should not force their way on the little guys. It is difficult to imagine a citizen who would seriously quarrel with any school that tried to stand for these values and to persuade its students to make these values operative parts of their character. At the same time, it is difficult to find many schools today that both formally articulate decency as an aim and precisely outline how the students can achieve it. (Sizer 1984, 121)

Schools sponsored by churches or synagogues need not be apologetic about efforts to teach decency or about the religious rootage of their commitments to the values of deep regard for each person and the care of each member of the community for the common good. Sizer's comment is worth pondering as a baseline for assessing what Lawrence Kohlberg used to call "the moral atmosphere" of our schools, religiously sponsored or otherwise.

How consistently, how clearly, how specifically and coherently do our schools articulate and teach the values we stand for? How clearly have administrators and faculties reached agreement and received authorization to make these standards and values integral in the operations of classrooms, cafeterias, coaching contexts, and in the teaching of courses and subject matter? To what degree are extracurricular organizations and activities formed and monitored around adherence to values of mutual respect, care for each other, the civil discussion of controversial matters, and the development of loyalty to the broad moral and ethical foundations of our schools?

"Values issues infuse every classroom" (Sizer 1984, 123). What are the consequences for our water supply of the chemicals we dispose of after experiments or demonstrations in science class? What values are taught by social studies teachers' characterization of Native American Indians as "them" and the implication that the first settlers of the American West were Europeans? Describing the Indians as the first of many human immigrants to North America sends quite a different message. "The way a biology teacher treats life in class—whether, for example, live frogs are purchased and pithed in quantity for students to dissect—signals important values. Mocking the squeamishness and reserve of students who do not want to kill frogs can deeply affect a young student. How sacred is life?" Sizer writes,

> Teaching virtues like tolerance and generosity is neither easier nor more difficult than teaching any subtle art, such as literary grace or musical style. It is done, when at all, largely by example or, better put, by the "surround," by the insistent influence of the institution itself living out those values. This process is helped by explicitness; the ways of the school need to be explained, over and over again. Where these ways are uncertain—such as how the school should handle a particular problem among its students—the issue must be debated. Explaining must be incessant: This is how we at this school define tolerance. This is what decency means here. These are the kind of attitudes we honor. These kinds of actions are intolerable. Of course, this explaining, together with the debate that accompanies it, is itself a fine form of questioning as well as of telling. It pushes students (and their teachers) back to the "whys" of their

community, to the questions about decent living that apply in all situations. (Sizer 1984, 124)

Sizer's proposal of decency as the minimal threshold of moral and faith development in our schools deserves serious attention, especially against the backdrop of the morally corrosive environment of what I have characterized as our "uncivil society." But for religiously sponsored schools the opportunities and calling go well beyond that threshold set of goals. What does it mean for schools that stand in ecclesial and faith traditions? In a time when we as a nation are trying to embrace diversity and pluralism, what does faithfulness to a Christian heritage mean? It seems to me that church-sponsored schools face at least three clusters of issues when we focus on their Christian foundations and identity.

1. How do we define the mission of the school as regards the religious education and the spiritual formation of its students? Answering this question requires thinking through the role and place of assemblies for worship and spiritual observance; it requires thinking through the role and place and the manner of teaching of and about religion in the curriculum; and it requires clarifying the role of a chaplain, priest, or minister related to the school as a figure who perhaps teaches, but also may provide spiritual direction and pastoral care.

2. How shall the school honor the religious and cultural diversity of the range of students, and their families, who are part of the student body? What policies shall govern the selection and retention of faculty, as regards their religious interests, commitments, or affiliations?

3. How shall the school prepare students for responsible citizenship in a religiously pluralistic society—one in which large and complex issues involving ethical decisions and choice will be on the common agenda for as long as they live? How do we empower and shape the virtues and strengths of leadership for such a society? How do we provide opportunities for firsthand, experiential learning related to several dimensions of our society's economy, its governance, its patterns of social relations, its dividedness along racial, class, ethnic, and religious lines?

Let me speak first about *defining the mission of the school as regards the religious and spiritual formation of its students.* Charles Taylor, a contemporary philosopher of great scope and range, published a magisterial book called *Sources of the Self* in 1989. From the standpoint of brilliant intellectual history in this book he explored the sources of moral formation in Western societies. One incisive thesis of the book is that we must understand that the core ethical goods around which our society is built have their rootage in understandings of God that come to expression in the biblical tradition. Taylor raises the question sharply whether we can maintain our cultural commitments to benevolence, justice, the rights of persons, and corporate care for the common good—core values of our society—if we allow them to become separated from their religious rootage.

We do not need Taylor's book to tell us that we live in a largely post-Christian era. Nor do we need him to tell us that most of the bloody conflicts in this world—and in our own society—arise out of the shrillness of assertive blends of religion with nationalism, ethnocentrism, or racism. Mainline denominations in this country have not been adequately attentive to these emergent facts. We continue to conduct ecclesial life and the shaping of our schools, I suspect, as though this were still—in most respects that mattered—a "Christian" society. Unlike our colleagues among Jewish educators, we typically do not have an intense recognition that our churches—mainline, mainstream, old-line churches—could be one or two generations away from becoming museums. Nor have we adequately reckoned with the spiritual emptiness and hunger that, curiously enough, draws our children and youth toward Dungeons and Dragons, toward *Star Trek*, and toward the mysterious, confused symbols of transcendence and death offered on MTV and through other expressions of popular culture.

We should consider more boldly the opportunity and responsibility of church-sponsored schools to provide for the religious and spiritual formation of our students. Academically this means defining a path of in-depth, progressive encounter with the Christian and biblical traditions. In the academic study of religion, place should be made for respectful study of other religious traditions, with opportunities for interaction with and honoring of the traditions of members of the school community who may be representations of other traditions than Christian. In terms of the common life of the school, it underscores the importance of a ritual and liturgical center to the life of the school. Schooling tends to neglect the right hemisphere of the brain: the stimulation of spiritual imagination, the formation of the deep going emotional patterns that underlie commitments to love of God and neighbor. In our various traditions, there are indispensable resources for addressing the spiritual potential and hungers of our students (and our faculties).

Now a word about *how to honor the religious and cultural diversity of the range of students, their families, and about the question of faculty diversity.* Some mainline traditions have long known a good deal about how to stand, committedly and informedly, in their traditions, while maintaining a principled and genuine openness to the traditions of others that are different. This occurs best when there is a certainty about who we are that makes possible a nonaggressive, nondefensive readiness for interactions with those who are "other." These are virtues that are necessary for what I call a "public church." These virtues provide material from which our schools can offer something uniquely valuable for multicultural, multireligious education. There is no point in centering religiously sponsored schools solely on the goals of excellence of education, with traces of Christian or denominational heritage being transmitted merely through a process of "seepage." One of the principal features that attracts families to religiously sponsored schools is the hope that their children will receive some kind of nonrigid, nondogmatic, but nonetheless determinate religious formation. To this end, it seems crucial that faculty and administration (as well as trustees and sponsoring churches) should be clear, in concert, and unapologetic regarding the teaching of religion and the provision for liturgical participation that are part of the life of the school. Where there is clear identity and purpose, there can be clear patterns of welcoming the stranger, honoring those who stand in other traditions, and providing space for persons within the community to grow and develop in—and if necessary, against—the centering faith tradition.

These points lead to the third cluster of issues I want to address: *how our schools can prepare students for responsible citizenship in a religiously pluralistic and ethically challenged society.* Richard Sennett, a sociologist, wrote some years ago, "It is a cruel thing to prepare 'soft' people for life in a 'hard' world" (Sennett 1971). It is important, as regards moral and faith development, for our schools to think through the question, "What kinds of virtues, awarenesses, faith, and skills do we want to help students form as they move toward adulthood in this society in the twenty-first century?" In this context, let me explore two clusters of qualities I hope we can nurture among the students in church-sponsored schools. The first cluster involves several paradoxical images: I would like us to form young women and men who can be

Tough-Minded Visionaries
and
Skillful and Resourceful Idealists.

That is to say, I want us to combine rigorous and broad-gauged preparation for understanding, influencing, and interacting with the *systems* of our contemporary world, with nurtured eyes and hearts that can attend to purposes, meanings, and values. I want us to form young people equipped with appreciation and empowered understandings of our systems, but who resist a fascination, lust, or intimidation that clouds questions of purpose, accountability, and compassion for persons and for creation. Education in the sciences and mathematics; grounding in the human sciences of philosophy, economics, and political theory; exposure to branches of sociology and psychology—are all necessary for the nurture young people need. But also literature and the in-depth and experiential study of their own and other religious traditions are required. The spiritualities of our great religious traditions provide the best point of convergent study and practice. The disciplines and skills of attending to the transcendent have striking similarities in our traditions. Starting there, and then widening to the world images, the ritual practices, the ethical teachings, and the ways of pursuing and honoring the sacral dimensions of life are essential for tough-minded visionaries and resourceful idealists.

The second cluster of qualities I hope we can nurture includes

Individuated Identity combined with Intimate Connectedness;
High Cognitive Operations combined with Emotional Integration;
Grounding in a Tradition combined with Preparation for Continuing Change.

I will not unpack each of these pairs of qualities in depth here. Suffice it to say that holding together *individuation* (not individualism) and *intimate connectedness* represents one of the challenges of adult maturation on which both feminist and male-oriented theorists of human development agree. Both sides of this tensional ideal are required in the balanced life.

Now a thought about *high cognitive operations* combined with *emotional integration:* This combination is required for what Gregory Bateson once called "deutero learning"—learning to learn. Both are prerequisite for understanding and operating on and within the matrix of systems in which we live. But how much of the tragedy of our interpersonal and international lives is bound up with the pairing of cognitive sophistication with emotional fragmentation? Unresolved childhood abuse or neglect; the masked shame of false selves; the determined aggressiveness of those rendered invisible in families or societies; the one-sided fixation on power and control—all point out the need for attention in our educational processes to emotional healing and integration.

Grounding in tradition and *preparation for continuing change* also have something of a paradoxical ring. It only appears paradoxical, however, if we have not reflected enough on what we call "openness." Openness, if it is a *virtue* at all, is a second-level virtue, not a primary one, like *prudence, courage, faith,* or *love.* If you have only openness, you don't have very much at all. A window stuck open is as useless as a window stuck shut. Properly speaking, openness becomes meaningful as a quality of a person or system that has integrity or structure. Openness—the readiness to deal with continuing change—depends upon there being a grounding in a way of seeing and being, a system of values, a structure of beliefs and knowledge. I hope our students will have rich grounding in tradition and, therefore, preparation for continuing, discerning response and initiative in relation to change.

TEACHING FAITHFUL CHANGE

Finally, there is a quality, I hope, for our children and youth that both encompasses the others I have mentioned and goes, for me at least, to what lies at the heart of the matter: I want our students in church-related schools to begin the process of *finding purposes for their lives that are part of the purposes of God.*

I want each girl or boy we work with to be part of an educational community in which she or he experiences being prized and regarded as a gifted child of God.

As our children and youth form their identities and shape their beliefs and values, I hope they can form deep going images of a God who is active in and through the processes of nature and history and of their lives.

I want our youth to come to image and trust that human expressions of love and fidelity, and human care for justice, do not go counter to the grain of the Universe, but rather are close to its very heart, the heart of God.

I want them to begin to think of their careers or the work they will do or the ways they will live as being rooted in their relation to God. I want them to know and understand that they have an *ontological calling*—a calling that comes with the very gift of their lives—to relationship and partnership with God.

I want them to develop a growing sense that in the *creating,* the *ordering,* and the *liberating-redeeming* work of God—which is often subtle and likely to be missed by TV cameras, but is sometimes as blatant as an avalanche—they can find purposes for their lives that are part of the purposes of God.

I want them to begin to trust that the world represented to them as permeated by the powers of evil, of human selfishness, of human greed and stupidity, is but one side of a larger reality.

I want them to understand and begin to discern the steel tendrils of the influence of goodness in this world. I want them to begin to sense the pulse and breathing of the divine mercy that sustains and renews the world each day.

I want them to sense the arbitrariness of our divisions of the sacred and the secular and to understand that the spirit of God is present in unexpected places and in transforming ways.

I want them to begin to be able to counter their (and our) disillusionment, cynicism, and despair at the incivility of our world. I want for them—and for us—the growing hope and conviction that truth is strong, that love is unconquerable, and that justice—as the social combination of truth and love—is robust and resilient and will be sustained by God, if human beings are faithful.

BIBLIOGRAPHY

Allport, Gordon
1955   *Becoming: Basic Considerations for a Psychology of Personality.* New Haven: Yale University Press.

Angelou, Maya
1970   *I Know Why the Caged Bird Sings.* New York: Random House.

Aries, Philippe
1962   *Centuries of Childhood.* Translated by Robert Baldock. New York: Alfred A. Knopf.

Augustine
1950   *The City of God.* Translated by Marcus Dods. New York: Modern Library.

Bakan, David
1966   *The Duality of Human Experience.* Chicago: Rand McNally.

Barbour, Ian G.
1989   "Creation and Cosmology." In *Cosmos as Creation: Theology and Science in Consonance,* edited by Ted Peters. Nashville: Abingdon Press.
1990   *Religion in an Age of Science.* Vol. I. New York: Harper & Row.

Bellah, Robert
1970   *Beyond Belief.* New York: Harper & Row.

Benedict, Ruth
1946   *The Chrysanthemum and the Sword.* Boston: Houghton Mifflin.

Berry, Thomas
1988   *The Dream of the Earth.* San Francisco: Sierra Club Books.

Bettelheim, Bruno
1977   *The Uses of Enchantment: The Meaning and Importance of Fairy Tales.* New York: Vintage Books.

Birch, Charles, and John B. Cobb Jr.
1981   *The Liberation of Life.* Cambridge: Cambridge University Press.

Bonhoeffer, Dietrich
1965   *Ethics.* Edited by Eberhard Bethge; translated by N. H. Smith. New York: Macmillan.

Bohm, David
1980   *Wholeness and the Implicate Order.* London: Routledge Kegan Paul.

Bonino, Jose-Miquez
1976   *Christians and Marxists.* Grand Rapids, Mich.: William B. Eerdmans.

Boys, Mary C., ed.
1989   *Education for Citizenship and Discipleship.* New York: Pilgrim Press.

Bradshaw, John
1988   *Healing the Shame That Binds You.* Deerfield Beach, Fla.: Health Communications.

Brewer, Connie
1991   *Escaping the Shadows, Seeking the Light.* San Francisco: HarperSanFrancisco.

Bridges, William
1980   *Transitions: Making Sense of Life's Changes.* Reading, Mass.: Addison-Wesley.

Brinton, Craine
1967   "Enlightenment." In *The Encyclopedia of Philosophy,* edited by P. Edwards. Vol. 2, pp. 519-25. New York: Macmillan.

Brock, Rita Nakashima
1988   *Journeys by Heart: A Christology of Erotic Power.* New York: Crossroad.

Broucek, Francis J.
1991   *Shame and the Self.* New York: Guilford Press.

Browning, Don S.
1991   *A Fundamental Practical Theology: Descriptive and Strategic Proposals.* Minneapolis: Fortress Press.

Brueggemann, Walter
1989   "The Legitimacy of a Sectarian Hermeneutic." In *Education for Citizenship and Discipleship,* edited by Mary C. Boys. New York: Pilgrim Press.

Cady, Linell E.
1991   "Resisting the Postmodern Turn: Theology and Contextualization." In *Theology at the End of Modernity,* edited by Sheila Greeve Davaney. Philadelphia: Trinity Press International.

Capps, Donald
1984   *Pastoral Care and Hermeneutics.* Philadelphia: Fortress Press.

Cassirer, Ernst
1951   *The Philosophy of the Enlightenment.* Translated by Fritz C. A. Koelln and James P. Pettegrove. Princeton, N.J.: Princeton University Press.

Chopp, Rebecca S.
1986   *The Praxis of Suffering: An Interpretation of Liberation and Political Theologies.* Maryknoll, N.Y.: Orbis Books.

Cone, James
1970   *Liberation: A Black Theology of Liberation.* Philadelphia: J. B. Lippincott.

Darwin, Charles
1965   *The Expresssion of the Emotions in Man and Animals.* Chicago: University of Chicago Press.

Davaney, Sheila Greeve, ed.
1991   *Theology at the End of Modernity.* Philadelphia: Trinity Press International.

Davies, Paul
1984   *Superforce: The Search for a Grand Unified Theory of Nature.* New York: Simon and Schuster.
1988   *The Cosmic Blueprint: New Discoveries in Nature's Creative Ability to Order the Universe.* New York: Simon and Schuster.

Dunn, Judy
1987   "The Beginnings of Moral Understanding: Development in the Second Year." In *The Emergence of Morality in Young Children,* edited by Jerome Kagan and Sharon Lamb. Chicago: University of Chicago Press.

Durkheim, Emile
1915   *The Elementary Forms of the Religious Life.* Translated by J. W. Swain. London: Allen & Unwin.

Ellis, Havelock
1936   "The Evolution of Modesty." In *Studies in the Psychology of Sex,* 3rd rev. ed. Vol. 1, part 1. New York: Random House.

Emde, Robert, William F. Johnson, and M. Ann Easterbrooks
1987   "The Do's and Don'ts of Early Moral Development: Psychoanalytic Tradition and Current Research." In *The Emergence of Morality in Young Children*, edited by Jerome Kagan and Sharon Lamb. Chicago: University of Chicago Press.

Erikson, Erik H.
1962   *Young Man Luther*. New York: W. W. Norton.
1963   Reprint. *Childhood and Society*. New York: W. W. Norton. Original edition, 1950.
1977   *Toys and Reasons*. New York: W. W. Norton.
1982   *The Life Cycle Completed*. New York: W. W. Norton.
1987   *A Way of Looking At Things*. Edited by Stephen Schlein. New York: W. W. Norton.

Fowler, James W.
1980   "Faith and the Structuring of Meaning," in *Toward Moral and Religious Maturity*, edited by James W. Fowler and Anton Vergote. Morriston, N.J.: Silver Burdett.
1984   *Becoming Adult, Becoming Christian: Adult Development and Christian Faith*. San Francisco: Harper & Row.
1985   Reprint. *To See the Kingdom: The Theological Vision of H. Richard Niebuhr*. Lanham, Md.: University Press of America. Original edition, Nashville: Abingdon Press, 1974.
1986a   "Faith and the Structuring of Meaning." In *Faith Development and Fowler*, edited by Craig Dykstra and Sharon Parks. Birmingham, Ala.: Religious Education Press.
1986b   "Dialogue Toward a Future in Faith Development Studies." In Dykstra and Parks, *Faith Development and Fowler*.
1987   *Faith Development and Pastoral Care*. Philadelphia: Fortress Press.
1989   "Faith Development in Early Childhood." In *Early Childhood and the Development of Faith*, edited by Doris Blazer. Kansas City, Mo.: Sheed and Ward.
1991   *Weaving the New Creation: Stages of Faith and the Public Church*. San Francisco: HarperCollins.
1995   Reprint. *Stages of Faith: The Psychology of Human Development and the Quest for Meaning*. San Francisco: Harper & Row. Original edition, 1981.

Fowler, James W., and Sam Keen
1980   *Life-Maps: Conversations on the Journey of Faith*. Edited by Jerome Berryman. Waco, Tex.: Word Books.

Franks, Lucinda
1993   "Little Big People." *The New York Times Magazine*, October 10, 28-34.

Freud, Sigmund
1900   *The Interpretation of Dreams*. Translated by James Strachey. New York: Avon.

Friedrich, Karl J., ed. and trans.
1949   *The Philosophy of Kant*. New York: The Modern Library.

Goldberg, Carl
1991   *Understanding Shame*. Northwale, N.J.: Jason Aronson.

Gutiérrez, Gustavo
1973   *A Theology of Liberation: History, Politics, and Salvation*. Maryknoll, N.Y.:
        Orbis Books.

Habermas, Jürgen
1987   *The Philosophical Discourse of Modernity: Twelve Lectures*. Translated by
        Frederick G. Lawrence. Cambridge, Mass.: MIT Press.
1989   *The Structural Transformation of the Public Sphere: An Inquiry into a Category
        of Bourgeois Society*. Translated by Thomas Burger. Cambridge, Mass.:
        MIT Press.

Hauerwas, Stanley
1988   *Christian Existence Today: Essays on Church, World, and Living in Between*.
        Durham, N.C.: Labyrinth Press.

Hick, John
1966   *Evil and the God of Love*. San Francisco: Harper & Row.

Hillman, James
1975   *Re-Visioning Psychology*. New York: Harper Colophon.

Hodgson, Peter
1989   *God in History*. Nashville: Abingdon Press.

Hunter, James Davison
1991   *Culture Wars: The Struggle to Define America*. New York: Basic Books.

James, William
1961   Reprint. *The Varieties of Religious Experience*. New York: Collier Books. Ori-
        ginal edition, New York, London, Bombay, and Calcutta: Longmans,
        Green and Co., 1902.

Jones, William R.
1973   *Is God a White Racist?* New York: Doubleday.

Jung, Carl
1933   *Modern Man in Search of a Soul*. New York: Harcourt, Brace, and World.

Kagan, Jerome
1984   *The Nature of the Child.* New York: Basic Books.

Kagan, Jerome, and Sharon Lamb, eds.
1987   *The Emergence of Morality in Young Children.* Chicago: University of Chicago Press.

Kaufman, Gordon D.
1993   *In Face of Mystery: A Constructive Theology.* Cambridge, Mass.: Harvard University Press.

Kegan, Robert
1982   *The Evolving Self: Problem and Process in Human Development.* Cambridge, Mass.: Harvard University Press.
1994   *In Over Our Heads: The Mental Demands of Modern Life.* Cambridge, Mass.: Harvard University Press.

Kohlberg, Lawrence
1981   *Essays on Moral Development.* Vol. 1: *The Philosophy of Moral Development.* San Francisco: Harper & Row.
1984   *Essays on Moral Development.* Vol. 2: *The Psychology of Moral Development.* San Francisco: Harper & Row.

Kohut, Heinz
1977   *The Restoration of the Self.* New York: International Universities Press.
1984   *How Does Analysis Cure? Contributions to the Psychology of the Self.* Edited by Arnold Goldberg, with Paul E. Stepansky. Chicago: University of Chicago Press.

Lewis, Helen Block
1971   *Shame and Guilt in Neurosis.* New York: International Universities Press.

Lindbeck, George
1984   *The Nature of Doctrine: Religion and Theology in a Postliberal Age.* Philadelphia: Westminster Press.

Lynd, Helen Merrell
1958   *On Shame and the Search for Identity.* New York: Harcourt, Brace, and World.

Magid, Ken, and Carole A. McKelvey
1987   *High Risk: Children Without a Conscience.* New York: Bantam Books.

McFague, Sallie
1987   *Models of God: Theology for an Ecological, Nuclear Age.* Philadelphia: Fortress Press.

1991   "Cosmology and Christianity: Implications of the Common Creation Story for Theology." In *Theology at the End of Modernity,* edited by Sheila Greeve Davaney. Philadelphia: Trinity Press International.

1993   *The Body of God: An Ecological Theology.* Minneapolis: Fortress Press.

Mahan, Brian James
1989   "The Ethics of Belief: An Interpretation and Evaluation of William James's Notion of Spiritual Judgment." Ph.D. diss., University of Chicago.

Marty, Martin E.
1981   *The Public Church.* New York: Crossroad.

May, Gerald
1982   *Will and Spirit: A Contemplative Psychology.* San Francisco: Harper & Row.

Metz, Johannes B.
1979   *Faith in History and Society.* New York: Crossroad.

Miller, Alice
1981   *The Drama of the Gifted Child: The Search for True Self.* Translated by Ruth Ward. New York: Basic Books.

1990   *The Untouched Key: Tracing Childhood Trauma in Creativity and Destructiveness.* Translated by Hildegarde Hannum and Hunter Hannum. New York: Doubleday.

Miller, Judith, and Laurie Mylroie
1990   *Saddam Hussein and the Crisis in the Gulf.* New York: Times Books.

Moltmann, Jürgen
1967   *The Theology of Hope: On the Ground and the Implications of a Christian Eschatology.* New York: Harper & Row.

1973   *The Crucified God: The Cross of Christ as the Foundation and Criticism of Christian Theology.* New York: Harper & Row.

More, Thomas
1992   *Care of the Soul: A Guide for Cultivating Depth and Sacredness in Everyday Life.* San Francisco: HarperCollins.

Morrison, Andrew
1989   *Shame: The Underside of Narcissism.* Hillsdale, N.J.: The Analytic Press.

Nathanson, Donald L.
1992   *Shame and Pride: Affect, Sex, and the Birth of the Self.* New York: W. W. Norton.

———, ed.
1987   *The Many Faces of Shame.* New York: Guilford Press.

Niebuhr, H. Richard
1960   *The Responsible Self.* New York: Harper & Brothers.

Nietzsche, Friedrich
1959   *The Portable Nietzsche.* Edited and translated by Walter Kaufmann. New York: Penguin Books.

Peacocke, A. R.
1979   *Creation and the World of Science.* Oxford: Clarendon Press.

Piaget, Jean
1962   *Play, Dreams and Imitation in Childhood.* New York: W. W. Norton.
1967   *Six Psychological Studies.* New York: Random House, Vintage.
1970   "Piaget's Theory." In *Carmichael's Manual of Child Psychology.* 3rd ed. Edited by Paul Mussen. Vol. 1. New York: John Wiley and Sons.
1976   *The Child and Reality.* New York: Penguin Books.

Piaget, Jean, and Barbel Inhelder
1969   *The Psychology of the Child.* New York: Basic Books.

Piers, Gerhart, and Milton B. Singer
1971   *Shame and Guilt: A Psychoanalytic and a Cultural Study.* New York: W. W. Norton.

Placher, William C.
1989   *Unapologetic Theology: A Christian Voice in a Pluralistic Conversation.* Louisville, Ky.: Westminister/John Knox Press.

Polanyi, Michael
1958   *Personal Knowledge: Towards a Postcritical Philosophy.* Chicago: University of Chicago Press.
1967   *The Tacit Dimension.* Garden City, N.Y.: Anchor Books.

Ricoeur, Paul
1967   *The Symbolism of Evil.* Translated by Emerson Buchanan. Boston: Beacon Press.

Rizzuto, Ana-Maria
1980   *The Birth of the Living God.* Chicago: University of Chicago Press.

St. Clair, Michael
1986   *Object Relations and Self Psychology: An Introduction.* Monterey, Calif.: Brooks/Cole.

Scheff, Thomas J., and Suzanne M. Retzinger
1991   *Emotion and Violence: The Role of Shame-Rage.* New York: Free Press.

Schneider, Carl
1992   *Shame, Exposure, and Privacy.* New York: W. W. Norton.

Schüssler Fiorenza, Elisabeth, and David Tracy, eds.
1984   *The Holocaust as Interruption. Concillium,* vol. 175. Edinburgh: T & T Clark.

Segundo, Juan L.
1976   *The Liberation of Theology.* Maryknoll, N.Y.: Orbis Books.

Selman, Robert L.
1974   "The Developmental Conceptions of Interpersonal Relations." Publication of the Harvard-Judge Baker Social Reasoning Project, vols. 1 & 2.
1976   "Social Cognitive Understanding." In *Moral Development and Behavior,* edited by Thomas Lickona. New York: Holt, Rinehart & Winston.

Sennett, Richard
1977   *The Fall of Public Man.* New York: Alfred A. Knopf.

Shengold, Leonard
1989   *Soul Murder: The Effects of Childhood Abuse and Deprivation.* New York: Fawcett Columbine.

Sizer, Theodore R.
1984   *Horace's Compromise: The Dilemma of the American High School.* New York: Houghton Mifflin.

Smedes, Lewis B.
1993   *Shame and Grace: Healing the Shame We Don't Deserve.* San Francisco: HarperSanFrancisco.

Sobrino, Jon
1978   *Christology at the Crossroads: A Latin American Approach.* Maryknoll, N.Y.: Orbis Books.

Soelle, Dorothee
1975   *Suffering.* Philadelphia: Fortress Press.

Stern, Daniel N.
1985   *The Interpersonal World of the Infant: A View from Psychoanalysis and Developmental Psychology.* New York: Basic Books.

Stroup, George
1982   *The Promise of Narrative Theology.* Atlanta: John Knox Press.

Taylor, Charles
1989   *Sources of the Self: The Making of the Modern Identity.* Cambridge, Mass.: Harvard University Press.

Toennies, Ferdinand
1963 ⸱ *Community and Society: Gemeinschaft and Gesellschaft.* Translated by Charles
       P. Loomis. New York: Harper & Row.

Tomkins, Silvan S.
1987 "Shame." In *The Many Faces of Shame,* edited by Donald L. Nathanson.
       New York: Guilford Press.

Tracy, David
1981 *The Analogical Imagination: Christian Theology and the Culture of Pluralism.*
       New York: Crossroad.

Tronick, E. et al.
1978 "The Infant's Response to Entrapment Between Contradictory Messages
       in Face-to-Face Interaction." *Journal of Child Psychiatry* 17:1-13.

Washington, Joseph
1967 *The Politics of God.* Boston: Beacon Press

Wink, Walter
1992 *Engaging the Powers: Discernment and Resistance in a World of Domination.*
       Minneapolis: Fortress Press.

Winnicott, Donald W.
1971 *Playing and Reality.* New York: Basic Books.

Wooden, Kenneth
1976 *Weeping in the Playtime of Others: America's Incarcerated Children.* New York:
       McGraw-Hill.

Wulff, David M.
1991 *Psychology of Religion: Classic and Contemporary Views.* New York: John Wiley
       and Sons.

Wurmser, Leon
1981 *The Mask of Shame.* Baltimore: John Hopkins University Press.